Best Hikes Washington, D.C.

Falcon Guides by Bill and Mary Burnham:

Hiking Virginia
Best Hikes Near Washington, D.C.
Florida Keys Paddling Atlas
Kayaking for Everyone
Car Camping for Everyone

Best Hikes
Washington, D.C.

The Greatest Views, Wildlife, and Forest Strolls

Second Edition

Bill and Mary Burnham

GUILFORD, CONNECTICUT

An imprint of The Rowman & Littlefield Publishing Group, Inc.
4501 Forbes Blvd., Ste. 200
Lanham, MD 20706
www.rowman.com

Falcon and FalconGuides are registered trademarks and Make Adventure Your Story is a trademark of The Rowman & Littlefield Publishing Group, Inc.

Distributed by NATIONAL BOOK NETWORK

Photos by authors unless otherwise noted
Maps by The Rowman & Littlefield Publishing Group, Inc.

British Library Cataloguing-in-Publication Information available

Library of Congress Cataloging-in-Publication Data available

ISBN 978-1-4930-3499-4 (paperback)
ISBN 978-1-4930-3500-7 (e-book)

∞™ The paper used in this publication meets the minimum requirements of American National Standard for Information Sciences—Permanence of Paper for Printed Library Materials, ANSI / NISO Z39.48-1992.

Printed in the United States of America

The authors and The Rowman & Littlefield Publishing Group, Inc., assume no liability for accidents happening to, or injuries sustained by, readers who engage in the activities described in this book.

Contents

Washington, D.C., Overview

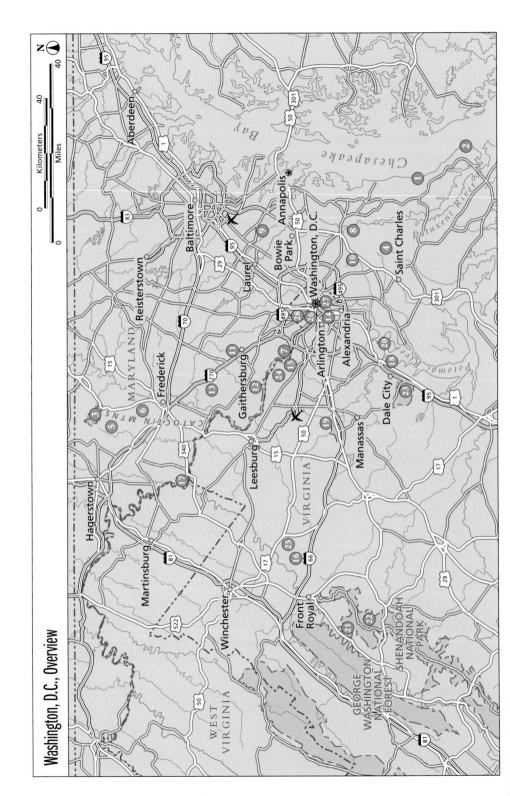

Introduction

Mary and I relish this opportunity to share with you our favorite hikes in metro Washington, D.C., the Blue Ridge, and the Coastal Plain with *Best Hikes Near Washington, D.C.* Although we've been hiking Virginia and Maryland for more than two decades, it was with fresh eyes that we explored freshwater marshes along the Patuxent River at Jug Bay and felt the rough sandstone beneath our hands and knees on Catoctin Mountain Park. We absorbed the majesty of a 96-foot free-falling waterfall in Shenandoah National Park and enjoyed the discovery of new places like the American Chestnut Land Trust Preserve.

We also savored the quiet scenes: hiking through the muggy morning mist the day after a heavy rain, our ears ringing with the shrill call of spring peepers; studying wildflowers; enjoying the company of trail friends; learning how locals find the treasured morel mushrooms. All these experiences and more helped us press on in discovering and presenting to you the very best day hiking in and around Washington, D.C.

The diversity of terrain, climate, culture, and environment encompassed in this compact region is mind-boggling. The Chesapeake Bay laps at your feet at Calvert Cliffs State Park in Maryland. (These high cliffs glistened with such intensity on a June day in 1608 that they served as a beacon for Capt. John Smith and his crew of fifteen men circumnavigating the Chesapeake Bay.) Barely 30 miles west as the crow flies, you land in the Zekiah Swamp in Charles County, Maryland, whose wet, mysterious woodlands briefly sheltered fugitive John Wilkes Booth, a man shunned after he assassinated President Abraham Lincoln in 1865.

WASHINGTON, D.C. AREA HIKING CLUBS

The Northern Virginia area (popularly known as NoVa) has several very active hiking clubs that schedule regular hikes not only in the NoVa region of Virginia, Maryland, and D.C., but also in nearby Shenandoah National Park. Some even provide transportation to the hike.

Capital Hiking Club, www.capitalhikingclub.org. Hikes and trips in Virginia, Maryland, and Pennsylvania.

Center Hiking Club, (301) 468-1896, www.centerhikingclub.org. Hikes and trips in Virginia, Maryland, and Pennsylvania.

Potomac Appalachian Trail Club (PATC), Vienna, (703) 242-0315, www.patc.net.

Wanderbirds Hiking Club, www.wanderbirds.org. Hikes in Virginia, West Virginia, Maryland, and Pennsylvania.

Washington Women Outdoors, Germantown, MD, (301) 864-3070, www.washington womenoutdoors.org. Outdoor adventures for women, including hiking, kayaking, rock climbing, and biking.

Author Bill Burnham with nephew Gregory Nardacci, the next generation

Continue west another 30 miles, across the Potomac River separating Maryland and Virginia, to find Prince William Forest Park in Prince William County, Virginia. Here, the Quantico and South Fork Quantico Creeks cascade over the "fall line," the geologic cleft that demarks the Coastal Plain from the Piedmont. Waterfalls cascade over one another on these creeks, as they do at places along the fall line north and south, at Great Falls of the Potomac and elsewhere.

Another 30 miles west finds the hiker in the foothills of the Blue Ridge. Small "hills" of resistant quartzite bedrock have withstood the weathering of time. Bull Run Mountains near Thoroughfare Gap and Wildcat Mountain near Warrensburg foreshadow more rugged mountain terrain that awaits just another 30 miles west in the Blue Ridge and Catoctin Mountain regions.

Great Falls

By straight line, our trip of 120 miles spans the Bay to the Blue Ridge. In between, we've left no stone unturned to document only the very best of the hikes found here.

Weather

Befitting its geographic diversity, weather in metro Washington, D.C., and outlying areas varies to the extremes. On a mild winter day along the Patuxent River in Calvert County, it may be snowing in Shenandoah National Park. Temperatures fluctuate throughout the year from midsummer highs of 90°F or more to winter low temperatures in the teens. Generally speaking, hikers will find coastal areas are tempered by Chesapeake Bay breezes, while higher elevations west and north swing from extreme high to extreme low temperatures depending on the season. It's not an exaggeration to state that in a matter of an hour, you can drive from shorts weather in the Piedmont to sweater weather in the Blue Ridge.

The best months for comfortable hiking temperatures are the "shoulder" seasons of spring and fall. Summertime becomes extremely humid; in spring and summer, fast-moving and often violent storms can alter your hiking plans within minutes. In Prince William Forest Park, a springtime storm altered the course of the Quantico River and its South Branch to such an extent that floodplains, once lush with grass, small shrubs, and skinny trees, were scoured clean by water that rose several feet in a matter of an hour. Tree trunks as thick as a bridge piling were tossed about like toothpicks. One need not have witnessed it in person, but only walk the trails in its aftermath, to gain a new appreciation for weather's powerful impact on the environment.

Many try to escape the height of city heat by heading to higher elevations or by seeking out coastal breezes. Or, you can pass up the hot sun and concrete of the capital by slipping into Rock Creek Park or its neighboring stream valley parks around Georgetown. Winter hiking on a cloudless blue day brings the reward of uncrowded trails and unobstructed views through a leafless forest. Summer thunderstorms with dangerous lightning are quick moving and dramatic, while fall might bring a tropical storm. Flash flooding may occur on some trails and along streambeds. Always check the NOAA weather reports on a weather-band radio or online before heading out.

Flora and Fauna

Mid-Atlantic forests are primarily broadleaf, deciduous trees. In moist pockets below 4,500 feet elevation, the Appalachian cove forest holds more than twenty species of trees: beech, sugar maple, and yellow poplar noticeable among these. Stands of eastern hemlock once made for impressive viewing; however, damage from the invasive woolly adelgid is now widespread. Evidence of its work is especially striking in Shenandoah National Park, where entire stands of hemlock are defoliated and dying. Even so, quiet, cool pockets of this venerable evergreen may still be found along isolated mountain streams.

The Appalachian oak-hickory forest rises to dominance with the Blue Ridge. Hickory is the successor of the American chestnut. In the early twentieth century, it was estimated one of every four trees in the Appalachians was a chestnut. Today, few grow taller than 6 feet before succumbing to the chestnut blight.

Virginia's Piedmont has traditionally supported agriculture. By the twentieth century, generations of farming left large swaths of barren land. Where forest returned, they are primarily bland white oak and Virginia and loblolly pine. In Virginia state and national forests, oak and poplar are managed for harvest. Willow oak, river birch,

White-tailed deer are common sightings on woodland trails.

hickory, and ash grow as well. Turkey, fox, deer, raccoon, and squirrel populate these pockets of rejuvenated woodlands.

Grasses, saltmeadow hay, and hearty shrubs such as wax myrtle populate coastal fringes. These are some of the most resilient plants in the world, able to withstand harsh winds and saltwater conditions. Inland from the beaches and dunes, lagoons mix a daily tidal wash with mainland runoff. Fish spawn here, and crustaceans such as fiddler crab live out early years on a nutrient-rich diet. On the mainland, forests of pines and oak typify the flat coastal region. In swampy areas, bald cypress and live oak are often draped with Spanish moss.

Violet

The forest understory provides the hiker with a seasonal palette of color. White dogwood and delicate pink redbud come before trees leaf out in early spring. Thousands of cherry trees bloom pale pink on the National Mall in April. Throughout the forest, the ubiquitous mountain laurel blooms in May, and its cousin the rhododendron in July.

Don't forget to look down: Wildflowers are profuse throughout the region in spring, from common purple violets, spring beauties, and white toothwort to the rarer Turks cap lily. G. Richard Thompson Wildlife Management Area is thought to hold the largest North American population of large-flowered trillium, a white tripetal flower. Beginning in late winter/early spring, look for naturalized daffodils around old homesteads. Since they don't grow naturally, wherever you see these cheerful harbingers of spring, you'll undoubtedly find the remains of a home foundation, a rock wall, a fence, or a well nearby.

Deer have rebounded from overhunting and habitat destruction of a century ago to rank as almost a nuisance in some areas. Black bear are found in the Blue Ridge and are quite common sightings in Shenandoah National Park. A hiker's footsteps may flush turkey or grouse. Raccoon are primarily nocturnal animals and are scavengers, so be mindful of dropping any trash or food crumbs. Bobcat and coyote are found throughout the region, but generally in larger areas of preserved forest.

The river systems host a wide range of life from the common brook trout to the endangered freshwater mussel. Salamander and crayfish can be seen in streams by the quiet observer. Wild trout streams, stocked ponds and lakes, and seasonal Chesapeake Bay runs of rockfish and croaker provide variety for anglers.

The region's wildlife has witnessed many successes under the federal Endangered Species Act, perhaps none as stirring as the return of a viable bald eagle population. Places like Mason Neck Wildlife Refuge and other preserves along the lower Potomac are renowned nesting and viewing sites. How apropos that sightings of our national bird, virtually extinct fifty years ago, are becoming more and more common around our nation's capital.

Wilderness Restrictions/Regulations

Public lands in the region fall into four broad categories: national parks and refuges; state parks, forests, and natural areas; private conservancy lands that are open to public use; and municipal parks.

Each entity has its own set of regulations. What's more, this book covers portions of three states and the District of Columbia, each with its own rules and operating procedures covering everything from pets to refuse (e.g., Maryland state parks are trash-free, requiring you to pack it out with you). But as you take advantage of this spectacular region, remember that our planet is very dear, very special, and very fragile. All of us should do everything we can to keep it clean, beautiful, and healthy, including following the Green Tips you'll find throughout this book.

You'll find varying degrees of public use among these designations. For example, hunting is allowed in some forests and parks, while wildlife refuges exist for the benefit of animals, not humans. Sections may be closed off to the public during breeding seasons. Conversely, federal, state, and municipal parks exist for humans, a fact reflected in their sometimes crowded conditions.

Signing in to the trail register at Cedarville State Forest (Hike 4)

In the following chapters, we've strived to give you the most accurate, thorough, and up-to-date information on regulations and public use. When in doubt, we give you contact information so you can call ahead.

Getting Around

AREA CODES

The Washington, D.C., area code is 202. Northern Virginia area codes are 703, 571, and 540. Area codes for Maryland areas covered in this book are 301 and 240. The area code for all of West Virginia is 304.

ROADS

For current information on Washington, D.C., road conditions, weather, and closures, contact the District Department of Transportation at (202) 727-1000, or visit http://ddot.dc.gov, where you can sign up for automatic road updates by e-mail.

◀ *Top: Jogger on the Mount Vernon Trail (Hike 14)*
 Bottom: The author pauses at the Jefferson Memorial (Hike 27).

For Virginia conditions contact the Virginia Department of Transportation (VDOT) twenty-four-hour Highway Helpline at (800) 367-7623 or visit www.vdot.state.va.us. For Maryland conditions contact the Maryland State Highway Administration at (410) 545-0300 or visit www.sha.state.md.us. For West Virginia's current road conditions, call (877) WVA-ROAD or visit www.wvdot.com.

BY AIR

Dulles International Airport (IAD) is 23 miles northwest of downtown Washington, D.C. Ronald Reagan Washington National Airport (DCA) is located in Arlington, Virginia, just across the Potomac River from D.C. The Web site for both is www.mwaa.com. Baltimore/Washington International Thurgood Marshall Airport (BWI) is located between the two cities. The Web site is www.bwiairport.com.

To book reservations online, check out your favorite airline's Web site or search one of the following travel sites for the best price: www.cheaptickets.com, www.expedia.com, www.previewtravel.com, www.orbitz.com, www.priceline.com, http://travel.yahoo.com, www.travelocity.com, or www.trip.com—just to name a few.

BY RAIL

Washington, D.C., is served by AMTRAK. Schedules and pricing are at www.amtrak.com or by calling (800) 872-7245. Washington Metropolitan Area Transit Authority (known as "the Metro") operates rail and bus service throughout D.C. and suburbs in Maryland and Virginia. Visit www.wmata.com or call (202) 637-7000. Virginia Railway Express (VRE) operates commuter rail service weekdays to Fredericksburg and Manassas. For more information visit www.vre.org or call (800) RIDE-VRE. Maryland Rail Commuter (MARC) operates commuter rail service weekdays along the Potomac River in Maryland with an important stop for hikers in Harpers Ferry, West Virginia. For more information visit www.mtamaryland.com or call (800) 543-9809.

BY BUS

In addition to Metrobus (see By Rail), Greyhound serves many towns in the region; call (800) 231-2222 or visit www.greyhound.com for more information.

VISITOR INFORMATION

For general information on Virginia, visit the Web site of the Virginia Tourism Corporation, www.virginia.org, or call (800) 321-3244. For general information on Maryland, visit the Web site of the Maryland Office of Tourism, www.visitmaryland.org, or call (866) 639-3526. For information on visiting Washington, D.C., visit the Web site of Destination DC, www.washington.org, or call (800) 422-8644. For general information on West Virginia, visit the Web site of the West Virginia Division of Tourism, www.wvtourism.com, or call (800) 225-5982.

How to Use This Guide

Take a close enough look, and you'll find that this guide contains just about everything you'll ever need to choose, plan for, enjoy, and survive a hike near Washington, D.C. Stuffed with useful D.C.–area information, *Best Hikes Washington, D.C.* features twenty-eight mapped and cued hikes. Here's an outline of the book's major components:

Each section begins with an **introduction to the region,** in which you're given a sweeping look at the lay of the land. Each hike then starts with a short **summary** of the hike's highlights. These quick overviews give you a taste of the hiking adventures to follow. You'll learn about the trail terrain and what surprises each route has to offer. Many chapters also include a **Kid Appeal** recommendation that provides parents with a quick reference for keeping their youngster engaged.

Following the overview you'll find the **hike specs:** quick, nitty-gritty details of the hike. Most are self-explanatory, but here are some details on others:

Distance: The total distance of the recommended route—one-way for loop hikes, the round-trip on an out-and-back or lollipop hike, point-to-point for a shuttle. Options are additional.

Approximate hiking time: The average time it will take to cover the route. It is based on the total distance, elevation gain, and condition and difficulty of the trail. Your fitness level will also affect your time.

A wild turkey

Canada Geese in wetlands of Mason Neck State Park (Hike 20)

Difficulty: Each hike has been assigned a level of difficulty. The rating system was developed from several sources and personal experience. These levels are meant to be a guideline only and may prove easier or harder for different people depending on ability and physical fitness.

> *Easy*—Five miles or less total trip distance in one day, with minimal elevation gain, and paved or smooth-surfaced dirt trail.

> *Moderate*—Up to 10 miles total trip distance in one day, with moderate elevation gain and potentially rough terrain.

> *Difficult*—More than 10 miles total trip distance in one day, strenuous elevation gains, and rough and/or rocky terrain.

Trail surface: General information about what to expect underfoot.

Seasons: General information on the best time of year to hike.

Other trail users: Such as horseback riders, mountain bikers, inline skaters, etc.

Handicapped accessibility: When available we describe the features that make a park or a trail accessible to people with disabilities.

Canine compatibility: Know the trail regulations before you take your dog hiking with you. Dogs are not allowed on several trails in this book.

Land status: National forest, county open space, national park wilderness, etc.

Fees and permits: Whether you need to carry any money with you for park entrance fees and permits.

Schedule: Information on when the hike area is open.

Facilities: Amenities available at the trailhead or along the route.

Maps: This is a list of other maps to supplement the maps in this book. USGS maps are the best source for accurate topographical information, but the local park map may show more recent trails. Use both.

Trail contacts: This is the location, phone number, and Web site URL for the local land manager(s) in charge of all the trails within the selected hike. Before you head out, get trail access information, or contact the land manager after your visit if you see problems with trail erosion, damage, or misuse.

Other: Other information that will enhance your hike.

Special considerations: This section calls your attention to specific trail hazards, like a lack of water or hunting seasons.

The **Finding the trailhead** section gives you dependable driving directions to where you'll want to park. **The Hike** is the meat of the chapter. Detailed and honest, it's a carefully researched impression of the trail. It also often includes lots of area history, both natural and human. Under **Miles and Directions,** mileage cues identify all turns and trail name changes, as well as points of interest. **Options** are also given for many hikes to make your journey shorter or longer depending on the amount of time you have. The **Hike Information** section provides information on local events and attractions, restaurants, hiking tours, and hiking organizations.

Don't feel restricted to the routes and trails that are mapped here. Be adventurous and use this guide as a platform to discover new routes for yourself. One of the

A hand-held GPS unit and a digital voice recorder are the authors' tools of the trade.

simplest ways to begin this is to just turn the map upside down and hike any route in reverse. The change in perspective is often fantastic, and the hike should feel quite different. With this in mind, it'll be like getting two distinctly different hikes on each map. For your own purposes, you may wish to copy the route directions onto a small sheet of paper to help you while hiking, or photocopy the map and cue sheet to take with you. Otherwise, just slip the whole book in your backpack and take it all with you. Enjoy your time in the outdoors and remember to pack out what you pack in.

How to Use the Maps

Overview map: This map shows the location of each hike in the area by hike number.

Route map: This is your primary guide to each hike. It shows all of the accessible roads and trails, points of interest, water, landmarks, and geographical features. It also distinguishes trails from roads, and paved roads from unpaved roads. The selected route is highlighted, and directional arrows point the way.

Map Legend

Transportation

==⬡95==	Freeway/Interstate Highway
==⬡1==	US Highway
==⬡4==	State Highway
==▭1431==	Other Road
== == ==	Unpaved Road
⊢—⊣—⊣	Railroad

Trails

▬▬▬▬	Selected Route
- - - - - -	Trail or Fire Road
⟶	Direction of Travel

Water Features

(shape)	Body of Water
∿	River or Creek
⁔ ⁔ ⁔	Marsh
�══	Waterfalls

Land Management

▭	Local & State Parks
⌐ ⌐	National Forest & Wilderness Areas

Symbols

✗	Airport
⌣	Bridge
■	Building/Point of Interest
⛺	Campground
⸸	Gate
♿	Handicap Parking Area
▲	Mountain/Peak
⛩	Observation Platform
Ⓟ	Parking
⊞	Picnic Area
🛈	Ranger Station
🚻	Restroom
⛰	Scenic View
▥	Steps
○	Towns and Cities
⓴	Trailhead
❓	Visitor Center

Trail Finder

Hike No.	Hike Name	Best Hikes for Beach/Coast Lovers	Best Hikes for History Lovers	Best Hikes for Waterfalls	Best Hikes for Geology/Fossils	Best Hikes for Children	Best Hikes for Dogs	Best Hikes for Great Views	Best Hikes for Bird Lovers	Best Hikes for Tree Huggers	Best Hikes for Handicapped Accessibility
1	American Chestnut Land Trust									●	
2	Calvert Cliffs State Park	●				●	●				
3	Catoctin Mountain Park		●		●	●	●	●			
4	Cedarville State Forest					●	●				
5	Cunningham Falls State Park			●		●	●	●			●
6	Gambrill State Park					●	●				
7	Great Falls Park, MD / Chesapeake and Ohio Canal National Historic Park		●	●	●	●	●	●			●
8	Jug Bay Natural Area (Patuxent River Park)	●				●	●		●		
9	Patuxent National Wildlife Refuge						●		●		●
10	Rosaryville State Park					●	●		●		
11	Seneca Creek Greenway Trail North (#1)				●	●	●			●	
12	Seneca Creek Greenway Trail South (#2)		●		●	●	●			●	

		1	2	3	4	5	6	7	8	9	10
13	Sugarloaf Mountain				•	•	•	•		•	
14	Arlington National Cemetery	•								•	
15	Great Falls Park	•			•	•	•		•		
16	G. Richard Thompson Wildlife Management Area		•				•				
17	Harpers Ferry, VA/MD/WV	•			•	•	•			•	
18	Leesylvania State Park	•				•	•			•	•
19	Manassas National Battlefield Park	•				•				•	
20	Mason Neck State Park	•		•			•			•	
21	Overall Run, SNP				•	•			•	•	
22	Piney River, SNP		•			•			•	•	
23	Prince William Forest Park	•	•			•	•	•			
24	Riverbend Park	•		•		•	•				
25	Sky Meadows State Park				•	•	•			•	
26	Georgetown Loop (Rock Creek Park South)	•				•	•			•	
27	National Mall Monuments	•					•			•	
28	Rock Creek Park North	•		•		•	•			•	

Maryland

Walk with us for a moment through Maryland. We begin at the water's edge, the riverine and bay environments where land and water mingle, where the purple-blossoming pickerelweed and broad-leafed arrow arum define an amazingly productive environment rich with frogs, snakes, and small mammals.

Walk west where the land shifts from flat coastal to a hilly Piedmont. It's a subtle transition all but obliterated by the region's dense population, yet dramatically underscored by the Great Falls of the Potomac. Look around the forests, too. The loblolly pines and sweet gum and holly that characterized the upland forest of the coastal plain are now oaks and hickory trees typical of the Piedmont.

Beyond Frederick, a long rampart of folded and faulted rock visible from and parallel to Route 15 marks the start of Maryland's mountain region. These are the Catoctin Mountains, part of the Blue Ridge complex that extends north into Pennsylvania and south into Tennessee.

In this broad sweep, from Chesapeake Bay shoreline to Blue Ridge rock outcrops, wildly different environments make every outdoor excursion a discovery. The coastal marshes attract wildfowl and shorebirds by the thousands in every season. The Potomac Gorge's micro-habitats with their attendant plants and insects have scientists declaring this region one of the most biologically diverse areas in the world. Stream valley parks follow the winding routes of streams like Seneca Creek, where flat bottomland forests and steep streamside hills make for sometimes—and surprisingly—rugged terrain.

In the cool mountain preserves amid the Catoctin Mountains, Maryland's tallest waterfall pours off the mountain side at McAfee Falls. The car- and house-size boulders of Cat Rock are a geologic monument to the powerful forces that shaped the mountains millions of years ago. And at Maryland Heights, near Harpers Ferry, you can witness the merging of two great rivers, the Shenandoah flowing from Virginia and the Potomac coming out of the West Virginia highlands.

◀ *Top: Bird watching at the American Chestnut Land Trust (Hike 1)*
Bottom: Marsh overlook at Jug Bay Natural Area (Hike 8)

Trailhead in Rosaryville State Park (Hike 10)

Human history is inseparable from the natural history here, and the physical character of each region helped shape customs and lifestyles. The coastal area was primarily agriculture, first with tobacco and later farm crops. The rivers were the highways, marked by wharfs and small towns. Speculators panned for gold in the hills outside Washington D.C. Expansionist dreams were embodied in construction of the C&O Canal. Mountain dwellers eked out a living marked by subsistence farming and charcoal production.

By and large, these habits and manners have all but faded in the day-to-day bustle and spread of suburbia. To all, that is, except the hiker. It is our happy lot to find the remains of old mills along the stream valley parks, like Black Rock Mill on the Great Seneca Creek. We can appreciate the backbreaking labor to build a charcoal pit or walk through the dark swamps that hid presidential assassin John Wilkes Booth in 1865.

We've walked only 100 miles or so from the water's edge to the mountains. A small region packed with so much to see.

1 American Chestnut Land Trust

Parkers Creek is the centerpiece of the American Chestnut Land Trust's 958-acre holdings in Calvert County. The creek's tidal salt marshes, upland forest of oak and hickory, and its many tributaries are billed as the last undeveloped watershed on the Chesapeake Bay's western shore. Of the described routes here, only those departing from Double Oak Farm (north tract) offer hikers glimpses of the stream. The south tract, covering old family farms, cemeteries, and a burgeoning beaver community, has its own special character as you explore muddy footpaths along Gravatt Stream and Jett Stream.

NORTH TRACT

Start: From the American Chestnut Land Trust's Double Oak Farm trailhead

Distance: Option 1: Horse Swamp Trail, 3.0-mile out-and-back; Option 2: Parkers Creek Loop, 4.1 miles

Approximate hiking time: 2 hours

Difficulty: Easy due to well-marked paths and only moderate elevation loss and gain. Of either hike, Horse Swamp Trail features terrain that is steeper—but even these are of short duration.

Trail surface: Both routes begin as mowed field paths but quickly adopt the character of the woodland that surrounds their namesake streams. Upland trails are old farm roads, while stream valley paths are single-track dirt paths that span low elevation and wetland via footbridges and boardwalks.

SOUTH TRACT

Start: From the American Chestnut Land Trust's Scientists Cliffs Road trailhead

Distance: Option 3: 4.7-mile loop

Approximate hiking time: 2 to 3 hours

Difficulty: Easy due to the short distance, minimum elevation gain, and wide, easy-to-follow paths

Trail surface: Old dirt farm roads characterize the upland paths. In the stream valleys, along Gravatt Stream and the Jett Stream, narrow footpaths have a woodsy and scenic character.

Seasons: Best in spring or autumn, seasons that coincide with the height of bird and beaver activity

Other trail users: Horseback riders, joggers, cross-country skiers, hunters

Canine compatibility: Leashed dogs permitted

Land status: Private land trust

Fees and permits: No fees required. Groups of more than 10 people are encouraged to apply for a group permit.

Schedule: Open dawn to dusk, 365 days a year.

Facilities: Picnic tables and a chemical toilet both trailheads.

Maps: *DeLorme Maryland/Delaware Atlas & Gazetteer:* Page 38 D3. USGS 7.5 minute series: *Prince Frederick, MD.* Trail maps are free and available at trail registers.

Trail contacts: American Chestnut Land Trust, Double Oak Road, Prince Frederick, MD 20678; (410) 414-3400; www.acltweb.org

Special considerations: The land trust requests that all visitors sign in at trail registers located at both parking areas. Groups are limited to 10 people or fewer. The land trust holds a special Deer Harvest Program each fall.

Finding the trailhead: Distance from Washington, D.C.: 49 miles

Double Oak Farm from the junction of MD 4 and MD 2 in Sunderland: Drive south on combined MD 2/4 (Solomons Island Road) for 8 miles. In Prince Frederick, turn left (east) on MD 402 (Dares Beach Road). In 2.4 miles, turn right (south) onto Double Oak Road. Follow this road for another 1.0 miles, and then veer left onto a gravel road. There is a metal gate (open during park hours) and signs for American Chestnut Land Trust property. Enter a gravel parking area adjacent to an equipment shed. Access to both Horse Swamp and the Parkers Creek Loop begins at a trailboard sign next to the equipment shed. Trailhead GPS: N38 32.821' / W76 31.982'

Scientists Cliffs from Prince Frederick: Continue south on MD 2/4 through Prince Frederick. Approaching the town of Port Republic, look for brown signs indicating the American Chestnut Land Trust. 5 miles from Prince Frederick, turn left (east) on Parkers Creek Road. Immediately cross over MD 765 (Old Solomons Island Road). Go 0.4 mile and turn right (south) on Scientists Cliffs Road. In another 0.8 mile, turn left (east) into the American Chestnut Land Trust parking lot. There is an equipment shed with a porch near the field. Gravatt Lane/Swamp Trail begins at a cable across a farm road near the entrance to the parking lot. Trailhead GPS: N38 30.752' / W76 31.112'

The Hike

The American Chestnut Land Trust (ACLT) is named for a tree that succumbed to the chestnut blight, a disease introduced to the United States in 1904. Within forty years, the blight had traveled down the Appalachian chain, destroying a climax forest that had stood for thousands of years. In mountain areas, American chestnut trees are often the standing white trunks, bare of any bark, ghostly white, like tree skeletons amid an otherwise healthy forest.

A note at the southern tract trailhead for the ACLT states simply: Losing this tree is a sad reminder that all things in Nature must be enjoyed and protected while they are here.

The same could be said for land that is owned or managed by the land trust. Upland farms on both sides of Parkers Creek protect what the trust describes as the "only pristine marsh on the western shore of the Chesapeake Bay." Although in its history this area has seen tobacco farms and related settlements, it is absent these activities today. Old fields are now thick forests of Virginia pine or the succession hardwood forest of maples, oaks, hickories, and black walnuts.

Choosing which tract to explore—the northern trails leave from Double Oak Farm, headquarters for the land trust; southern trails leave from an unattended trailhead on Scientists Cliff Road—is a choice between experiencing Parkers Creek firsthand or exploring a dynamic farms-to-woodland habitat. And thanks to the new 2.2 mile North-South Trail—and a raft to cross Parkers Creek—hikers can join these two environments into a single experience.

Both the Horse Swamp Trail and the Parkers Creek Loop, accessed via the northern tract, are easy routes that descend to overlooks over the stream. In the fall, the marsh grass is golden brown. Come springtime, it shows a fresh green tint. At the junction of Old Parkers Creek Road, where a bridge once spanned the creek, it is

Remains of an ancient American Chestnut

ACLT's southern tract harbored Maryland's largest American chestnut tree. The specimen finally succumbed to the blight that has virtually wiped out the tree from East Coast forests, although its ancient, decayed trunk and root system still sends up young shoots. GPS: N38 30.969' / W76 31.139'

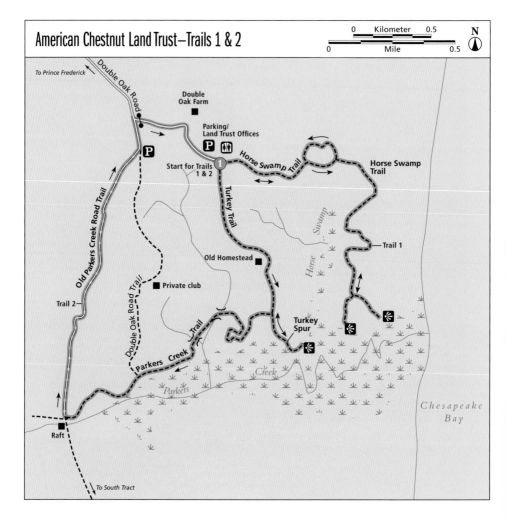

possible to sit, in the closing hours of the day, and wait for the loud slap sound of a beaver tail. A hand-pulled raft lets hikers cross the creek here and continue their exploration of the watershed. The forest floor bursts with mayapple in spring and large specimens of jack-in-the-pulpit. The handful of small tributaries crossed on Parkers Creek Trail show the broad leaves of three typical freshwater marshes: arrow arum, spatterdock, and pickerelweed. The last shows characteristic purple flowers in spring. All three plants are valuable food sources for wood ducks and other waterfowl, including migratory shorebirds like the sorrel and black rail.

From the southern tract trailhead on Scientists Cliff Road, Gravatt Lane offers the quickest access to what's interesting. Splitting from it onto Swamp Trail, you descend to follow a small tributary. At the cutoff for the chestnut tree memorial, continue walking to visit the marshy backwaters of another Parkers Creek tributary. By late spring, the mayapple leaves have taken on a yellowish hue, adding a new color to the brown- and tan-tinged understory thick with fallen leaves.

The marsh boardwalk extends out for several hundred feet over ground that is knee-high in water in spring but considerably less wet come late summer and fall. A morning chorus of bullfrogs—a descending, bowlike note—and songbirds keep up at a steady pace. Scarlet tanagers, red-eyed vireos, and wood thrushes are present. The wood thrush is especially present as evening falls, its multi-pitched, multi-syllable call filtering down from the darkening woods.

Miles and Directions

Trail 1: Horse Swamp

0.0 START from a trailboard map at the Double Oak Farm trailhead parking lot. Follow Horse Swamp Trail, a mowed path, through a field, passing the trailhead for Turkey Trail en route. At the far side of the field, follow the yellow-blazed trail into the woods and descend on a wide dirt path. (*Note:* Turkey Trail is the first leg of the Parkers Creek Loop.)

0.5 Veer right at a junction with the return leg of Horse Swamp Trail.

0.6 Stay straight, cross Horse Swamp on a footbridge.

1.5 Reach a fork in the trail. Both spurs, to the right and left, lead to overlooks of Parkers Creek. (*FYI:* Views from both overlooks are limited in summertime due to the trees and leaves blocking them.)

1.7 After exploring both spurs and overlooks, retrace your path by hiking north on Horse Swamp Trail.

2.4 Cross Horse Swamp on a footbridge and turn right (north). Cross a 30-foot-long boardwalk, and then start climbing the hillside.

2.5 Turn right onto the northern leg of the loop.

2.6 Bear right (south) as the Horse Swamp Trail finishes its loop.

3.0 HIKE ENDS at the Double Oak Farm trailhead parking lot.

Trail 2: Parkers Creek

0.0 START from the junction of Horse Swamp Trail and Turkey Trail, 60 feet east of the Double Oak Farm trailhead parking lot. Turn right (south) on Turkey Trail. (*FYI:* A number of signs alongside this trail help interpret the natural surroundings and the historic Scales/Simmons home site.)

0.5 The trail levels briefly at the site of an old homestead, then continues its descent to Parkers Creek.

0.6 Stay straight (south) at the junction with Parkers Creek Trail and merge onto Turkey Spur, an out-and-back trail that descends to the marshy fringes of Parkers Creek.

0.9 Spur trail ends. Turn around and return to Parkers Creek Trail.

1.2 Turn left (west) onto Parkers Creek Trail.

1.6 Descend into a gully and cross a tributary of Parkers Creek. Ahead, another footbridge and corduroys (hewn logs laid side by side) help you navigate over low, wet sections of trail.

2.2 Stay straight (west) on Parkers Creek Trail at a junction with Double Oak Road Trail on the right.

2.4 Turn right (north) onto Old Parkers Creek Road Trail. (*Side trip:* Turn left and descend to the creek. A small four-person raft allows you to cross Parkers Creek, max capacity 500 lbs, where a 2.2 mile trail heads south and links hikers with trails in the south tract of ACLT. This trail is described as "challenging" with steep climbs and six stream crossings.)

3.7 Emerge from woods onto Double Oak Road. Turn left (north) and walk up the paved road.

3.8 Turn right onto the gravel driveway that leads to the Double Oak Farm headquarters.

4.1 HIKE ENDS at the Double Oak Farm trailhead parking lot.

Trail 3: South Trails

0.0 START from the Scientists Cliffs Road trailhead, at the south end of the parking area. Gravatt Lane/Swamp Trail is blocked to traffic by a cable. Follow Gravatt Lane straight (north) down a tree-shaded farm road that divides fields on your left and right. (*Note:* Avoid trailheads for Bloodroot and Flint Trails, which veer left [west] and cross the field to the woodland beyond.)

0.2 Turn right (east) and pass a wooden outhouse on your right. (*Note:* Wallace Lane continues straight to a junction with Bloodroot Trail in 0.1 miles.)

0.3 Veer right (east) on Swamp Trail at a fork.

0.7 Stay straight (north) on Swamp Trail at a junction with the Chestnut Trail on the left. (*FYI:* Signs here indicate the trail ahead is closed at the Beaver Dam.)

1.0 Stay straight (north) on Swamp Trail past an unmarked trail that branches left.

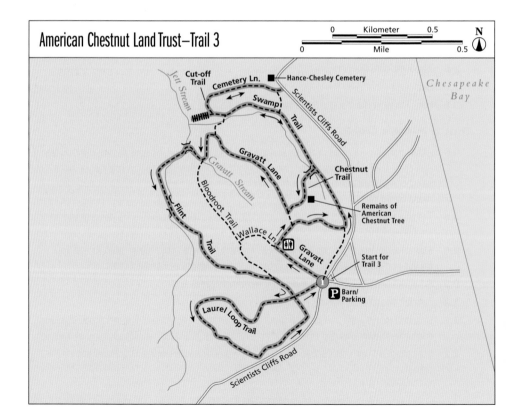

American Chestnut Land Trust–Trail 3

Hance-Chesley Cemetery

1.05 Stay straight (north) on Swamp Trail as an unmarked trail branches right. (*Note:* This is the access trail to Cemetery Lane.)

1.1 Reach the end of the boardwalk, turn around, and return to the Cemetery Lane access trail.

1.15 Turn left on the Cemetery Lane access trail and climb to the top of a small ridge.

1.2 Turn right on Cemetery Lane.

1.5 Reach the Hance-Chesley Cemetery. Explore, then retrace your steps to the Swamp Trail.

1.8 Turn left (south) on the Swamp Trail.

2.3 Turn right (west) on the Chestnut Trail. The landmark chestnut tree is marked on the left side of the trail as you climb. (It succumbed to the chestnut blight that affects all American chestnut trees; suckers, or shoots, now stem from the rotted trunk.)

2.4 Turn right (north) on Gravatt Lane.

2.9 Cross Gravatt Stream on a footbridge, then turn right (north) on the Flint Trail. Ahead, the trail crosses small streams three times on footbridges.

3.3 Bear right on Flint Trail to cross a boardwalk over a wetland. Avoid an unmarked, less-defined trail that forks left and climbs the hillside.

3.6 Turn right (south) on Bloodroot Trail.

3.7 Reach a Y junction and turn right (west) on Laurel Loop Trail.

4.0 Cross a stream on a footbridge and begin climbing the hillside opposite.

4.6 Turn right (east) on Bloodroot Trail. Descend to a field and cross diagonally right, heading toward the road.

4.7 HIKE ENDS at the Gravatt Lane/Swamp Trail trailhead.

Hike Information

Local information: Calvert County Tourism, 175 Main St., Prince Frederick; (410) 535-3825; www.choosecalvert.com

Chesapeake Bay Gateways Network, Annapolis, MD; www.findyourchesapeake .com. This is an initiative of the National Park Service Chesapeake Bay Program Office, including more than 150 parks, wildlife refuges, museums, and hiking, biking, paddling, and driving trails that promote the Chesapeake Bay's natural and cultural history.

Local events/attractions: Double Oak Farm, trailhead for Horse Swamp and Parkers Creek hikes, features an education garden demonstrating natural home gardening, historical and Native American farming techniques. Farm produce is donated to a local food pantry and volunteer gardeners are welcome.

Good eats: Jerry's Place Restaurant, 1541 Solomon's Island Road, Prince Frederick; (410) 535-3242; www.jerrys-place.com

Hike tours: Volunteers and staff members lead guided nature hikes and canoe trips seasonally.

GREEN TIP

All Maryland State Parks and State Forests are "trash free." That means there are no garbage pails or waste containers provided for visitors. Whatever trash you bring in or find, you must take away.

2 Calvert Cliffs State Park

A shallow sea once covered all of southern Maryland. When it receded ten to twenty million years ago, the steep shoreline now known as Calvert Cliffs was exposed and began to erode. The cliffs are still eroding today (making them dangerous to walk on), continually revealing the East Coast's largest assemblage of fossils—over 600 species of sharks, whales, rays, and seabirds that were the size of small airplanes!

Start: From the Red Trail parking area at the edge of a small pond
Distance: 4.6-mile loop
Approximate hiking time: 3 hours
Difficulty: Easy due to a minimum of elevation gain; well-marked, graded trails; and easy terrain
Trail surface: A combination of boardwalk and sandy roads mark the main stem of the trail network. Dirt footpaths alternate between low streamside terrain and upland forests.
Seasons: June through Sept, when a hot hike out to the bay is relieved with a little bit of wading along the shoreline
Other trail users: Bikers, hunters, cross-country skiers, runners, horseback riders, anglers
Canine compatibility: Dogs permitted
Land status: State park
Fees and permits: Per-vehicle entrance fee

Schedule: Sunrise to sunset daily. During summer weekends and holidays when the park reaches maximum capacity, it closes to new visitors for the day.
Facilities: Restrooms, picnic areas, playground
Maps: DeLorme *Maryland/Delaware Atlas & Gazetteer:* Page 31 B4. USGS: *Cove Point, MD. Calvert Cliffs State Park Trail Guide* is available as a download on the park's web page; for purchase online at www.shopdnr.com/southern marylandtrailguides.aspx; or by mail from the Maryland Department of Natural Resources, Maryland Park Service, Attn: Trail Guides, 580 Taylor Ave., Annapolis, MD 21401.
Trail contacts: Calvert Cliffs State Park, c/o Smallwood State Park, 2750 Sweden Point Rd., Marbury, MD 20658, (301) 743-7613; physical location of Calvert Cliffs: 10540 H. G. Trueman Parkway, Lusby, MD; http://dnr .maryland.gov/publiclands/Pages/southern/ calvertcliffs.aspx

Finding the trailhead: Distance from Washington, D.C.: 56 miles
   From Prince Frederick: Drive south on MD 2/4. In 14 miles, turn left onto H.G. Trueman Parkway and immediately enter the state park and follow the one-way road to the pay station. Continue past a maintenance shed and bathroom on the right, and descend to a parking area at the edge of a pond. Trailhead GPS: N38 23.695' / W76 26.091'

The Hike

In the annals of great North American explorations, many are familiar with the exploits of Lewis and Clark, who explored land from the Mississippi to the Pacific from 1804 to 1806. But nearly 200 years earlier, Capt. John Smith led a crew of fourteen men out into the Chesapeake Bay in the summer of 1608. Using a small boat

Calvert beach

powered by sail and oars, they left Jamestown Settlement and sailed into the Chesapeake Bay. Their journey touched on the eastern shore of Virginia and Maryland, and the western shore from the top of the Bay to Hampton Roads in the south. The reaches of great rivers like the Patuxent, Potomac, Rappahannock, and other smaller streams were explored as far as the flat water would allow.

Smith's goals were derived from a charter from the London Company, which financed the Jamestown project. One was to locate a "northwest passage" to India. Another was to explore and document as much land, creeks, and bays as possible, and to claim those lands for the English crown. As a result, Smith compiled most of the information known about Native Americans and the ecology of the Chesapeake Bay region in the 1600s.

It's all about the shark's tooth. A short stretch of Bay shoreline is open to the public, and it attracts kids of all ages searching for the elusive prehistoric prize: a shark's tooth. Stick to the Red Trail for the most direct route to and from the water. Best collecting is usually after a storm, when the supply of shells and other fossils is replenished. Low tide, when more beach is exposed, is the best time to look for fossils.

So it is with Calvert Cliffs. After exploring the Nanticoke River, Smith abandoned further exploration of the Eastern Shore and struck west to cross the Bay. He used as a landmark a set of tall cliffs that were lit up by the morning sun on the day of the crossing.

"Finding this eastern shore shallow broken isles, and for the most part without fresh water, we passed by the straits of Limbo for the western shore. So broad is the Bay here we could scarce perceive the great high cliffs on the other side. By them we anchored that night and called them Rickard's Cliffs." (Capt. John Smith's journal)

Smith named locations for local Native American tribes but also for men on his voyage. So it is that what is known today as Tangier Island was originally named Russell Isles for the doctor who accompanied them. The source of Rickard's Cliffs is thought to be Smith's mother (who was not on the trip), who came from "Rickards, at the Great Heck, in Yorkshire" (England).

The cliffs that line the Maryland shore are a geologic phenomenon. They were formed between ten and twenty million years ago and contain some of the largest Miocene fossil deposits in the world. The Red Trail is the "superhighway" for fossil seekers at Calvert Cliffs State Park. Access to the cliff line of these 130-foot-high banks is blocked because of erosion problems; walking the base of the cliff line is prohibited as well due to landslides.

As a geologic feature, the cliffs that can be glimpsed at the mouth of Grays Creek in Calvert Cliffs State Park are one piece of a line that continues north to Chesapeake Beach. They are justly famous. According to the Maryland Geological Survey, the first fossil described from North America was found in deposits of the St. Mary's Formation, which constitutes the youngest geologic formation present at Calvert Cliffs. That record was published in an English journal in 1865, some 257 years after John Smith had used the cliffs as a beacon to help his corps of explorers cross the Chesapeake Bay.

Miles and Directions

0.0 START from a parking lot and trail signboard at the edge of a pond. Locate the Red Trail trailhead and follow this dirt and crushed-rock path to a boardwalk along the pond's south shoreline. A sign at this trailhead points toward the Cliff Trail and the parking area.

0.1 Veer right and avoid a footpath that leads uphill to the left.

0.2 Turn right where the Red Trail, until now a sandy footpath, merges with a gravel-lined forest road.

0.3 Turn right off the gravel road and follow the Red Trail, which is now a dirt footpath.

0.35 Stay straight as the Yellow Trail intersects with the Red Trail on the right. (*Note:* This junction marks the return portion of this route.)

0.6 Stay straight as a dirt road merges with the Red Trail on the left.

0.7 Stay straight as the Blue Trail merges with the Red Trail from the right. The trail here is hard-packed sand, and the footing is uneven over exposed tree roots.

1.4 Pass a boardwalk that leads to a viewing platform on Grays Creek.

Calvert Cliffs State Park

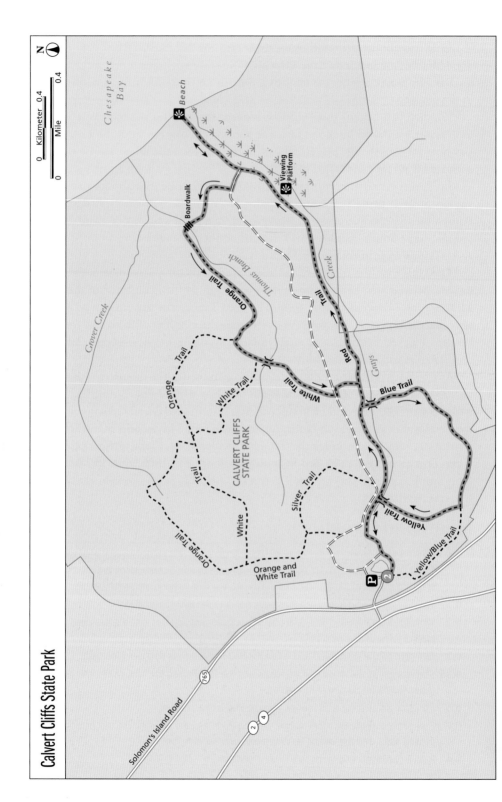

1.6 At a junction with a gravel service road, turn right (east).

1.8 The Red Trail ends at the Chesapeake Bay. After exploring the beach at the mouth of Grays Creek, begin to retrace your steps on the Red Trail. (*FYI:* The high cliffs to the left [north] are closed to the public due to erosion and landslides.)

2.0 Stay right on the gravel road as the Red Trail branches left (west) as a footpath.

2.1 After a brief climb, the service road levels at a left bend. Turn right here onto the Orange Trail, a wide dirt footpath.

2.3 Cross Thomas Branch on a boardwalk.

2.8 At a fork in the Orange Trail, bear left onto an unmarked footpath that descends through the woods. Within 0.1 mile, merge onto the White Trail, which enters from the right.

3.2 Turn left (east) onto a gravel service road. Walk 50 feet and turn right (south) onto a wide footpath that leads downhill. An arrow at this trail junction reads ACCESS TO RED TRAIL.

3.3 Turn right (west) onto the Red Trail.

3.4 Veer left (south) onto the Blue Trail. Immediately cross Grays Creek on a footbridge. The trail is a sandy footpath, and mileage markers are in descending order as you head south through the woods.

Boardwalk over bog

4.0 Turn right (north) onto the Yellow Trail. The trail begins to descend along a seasonal tributary of Grays Creek.

4.3 Turn left (west) on the Red Trail.

4.6 HIKE ENDS at the trailboard and parking area at the edge of a pond.

Hike Information

Local information: Calvert County Tourism, 175 Main St., Prince Frederick, MD; (410) 535-3825; www.choosecalvert.com

Solomons Information Center, 14175 Solomons Island Rd. S., Solomons, MD; (410) 326-6027

Local events/attractions: Calvert Marine Museum, 14200 Solomons Island Road, Solomons, MD; (410) 326-2042; www.calvertmarinemuseum.com. Premier museum about life on the Chesapeake Bay.

Good eats: The Ruddy Duck Brewery & Grill, 13200 Dowell Road, Solomons, MD; (410) 394-3825; www.ruddyduckbrewery.com

Organizations: Friends of Calvert Cliffs State Park, Lusby, MD; (410) 394-1778

GREEN TIP
If you see someone else littering, muster up
the courage to ask them not to.

3 Catoctin Mountain Park

Easy strolls and rugged climbs typify the diversity on the 25 miles of trails through the 5,770-acre park, located on the easternmost ridge of the Blue Ridge Mountains. Park overlooks include Hog Rock, the highest point, and Chimney Rock, the most challenging ascent. Trails are not blazed, but they have signs at intersections. Interpretive trails have descriptive signage detailing evidence of several early industries within the park: charcoal making, a sawmill, and a whiskey still.

Start: At a parking lot on MD 77 near two tall stone pillars marking the driveway entrance for the national park's headquarters

Distance: 8.9-mile lollipop, with options for up to 12 miles

Approximate hiking time: 4 hours

Difficulty: Moderate due to length, but has well-graded hiking paths and only short, vigorous climbs

Trail surface: A single-track dirt woods path, uneven with many rocks and roots, gives way to graded dirt trails as you hop from one spectacular view to the next. The descent off Hog Rock has several steep stretches where erosional forces make for some tricky footing.

Seasons: May through Oct, although Oct is the busiest month due to leaf peeping. Cross-country skiing is popular when conditions permit.

Other trail users: Hikers and cross-country skiers in winter. There is a 6-mile horse trail open April 15 to Dec 1.

Handicapped accessibility: The Spicebush Nature Trail is a 0.25-mile paved loop in the Chestnut Picnic Area. Signs describe general forest ecology. The Sawmill exhibit near Owens Creek Campground has an accessible wooden ramp system from the parking lot to the sawmill, with interpretive signs and resting platforms along the way.

Canine compatibility: Leashed dogs permitted

Land status: National park

Fees and permits: None

Schedule: Open year-round during daylight hours. Visitor center opens daily at 9 a.m. There are temporary closures of portions of the park trails and roads due to the presidential retreat, Camp David, and/or winter weather conditions. Owens Creek Campground is open May through mid-Nov; Camp Misty Mount family cabins are open mid-April through Oct.

Facilities: Visitor center, bookstore, restrooms, picnic areas, campground, cabins

Maps: DeLorme *Maryland/Delaware Atlas & Gazetteer:* Page 72 B2. USGS 7.5 minute series: *Blue Ridge Summit, PA* and *Catoctin Furnace, MD.* National Park maps online, www.nps.gov/cato/planyourvisit/hiking.htm. Maryland's map for Cunningham Falls State Park can be viewed and printed online at http://dnr.maryland.gov/publiclands/pages/western/cunningham.aspx. See also the Potomac Appalachian Trail Club's (PATC) Maps 5 and 6, which cover the Appalachian Trail through Maryland, all of Catoctin Mountain Park and Cunningham State Park.

Trail contacts: Catoctin Mountain Park, 6602 Foxville Rd., Thurmont, MD 21788-1598; (301) 663-9388; www.nps.gov/cato

Special considerations: Camp David, the president's retreat, is located within the park. Due to security during presidential visits, there may be temporary road and trail closures. Visit the Web site for updates.

Finding the trailhead: Distance from Washington, D.C.: 64 miles

From I-495 (Capital Beltway): Take I-270 north for 32 miles to Frederick, MD. Take exit 13B and get on US 15 north, a left exit. Drive 17 miles north to Thurmont, MD. Take MD 77 West/ Catoctin Mountain Park. Go 3 miles and turn right onto Park Central Road. Entrance to visitor center is on the right. Trailhead GPS: N39 37.586' / W77 26.501'

The Hike

The mountain-building activity that created the Appalachian Mountains over the last 250 million years has left us with plenty of evidence of these cataclysmic activities. Mostly, the mountains tell a story in exposed rock formations, what they're made of, and how they're situated.

Less than a mile up the trail to Chimney Rock, hikers have a chance to see another clue of the mountain-building activity: a steep slope covered with white rocks. It's a stone stream, a geologic expression of the force that heat and freezing temperatures have had on the famous rocks of Catoctin Mountain Park.

▶ **KID APPEAL**

Interpretive signs on the 0.5-mile Charcoal Trail tell the story of charcoal making in the 1800s. Hundreds of woodcutters were employed to produce the charcoal, which in turn fueled the Catoctin Iron Furnace. The trail starts at the Thurmont Vista parking lot on Park Central Road.

In the period of the last ice age, some 10,000 years ago, geologists say glacial sheets of ice came no farther south than central Pennsylvania. However, the effects of this climate change did extend farther south. That explains refugees of colder climates—like spruce and fir trees—found at the highest elevations of Appalachian mountains.

Catoctin was only 100 miles from the edge of the ice sheet and, as such, had a climate that is described as near glacial: permafrost, tundra, and fluctuations of freezing and thawing temperatures. Ideal conditions, in other words, for rocks like the sturdy quartzite, which makes up the citadel-like fortress known as Chimney Rock, to break up along fault lines. These broken-up bits then begin a slow migration downslope. A gradually warming climate, the retreat of the glaciers, and a stabilizing of temperatures brought an end to the conditions that facilitated the rock streams "slipping" down the slope. And so, as you scramble the rocks, the lichen and moss, as well as the small understory elms and beeches growing amid it, indicate a stabilization—a rock stream, frozen in time.

A hiker following this route will pass a threshold (unmarked, undeclared, and usually unnoticed), like the Continental Divide, that signals a shift in the underlying bedrock. The trail from Wolf Rock descends almost to Park Central Road, and thereafter

The presidential retreat, Camp David, is within the park. Portions of the television series *The West Wing* were filmed here. The retreat is closed to the public and cannot be seen from any roads, but there is a Camp David Museum in the historic Cozy Restaurant in Thurmont.

HOG ROCK NATURE TRAIL

As you reenter the woods opposite the Hog Rock parking area, look for a box nailed to a tree that holds a printed interpretive pamphlet. It describes the typical species, each assigned a number, that have repopulated the hills of Catoctin Mountain Park in the one hundred years since it was denuded of timber for the charcoal industry. A short 0.4-mile loop at Hog Rock Overlook has numbered posts that correspond with the sheet.

it climbs to Blue Ridge Summit Overlook. Undetected is a change in the underlying bedrock, from the white quartzite of Chimney Rock and Wolf Rock to the Catoctin greenstone. It is from this park that the stone received its name, and it's fitting as you look off Hog Rock, on the second leg of this route, that the stone beneath your feet is, in name and spirit, one and the same.

Catoctin Mountain Park has more recent stories to tell as well, and an excellent series of interpretive trails brings the park's past to life. As you descend from Wolf Rock to a four-way junction, consider a side trip to the Charcoal Trail, a 0.5-mile loop that describes how an industry built on timber denuded the hillsides of nearly every living tree.

Miles and Directions

0.0 START at a parking lot on MD 77 near two tall stone pillars that mark the driveway entrance to the national park's headquarters. Walk 250 feet west along the highway shoulder (with traffic) to a wood trail sign for Chimney Rock, Wolf Rock, and the visitor center. Enter the woods on a dirt woodland path and begin climbing.

0.3 Pass the lower trailhead for Crows Nest Loop on the right as the trail begins a series of switchbacks and crosses a stone stream indicated by the sheet of loose rock that covers the uphill slope.

0.6 Bear left (north) and uphill at a junction with the upper trailhead for Crows Nest Loop.

1.0 Circle around house-size rock formations as the trail rises to a spur trail on the left leading to the citadel-like tower of Weaverton quartzite that make up Chimney Rock. Turn left on the spur trail to reach the rock formation.

1.5 A spur trail branches right to Wolf Rock. (*FYI:* Views from this rock outcrop are blocked by the trees, but it remains a popular spot as it is the only area in the park where rock climbing is permitted.)

2.5 Continue northward. Turn right on a short spur trail to a rest area at Thurmont Vista. Views are eastward to the small town of Thurmont and the wider Frederick Valley.

2.9 Turn right at a four-way intersection, following signs for Hog Rock. (*Bailout:* Turn left [south] and hike 0.5 mile to a four-way trail junction. Here, turn left, hike uphill, and return to the trailhead via Wolf Rock and Chimney Rock.)

3.6 After a short, steep climb, the trail levels atop Blue Ridge Summit. (*FYI:* In summertime, views northward are limited from rocks that parallel the trail for the next 0.1 mile, but the summit is nonetheless a fascinating spot to investigate the hardy ferns, mosses, and chestnut oaks that grow on these rocks.)

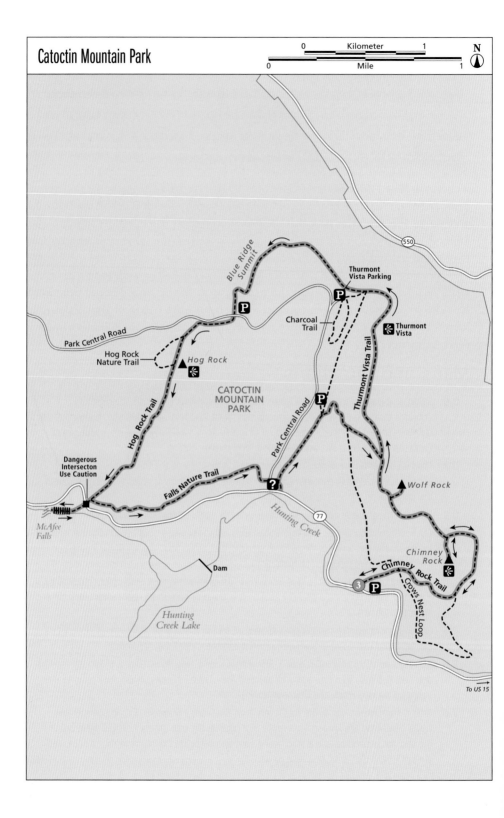

Catoctin Mountain Park

0 — Kilometer — 1
0 — Mile — 1

N

550

Blue Ridge Summit

Thurmont Vista Parking

P

Charcoal Trail

P

Thurmont Vista

Park Central Road

Hog Rock Nature Trail

Hog Rock

CATOCTIN MOUNTAIN PARK

Thurmont Vista Trail

Hog Rock Trail

Dangerous Intersecton Use Caution

P

Falls Nature Trail

?

Park Central Road

Wolf Rock

McAfee Falls

Hunting Creek

77

Chimney Rock

Chimney Rock Trail

Dam

3 **P**

Crows Nest Loop

Hunting Creek Lake

To US 15

3.9 Walk straight through the Hog Rock parking lot, cross Park Central Road, and reenter woods on a dirt woods path.

4.2 Reach Hog Rock Overlook on the left. This exposed quartzite rock formation has all-season views eastward and is shaded by an unusually tall shagbark hickory tree. (*Option:* From this overlook continue straight on Hog Rock Trail, or turn right [west] onto Hog Rock Nature Trail, an interpretive trail that rejoins Hog Rock Trail in 0.4 mile.) Continue south on Hog Rock Trail.

5.2 Turn left (east) on Falls Nature Trail. (*Side trip:* Continue straight on Hog Rock Trail to where it ends at MD 77. Turn left and walk 50 paces east on the road shoulder, against traffic. Cross to the south side of the highway and enter a parking lot for McAfee Falls [also known as Cunningham Falls], which is reserved for handicapped visitors. Inside the parking area, follow a boardwalk leading 0.3 mile to the falls area.) (*Caution:* This MD 77 crossing occurs at a blind corner for vehicles traveling in both directions.)

6.2 Enter the national park visitor center's west parking lot. Turn left and walk through the parking area, across Park Central Road into the east parking lot, and head for the far left corner. Climb a short flight of stone steps and enter the woods on the Thurmont Vista Trail.

6.8 Turn right (east) and hike uphill.

7.3 Merge right onto Chimney Rock Trail.

8.9 HIKE ENDS at the Chimney Rock trailhead.

The first youth Job Corps Center was established here in 1965 as part of President Lyndon Johnson's War on Poverty.

Hike Information

Local information: Tourism Council of Frederick County, 19 E. Church St., Frederick, MD; (301) 600-4047; www.fredericktourism.org

Local events/attractions: The Covered Bridge Driving Tour, www.frederick tourism.org/driving_coveredbridges.html. Passes three historic bridges on Old Frederick Road.

Good eats: Fitzgerald's Shamrock Restaurant, 7701 Fitzgerald Road, Thurmont, MD; (301) 271-2912; www.shamrockrestaurant.com/

Local outdoor stores: The Trail House, 17 S. Market St., Frederick, MD; (301) 694-8448; www.trailhouse.com. Has hiking supplies and maps.

Hike tours: TeamLink/Shenandoah Mountain Tours, Frederick, MD; (301) 695-1814; www.teamlinkinc.com

4 Cedarville State Forest

Cedarville State Forest protects Zekiah Swamp Run, ranked Maryland's most ecological diverse stream, notable for its rare and endangered plants. From its source in a moist bog of sphagnum moss, the stream moves sluggishly under a canopy of maples, sweetgum, and river birch. At its source grows the carnivorous roundleaf sundew and the northern pitcher plant.

Start: From a parking lot at the state forest visitor center

Distance: 13-mile loop

Approximate hiking time: 5 hours

Difficulty: Difficult due to length; terrain is easy.

Trail surface: Dirt footpaths and old forest roads traverse a heavily wooded area, with short stretches through the watershed of two major streams. Low areas adjacent to streams may be flooded in periods of heavy rain.

Seasons: April through Aug

Other trail users: Mountain bikers, horseback riders, hunters

Handicapped accessibility: Disabled hunting access and archery range

Canine compatibility: Dogs permitted

Land status: State forest

Fees and permits: Per-vehicle entrance fee

Schedule: Daily dawn to dusk

Facilities: Restrooms, visitor center, campground, playground, picnic pavilions, archery range, fish hatchery, visitor center

Maps: DeLorme *Maryland/Delaware Atlas & Gazetteer:* Page 37 C6. USGS 7.5 minute series: *Brandywine, MD.* Custom topographic maps are sold at the state forest's visitor center, or online at www.shopdnr.com/southern marylandtrailguides.aspx.

Trail contacts: Cedarville State Forest, 10201 Bee Oak Rd., Brandywine, MD 20613; (301) 888-1410; http://dnr.maryland.gov/public lands/Pages/southern/cedarville.aspx

Special considerations: Be aware of hunting seasons, competitive archery ranges on the Blue Trail, trail washouts after heavy rains, and sharing the trail with mountain bikers, the Orange Trail in particular.

Finding the trailhead: Distance from Washington, D.C.: 24 miles

From I-495 (Capital Beltway): Take exit 7A, MD 5 South, toward Waldorf. In 9.5 miles MD 5 merges onto US 301 South. In 2.1 miles, turn left on Cedarville Road (see State Forest sign). In 0.3 mile, Cedarville Road veers right. In 2 miles turn right into forest entrance on Bee Oak Road. In 0.9 mile reach the visitor center parking lot and honor pay station. Trailhead GPS: N38 38.817' / W76 49.814'

The Hike

As the Great Depression settled over America in the 1930s, the U.S. Government started buying land rendered useless by decades of abusive farming and timbering. Faced with thousands of men without jobs and a crippled economy, Franklin Delano

Top: Old charcoal kiln built by the Civilian Conservation Corps ▶
Bottom: Lunch break overlooking Cedarville Pond

Roosevelt created make-work programs: the Civilian Conservation Corps (CCC) and Works Project Administration (WPA).

Spurred by the federal government, Virginia and Maryland began a program to buy abused farmland, often for pennies on the dollar. That is how Cedarville State Forest was created. In the Coastal Plain, the government bought land that surrounded two stream valleys, Wolf Den Branch and Zekiah Swamp. They reclaimed abused farmland, planted trees, and built roads that hikers walk today beneath pine and hardwood forests.

Hiking one of those forest roads is a good time to ruminate. The path ahead is clear, and the mind wanders to what might lie off to the left and right. A gully forms alongside the road, dry in late summer. The hillside to the right steepens, and, in the crease between two hills, Wolf Den Branch gains strength.

Thanks to Cedarville State Forest, Zekiah Swamp was saved. Its headwaters originate in the forest and flow 21 miles toward the Wicomico River. Of some eighty-four streams surveyed in Maryland, Zekiah Swamp is rated the number one stronghold stream for its rare and endangered plants and animals, according to a survey by Maryland's Department of Natural Resources from 2000 to 2004.

There are two types of bogs on the East Coast: northern bogs and pocosins. The headwaters of Zekiah Swamp is classified as a northern bog. Here thrives the northern pitcher plant (*Sarracenia purpurea*), which captures insects in pools of water in its leaves, then digests them with the aid of a bacteria.

You can see an example of this rich bottomland as the trail descends alongside Wolf Den Branch. After heavy rain, the trail is washed out by a tributary that crosses it and spreads out across the flat ground. Small hummocks of grass poke out here and there, making it possible to hopscotch through the sheet flow of water. Signs of considerably more flow force can be seen in the piles of twigs and leaf debris pressed against the upstream side of trees.

In Cedarville, Zekiah Swamp wells up through the sphagnum and forms a freshwater swamp forest. The hillsides are low, and the riverbed isn't a deep channel. This is more of a spreading stream than a channelized stream. Water moves slowly, and the hiker is encouraged to move slowly as well, the better to appreciate this special scenery.

Miles and Directions

0.0 START from a trail register at the head of Holly Trail, a single-track woods path blazed orange. Follow the trail through a forest of young holly, ash, and elm.

0.2 Turn left (south) onto Orange Trail at a T junction. (*Note:* At the end of this hike, you will approach this same junction from the right.)

0.9 Cross Hidden Springs Road, turn right (south) and walk along the shoulder. After 500 feet, turn left (east) and reenter the woods.

1.2 Bear right (south) at a fork in the trail onto white-blazed White Trail. In a few feet, turn right onto gravel Sunset Road. Walk 0.1 mile, turn left, and reenter the woods on the White Trail, a single-track dirt path through a young pine forest. (*Note:* For the next 8 miles, this route passes through an area of the forest where hunting is permitted. See *Special considerations* on page 38 for more information.)

1.9 Turn left (south) onto a dirt road. In 0.1 mile, swing left (east) on White Trail.

2.4 Veer left on White Trail as it takes a northward track. After an initial climb, the trail begins a steady descent to Wolf Den Branch. (*FYI:* After heavy rains, low-elevation sections of this trail can be washed out.)

3.2 Stay right as White Trail merges with Sunset Road, which descends from the left. Walk 200 feet on this dirt road, then turn right onto Blue Trail, which is a single-track dirt path. In 200 feet, cross Wolf Den Branch on a footbridge. In a few feet, there is another footbridge over a wetland area. Thereafter, Blue Trail climbs to traverse a hillside offering good views down a rich stream bottomland forest.

4.2 Enter a field that appears recently timbered. Young pine saplings are starting to colonize this disturbed area.

4.3 Pass through a competitive archery range.

4.8 Turn right (south) on a gravel fire road and cross Zekiah Swamp Run. Ahead is a parking area, outhouse, and picnic areas next to Cedarville Pond.

4.9 Turn right (southwest) on Green Trail. For the next 0.5 mile, the trail swerves in and out of small gullies formed by seasonal streams that feed Zekiah Swamp Run.

6.4 Continue straight (southeast) and merge onto Brown Trail. (*Note:* Here, Green Trail turns left [north] and returns to Cedarville Pond. While it can be used as a bailout, hikers risk missing one of this loop's more scenic areas along Brown Trail.)

6.8 Descend to cross a wetlands on a wooden footbridge. This swamp, alive with frog calls and birdsong, is the headwater of Cedarville Pond and is worthy of a long break to soak in the scenery. Beyond here, the trail briefly parallels the wetlands, then climbs back into a dry forest of young hardwoods.

7.1 Turn left, continuing on Brown Trail, at a T junction with a gated forest road that fades, overgrown with grass, into the woods on the right. In 0.1 mile, turn left on Brown Trail as the old road continues straight.

7.7 Emerge from the woods at the base of Cedarville Pond. Continue straight to the gravel forest road, turn right, and cross Zekiah Swamp Run.

7.9 Turn right (north) onto Blue Trail. Within 0.1 mile, cross over Mistletoe Road, a dirt road that provides disabled hunters access. The next 1.4 miles of trail is another trip highlight: The scenic footpath winds, dips into, and rises up out of small seasonal streams under a canopy of the mixed hardwood forest.

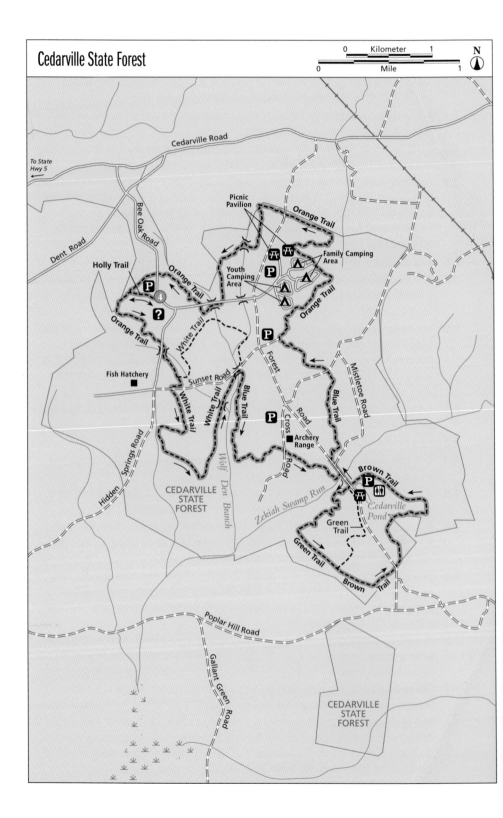

Cedarville State Forest

9.1 Turn right onto the combined Orange Trail–Blue Trail.

9.3 Bear right on Orange Trail where Blue Trail splits left. Begin a climb on a gentle grade on an old dirt and gravel road that is reverting to woodsy trail.

9.9 Pass the Family Camping Area. Here, Orange Trail merges onto a dirt and gravel road. Pass two campground access roads that merge on the left; stay right at each junction. As you pass out of the camping area, there is a large fire circle on the right, and still farther, a picnic pavilion on the left.

10.1 Bear right as Orange Trail departs the camp road at a Y junction. A young pine plantation now flanks the trail on your left.

11.3 Emerge onto a power line easement and swing right. Over the next 0.1 mile, the trail alternates between the open air of the easement and the canopy of the adjacent forest, and it crosses a small stream on a footbridge.

11.9 Cross Bee Oak Road and reenter the woods directly opposite. (*Caution:* In the next 0.5 mile, Orange Trail will cross Bee Oak Road three times. Watch for traffic at each crossing.)

12.5 Cross Bee Oak Road for the final time; enter the woods directly opposite.

12.7 Turn left onto Holly Trail.

13.0 HIKE ENDS at the visitor center parking area.

Hike Information

Local information: Prince George's County, Maryland, Conference and Visitor's Bureau, Largo, MD; (301) 925-8300; www.visitprincegeorges.com

Good eats: Cedarville Carry Out, 1800 Cedarville Rd., Brandywine, MD; (301) 579-2888. Less than 2 miles east of the park; open 5:00 a.m. to 3:00 p.m., so you can get a hearty breakfast and pick up a sandwich for the trail.

Local outdoor stores: Beacon Surplus All-in-One Outdoor Store, 3256 Leonardtown Rd., Waldorf, MD; (301) 645-0077; www.beaconsurplus.com

Dick's Sporting Goods, 11080 Mall Circle Rd., Waldorf, MD; (301) 885-1762; www.dickssportinggoods.com

Organizations: Friends of Cedarville State Forest (FCSF); (800) 784-5380

5 Cunningham Falls State Park

The views from three high points on this hike are matched only by the impressive McAfee Falls, Maryland's highest. This route, following narrow woods paths and old dirt roads that date to a bygone era of timbering and charcoal making, is designed to give hikers plenty of time to savor just how far Cunningham Falls State Park, and adjacent Catoctin Mountain Park, have come in less than one hundred years, from a denuded landscape to a small pocket of wildness.

Start: From a trailhead opposite the Manor House Visitors Center and aviary

Distance: 13.5-mile lollipop

Approximate hiking time: 6 hours

Difficulty: Difficult due to length and moderate inclines, highlighted by several strenuous but short inclines

Trail surface: Forested trails, boardwalk, open rock

Seasons: Best in winter and spring, when views are open and crowds thinned out

Other trail users: Hikers only

Handicapped accessibility: A 0.25-mile boardwalk trail provides the shortest and easiest access to Cunningham Falls. Parking lot on MD 77 is reserved for vehicles displaying the handicapped symbol.

Canine compatibility: Leashed dogs permitted on trails and camping loops; in the William Houck Area, dogs are prohibited from the beach Memorial Day through Labor Day.

Land status: State park, national park

Fees and permits: Entrance fee

Schedule: Open daily, 8:00 a.m. to dusk April through Oct; 10 a.m. to dusk Nov through Mar.

Facilities: Restrooms, campground, cabins, picnic area, boat ramp, visitor center, amphitheater

Maps: DeLorme *Maryland/Delaware Atlas & Gazetteer:* Page 72 B2. USGS 7.5 minute series: *Catoctin Furnace, MD* and *Blue Ridge Summit, PA.* Maryland's map for Cunningham Falls State Park can be viewed and printed online at http://dnr.maryland.gov/public lands/pages/western/cunningham.aspx. See also the Potomac Appalachian Trail Club's (PATC) Maps 5 and 6, which cover the Appalachian Trail through Maryland, all of Catoctin Mountain Park and Cunningham State Park.

Trail contacts: Cunningham Falls State Park, 14039 Catoctin Hollow Rd., Thurmont, MD 21788; (301) 271-7574; http://dnr.maryland .gov/publiclands/pages/western/cunningham .aspx

Special considerations: Fall deer hunting is permitted on 3,500 acres of undeveloped wildlands. There will be signs warning hikers, but trails generally remain open.

Finding the trailhead: Distance from Washington, D.C.: 61 miles

From I-495 (Capital Beltway): Take I-270 north for 32 miles to Frederick, MD. Take exit 13B and get on US 15 North, a left exit. Go 12.5 miles to the park's Manor Area entrance on left. Trailhead GPS: N39 35.262' / W77 26.155'

The Hike

The Catoctin Trail from the Manor Area to the flat top of Bob's Hill begins as a narrow dirt footpath and, as it climbs, gradually widens to road width. Banks form on both sides, sometimes reaching as high as your head, creating a "sunken" effect. Mountain laurel is profuse in the understory of the young forest that covers the mountain slope.

Some 200 years ago, the scene would have been strikingly different. In the warmer months, a breeze would carry the pitch tar smell of a charcoal pit across the mountain. Come winter, the ax blow would ring through the forest. A horse-drawn sled laden with timber, cut into 4-foot lengths of varying widths, would trundle down this road, bringing a fresh supply for the collier (charcoal maker). A metal-lined wagon pulled by six mules would carry a load of charcoal to the blast furnace at Catoctin.

Iron furnaces operated at Catoctin from 1776 to 1903, and for the first one hundred years, were entirely fueled by charcoal, which is made from charred wood. That wood came from the vast forest that covered Catoctin Mountain. It would be hard to overemphasize the impact this industry had: Any wood made good charcoal, and so the elm, hickory, oak, and chestnut fell to the woodsman's ax. Into the twentieth century, as many as 500 men swarmed over these hills, cutting timber for railroad ties and other wooden necessities. In 1936, a former superintendent of Catoctin Mountain Park described there being "barely a tree over the size of a fence post."

The scenery is markedly different today. A young forest of hickories, elms, and other hardwoods of the Appalachian forest cover mountain slopes at lower elevations. Atop Bob's Hill and neighboring Cat Rock, thinner, well-drained soils support chestnut oaks and pitch pine.

The regeneration started in 1936, when the federal government bought 10,000 acres on Catoctin Mountain for redevelopment. Similar projects were undertaken throughout Appalachia—in Shenandoah, some 180,000 acres were purchased to help restore the Blue Ridge Mountains to a "natural" park. The plans for Catoctin were different. Here, the goal was to develop a recreational site. Men with the WPA began the work of removing blighted chestnut trees, destroying old farm buildings, and obscuring miles of logging roads and farm fences. The CCC followed by constructing trails, a custodian's residence, retaining walls, a bathhouse, and trail shelters. More than 1,500 trees were planted.

Cunningham State Park was created from lands from this federal project in 1954. Evenly split at 5,000 acres with adjacent Catoctin Mountain Park, Cunningham lays claim to Maryland's highest waterfall on Hunting Creek, as well as two striking

▶ **KID APPEAL**
The playground in the Manor Area was made by volunteers from 3,000 recycled tires that would have otherwise ended up in a landfill. Nice talking point for a recycling lesson. After hiking, cool off with a swim in Hunting Creek Lake. Lifeguards are on duty Memorial Day through Labor Day.

outlooks, atop Bob's Hill and Cat Rock. In summertime, views encompass a lush green woodland that white-tailed deer, turkey, fox, and squirrel call home. It's scenery made all the more satisfying knowing how far this landscape has changed in less than one hundred years.

Miles and Directions

0.0   START from a trailhead opposite the Manor Area Visitor Center. Follow the white-blazed trail 400 feet uphill, then merge right (north) onto the blue-blazed Catoctin Trail.

0.3   Bear left (northwest) on a gradual uphill grade as yellow-blazed Bob's Hill Trail merges with Catoctin Trail on the right. Over the next 1.2 miles, the trail will gain 1,000 feet of elevation. (*Note:* The state park topographic map describes this trail section as the combined Catoctin, Bob's Hill, and Cat Rock Trails, but only blue blazes of the Catoctin are visible.)

1.5   Side trails to North and South Bob's Hill Overlooks (1,700 feet) branch right and left, respectively. The north overlook is within 100 feet of the Catoctin Trail; the south overlook is approximately 500 feet and features better views.

2.6   Turn right (northeast) onto yellow-blazed Catoctin–Cat Rock Connector Trail.

4.0   A series of sharp switchbacks lead steeply downhill to a T junction with a side trail to Cat Rock Overlook (1,560 feet). Turn right and walk 0.1 mile to the overlook, then return to this junction to follow Cat Rock Trail straight (north). (*FYI:* Cat Rock is an impressive five-story-tall tower of car-size quartzite boulders with west views. Use caution when climbing the exposed rock.)

4.4   Continue straight on Cat Rock Trail past a junction with Old Misery Trail (red blazes) on the left.

5.0   After a long descent, exit from Cat Rock Trail into a trailhead parking area on MD 77. At the trailboard, turn left, walk west through the parking lot, and reenter woods on an unmarked fisherman's path that parallels Little Hunting Creek beneath shady hemlocks. (*Note:* The topography will steepen on your left side and pinch the trail and creek together. At this point, look for a convenient spot to rock-hop across Little Hunting Creek, and continue the westward trek on a fisherman's path on the north stream bank.)

6.1   Climb up the north stream bank to the road shoulder of MD 77, cross the highway, and enter Catoctin Mountain Park via the paved Park Central Road. Turn left into the west parking area, walk to the far right corner, and reenter the woods on a single-track woodland trail. Within a few feet, cross a small footbridge.

7.1   Falls Nature Trail ends at a T junction with Hog Rock Trail. Turn left and descend to MD 77. On the road shoulder, turn left and walk 50 paces east, against traffic. Cross to the south side of the highway and enter a parking lot for McAfee Falls reserved for handicapped access. Inside the parking area, turn right to reach a boardwalk leading to the falls area. (*Caution:* This MD 77 crossing occurs at a blind corner for vehicles traveling in both directions.)

7.4   The boardwalk ends at an overlook of McAfee Falls. To reach the south stream bank, or to rock-scramble about the falls, retrace your footsteps along the boardwalk for 250 paces, hop off the uphill side, and follow any number of foot-worn paths to the exposed rock base of the falls. After admiring the 78-foot drop of Maryland's highest waterfall, rock-hop across Little Hunting Creek and regain the south stream bank in the area of another boardwalk overlook.

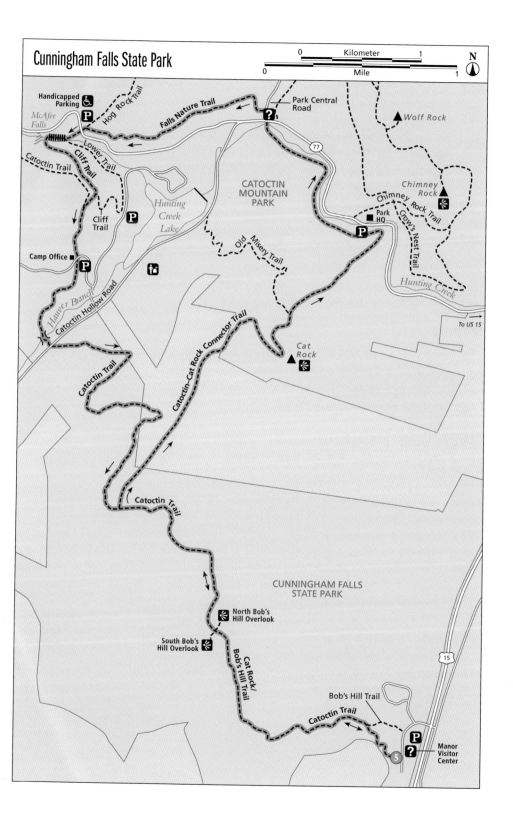

Cunningham Falls State Park

Kilometer
0   1

Mile
0   1

N

Handicapped Parking ♿ P

McAfee Falls

Hog Rock Trail

Falls Nature Trail

Park Central Road ?

Wolf Rock ▲

Lower Trail

Catoctin Trail

Cliff Trail

77

CATOCTIN MOUNTAIN PARK

Chimney Rock ▲

Chimney Rock Trail

Park HQ ■ P

Crow's Nest Trail

Cliff Trail

P

Hunting Creek Lake

Old Misery Trail

Camp Office ■ P

Catoctin Hollow Road

Hauver Branch

Hunting Creek

To US 15

Catoctin–Cat Rock Connector Trail

Cat Rock ▲

Catoctin Trail

Catoctin Trail

CUNNINGHAM FALLS STATE PARK

North Bob's Hill Overlook

South Bob's Hill Overlook

Cat Rock/ Bob's Hill Trail

15

Bob's Hill Trail

Catoctin Trail

P

5

? **Manor Visitor Center**

7.5 Veer right and uphill on yellow-blazed Cliff Trail. (*Note:* Lower Falls Trail [red blazes] continues straight for 0.5 mile to a parking area.)

7.7 Turn left (east) at a T junction onto blue-blazed Catoctin Trail. For 0.2 mile, Cliff and Catoctin Trails share this woodland path.

7.9 Veer right (south) on Catoctin Trail where it splits from the Cliff Trail. (*Note:* This junction is easily missed, especially in summertime when the trails are overgrown. Look for a waist-high wooden post that signals the split.)

8.3 Cross camp road (ranger station on the right). (*FYI:* There are bathrooms, a soda machine, and a freshwater spigot at the ranger station.)

8.8 Cross Catoctin Hollow Road, reenter the woods on a blue-blazed dirt footpath, and immediately begin climbing.

10.7 Continue straight past a junction for Cat Rock Trail (yellow blazes) on the left. (*Note:* The route from here to Manor House is on the combined Catoctin/Cat Rock/Bob's Hill Trail, but only blue blazes of the Catoctin Trail are visible.)

11.8 Side trails to North and South Bob's Hill Overlooks branch left and right, respectively.

13.5 HIKE ENDS at the Manor Area Visitor Center.

OPTIONS

Chimney Rock. Cross MD 77 and Little Hunting Creek and enter a parking area. Next to a wood trailboard, enter the woods on a dirt woods path. It is 1.2 miles, mostly uphill, to Chimney Rock, another formation of Weaverton quartzite that rivals Cat Rock with its ruggedness and views.

Hike Information

Local information: Tourism Council of Frederick County, Frederick, MD; (301) 644-4047; www.fredericktourism.org

Local events/attractions: The Annual Maple Syrup demonstration takes place two weekends in March in the William Houck Area. Sausage and pancake breakfast served. Suggested donation.

Good eats: Cactus Flats, 10026 Hansonville Rd., Frederick, MD; (301) 898-3085. Just 6 miles south of the Manor Area on US 15 is a funky roadhouse stop for beer and burgers.

Local outdoor stores: The Trail House, 17 S. Market St., Frederick, MD; (301) 694-8448; www.trailhouse.com. Has hiking supplies and maps.

Hike tours: TeamLink Mountain/Shenandoah Mountain Guides, Frederick, MD; (301) 695-1814; www.teamlinkinc.com

Organizations: Friends of Cunningham Falls State Park, Inc., 14039 Catoctin Hollow Rd., Thurmont, MD 21788

6 Gambrill State Park

Gambrill State Park protects the lower third of the Catoctin Mountain chain. The Catoctin Trail, one of Maryland's premier long-distance footpaths, begins here. The park and its trails date back to civic-minded residents of Frederick, Maryland, who bought the land for protection and recreation. It is a tradition that continues today with active involvement in trail maintenance by Frederick-area hikers, mountain bikers, and equestrians. At 7.4 miles, this is the longest trek that can be pieced together through the park. With so many interconnecting trails, however, options abound for making this as long or as short as time and energy permit.

Start: From the trail system parking lot on Gambrill Park Road, 0.4 mile north of the park entrance

Distance: 7.4-mile loop

Approximate hiking time: 4 hours

Difficulty: Moderate due to minimal elevation gain and well-graded trails

Trail surface: Dirt footpaths, old forest roads, gravel roads, and open-face rock

Seasons: Sept through May

Other trail users: Mountain bikers, joggers, horses, and cross-country skiers

Handicapped accessibility: Park trails are not handicapped accessible, but the North and South Frederick Overlooks are.

Canine compatibility: Leashed dogs permitted

Land status: State park

Fees and permits: Per vehicle day use fee; camping fees.

Schedule: April through Oct, 8:00 a.m. to sunset; Nov through Mar, 10:00 a.m. to sunset daily

Facilities: Picnic areas, restrooms, nature center, campground with electric hook-ups, bathhouse, dump station and four rustic cabins (reserve camping at https://parkreservations.maryland.gov).

Maps: DeLorme *Maryland/Delaware Atlas & Gazetteer:* Page 72 D2. USGS 7.5 minute series: *Middletown, MD.* See also National Geographic's TOPO! software, Mid-Atlantic Region, Disc 4. A state park–issued topographical map is available online for a fee at www.shopdnr.com/westernmarylandtrailguides.aspx

Trail contacts: Gambrill State Park, 8602 Gambrill Park Rd., Frederick, MD 21702; (301) 271-7574; www.dnr.state.md.us/publiclands/Pages/western/gambrill.aspx.

Finding the trailhead: Distance from Washington, D.C.: 50 miles

From US 70 in Frederick: Take exit onto US 40. In 6 miles turn right onto Gambrill Park Road. Cross over Shookstown Road, pass the Rock Run Area on the left, and, in 1.2 miles from US 40, turn right into the trail parking lot, marked by a wooden sign reading GAMBRILL STATE PARK TRAIL SYSTEM PARKING LOT. Trailhead GPS: N39 27.722' / W77 29.465'

The Hike

Half the fun of exploring a park as popular and well used as Gambrill State Park is to take every unmarked side trail in the spirit of "what if." What if this trail links up with another, and I've found a shortcut? What if I see a bear? What if . . . ?

What if you're walking uphill on a rocky footbed beneath a power line? It tops out at a grass road that swings left and continues climbing. In May, the clearing off to the left of the road is visited by wild turkeys. Farther still, the grass road rises to meet the paved road leading to a radio tower. Here, it is faster to retrace your steps back beneath the power line easement and rejoin the trail.

There are two poisonous snakes in Maryland, the northern copperhead and the timber rattler. On warm spring days, they emerge to bask in the heat of the exposed rock that mark so many overlooks and outcrops throughout Gambrill State Park. They also like power line easements, as in the case of the timber rattler that blocked my descent back toward the Yellow Poplar Trail. Timber rattlesnakes dine on small mammals, some birds, and maybe a frog here and there. They enjoy the rocky ridgetops and forested swamps. This one seemed to prefer the rocky ridge; unwilling to budge, it forced me off trail onto a bushwhack across a dry forest of oak and hickory until I crossed paths again with Yellow Poplar Trail.

Among the highlights along this north–south route are the many wildflowers. From its trailhead, the Catoctin Trail swings north to traverse a dry forested slope. A sharp eye will catch, in the leaf litter alongside the trail, the delicate spotted wintergreen. Its serrated-edged leaves, narrow and pointed at the tip, have a white streak

Rattlesnake in the trail

Catoctin Mountain Trail runs through the park.

down the center vein that could almost pass for hand-painted. Two thin stems rise from the vortex of leaves at the base. Each stem is capped by a small yellow flower. In early spring, the stems may be red or yellow, and the buds may be closed, resembling small BB-gun–like pellets.

And just as quickly, 0.1 mile north on the trail, the dry forest upslope is covered with fiddlehead ferns. Somewhere up that slope, a seep or stream is keeping the ferns watered well.

Save for the developed overlooks at High Point, the rock outcrops and vistas are not as spectacular at Gambrill State Park as they are farther up the mountain chain at Cunningham State Park and Catoctin Mountain Park. But evidence abounds in what these three locales share: the quartzite bedrock that forms so many of the Catoctin Mountains's signature outcrops. Gambrill, together with land owned by the City of Frederick, and the state and national parks to the north, protect a beautiful woodland and significant geologic feature.

Miles and Directions

0.0 START from an information map board in the trail system parking area on Gambrill Park Road. Choose the Catoctin Trail/Black Locust Trail/Red Maple Trail trailhead, marked by a sign on a wooden post reading WELCOME TO THE CATOCTIN HIKING TRAIL. Walk east on this wide dirt footpath, following a triple sequence of light blue, black, and red blazes. In 300 feet past the trailhead, red-blazed Red Maple Trail splits right (south). Continue straight (east) on combined Catoctin Trail/Black Locust Trail.

0.6 Bear right (north) as Green Ash Trail merges with the Catoctin Trail.

1.1 Stay straight (north) on the Catoctin Trail as Green Ash Trail and Black Locust Trail branch left to climb back to the park road.

1.3 Climb to a T junction with Yellow Poplar Trail via two switchbacks. Turn right (north) and follow combined Catoctin Trail/Yellow Poplar Trail, a wide dirt two-track road.

1.6 Catoctin Trail and Yellow Poplar Trail split at a T junction. Turn left (west) and follow yellow-blazed Yellow Poplar Trail, which is a two-track dirt road. In 0.1 mile, the route veers off the road and becomes a narrow footpath.

1.7 Cross a gravel road that links Gambrill Park Road to a radio tower. The trail reenters the woods via steps hewn from logs and rocks. An impressive set of Catoctin greenstone outcrops is visible in woods to the right.

2.1 Turn left (north) at a T junction and continue on Yellow Poplar Trail as it descends to a seasonal stream. Cross the stream and pass a pond on the right.

2.3 The trail departs the forest and follows a power line easement north. (*Note:* A sign here indicates that you've been hiking the Lower Yellow Loop.)

2.4 Turn right (northeast) at a T junction to begin the Upper Yellow Loop, which is a popular mountain bike route. (*Option:* You can shave 2 miles off this loop by turning left here and descending to Gambrill Park Road via the Lower Yellow Loop.)

3.2 Take a hard left (south) and avoid an unmarked footpath that continues straight (west). The trail, which is a narrow dirt footpath, soon climbs several long switchbacks through what was once an old U.S. weather station.

4.0 Cross Gambrill Park Road.

4.4 Continue straight as a spur trail branches left (this is the shortcut described in the Option at mile 2.4). As the Yellow Poplar Trail descends gently, the trail footing is rough with exposed rocks.

5.5 Turn right (west) and descend on combined Yellow Poplar/Black Locust Trail, following both yellow and black blazes. The next 0.5 mile is marked by nice wintertime views west off Catoctin Mountain. (*Side trip:* A left onto Black Locust Trail leads approximately 90 yards up to the park road and the North Frederick Overlook, which has easterly views.)

5.7 Continue straight (south) past a spur trail that branches left (east) and climbs to the park ranger station.

6.0 At a four-way trail junction, turn right (west) and follow Yellow Poplar Trail downhill on a narrow dirt footpath.

6.6 Turn right (south) on Red Maple Trail. It descends 0.1 mile to the Rock Run Area and campsites.

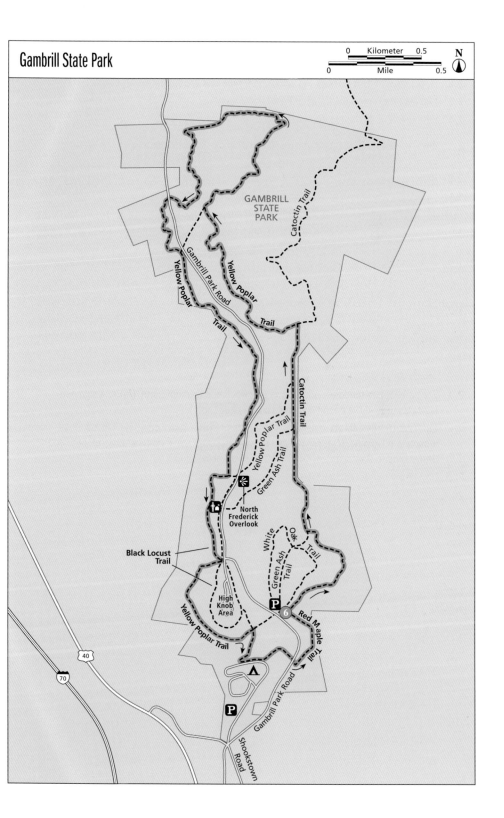

Gambrill State Park

GAMBRILL
STATE
PARK

Catoctin Trail

Yellow Poplar

Gambrill Park Road

Yellow Poplar

Trail

Yellow Poplar

Trail

Catoctin Trail

Yellow Poplar Trail

Green Ash Trail

North
Frederick
Overlook

Black Locust
Trail

White

Oak

Green Ash

Trail

Trail

High
Knob
Area

Yellow Poplar Trail

P
6
Red Maple Trail

A

P

Gambrill Park Road

Shookstown
Road

40

70

0   Kilometer   0.5

0   Mile   0.5

N

7.0 Cross the park road and climb the road embankment on the opposite side. A double red blaze marks your left (northeast) turn up a gravel driveway. After a brief climb, follow red blazes straight as it reenters the woods as a wide and graded path.

7.3 Turn left (west) onto the Catoctin Trail.

7.4 HIKE ENDS at the trail system parking lot.

Hike Information

Local information: Visit Frederick Visitor Center, 151 S. East St., Frederick, MD, 21701; (301) 600-4047; www.visitfrederick.org

Local events/attractions: Rose Hill Manor Park/The Children's & Farm Museum, 1611 N. Market St., Frederick, MD; (301) 600-1650; www.rosehillmuseum.com. Living-history museum interprets early American life through historic tours and events.

Good eats: The Main Cup has gourmet sandwiches and a bar, 14 W. Main St., Middletown, MD, (301) 371-4433; www.themaincuprestaurant.com.

Organizations: Friends of Cunningham Falls State Park and Gambrill State Park, 14039 Catoctin Hollow Rd., Thurmont, MD 21788; www.cunninghamgambrill.org

Local outdoor stores: The Trail House, 17 S. Market St., Frederick, MD; (301) 694-8448; www.trailhouse.com

GREEN TIP
Avoid sensitive ecological areas. Hike and rest at least
200 feet from streams, lakes, and rivers.

7 Great Falls Park, MD / Chesapeake and Ohio Canal National Historic Park

A public relations effort by Supreme Court Justice William O. Douglas in 1954 saved the Chesapeake and Ohio Canal and towpath from a different fate: The National Park Service had proposed paving the route as a scenic roadway on par with Skyline Drive. Instead, the towpath and canal are preserved, mostly in their original state. Between Georgetown and Great Falls, it serves as a recreational release valve for metropolitan Washington. It also makes an ideal spine for a day hike that veers off course at every opportunity to explore wooded hillsides, small stream valleys, floodplain forests, and dramatic rock cliffs overlooking the mighty Potomac River.

Start: From the Carderock Recreation Area, north parking lot

Distance: 9.1-mile loop

Approximate hiking time: 3 to 4 hours

Difficulty: Difficult due to a combination of distance, several bushwhack options, and extremely rocky, technical terrain along the Billy Goat Trail on Bear Island

Trail surface: The C&O Canal is a hard-packed dirt and stone path. Woodland dirt footpaths and old dirt mining roads characterize trails along the Gold Mine Loop. Billy Goat Trail, especially the section on Bear Island, features technical terrain across large and exposed rock faces.

Seasons: Autumn for the foliage colors, and winter for unobstructed views

Other trail users: Joggers, bicyclists, rock climbers, and kayakers (carrying their boats down to the river from Old Angler's Inn parking area)

Handicapped accessibility: Overlooks on Olmsted Island of the Potomac River at Mathers Gorge are accessible via a series of bridges and boardwalks.

Canine compatibility: While generally leashed dogs are permitted, it's not practical for this described route because of the national park bans on pets on Olmsted Island, Bear Island, and "Section A" of the Billy Goat Trail.

Land status: National historical park

Fees and permits: The only location in the park that collects entrance fees is Great Falls Entrance Station on MacArthur Blvd. All other access to the park is free.

Schedule: Dawn to dusk daily, 365 days a year. Great Falls Tavern is open 9:00 a.m. to 4:30 p.m. Wed through Sun; closed Mon, Tues, and on Thanksgiving, Christmas Day, and New Year's Day.

Facilities: Restrooms are located at the trailhead and Great Falls Tavern. There are picnic tables, a snack bar, visitor center, and bookstore at Great Falls Tavern. Hiker-biker and drive-in campsites are available every few miles up and down the canal, open year-round.

Maps: DeLorme *Maryland/Delaware Atlas & Gazetteer:* Page 46 B2. USGS 7.5 minute series: *Falls Church, VA/MD.* Potomac Appalachian Trail Club's Map D: *Trails of the Potomac Gorge Area* available from the PATC (see *Trail contacts*). A variety of trail maps and walking guides can be downloaded from the park website.

Trail contacts: Chesapeake and Ohio Canal National Historical Park, Great Falls Tavern Visitors Center, 11710 MacArthur Blvd., Potomac, MD 20854; (301) 767-3714; Park main number: (301) 739-4200; www.nps.gov/choh

Potomac Appalachian Trail Club (PATC), 118 Park St. SE, Vienna, VA 22180; (703) 242-0315; www.patc.net

Special considerations: Springtime flooding on the Potomac may force temporary closure of Billy Goat Trail on Bear Island with little or no advance notice. If so, finish the described route by using the C&O Canal towpath.

Finding the trailhead: Distance from Washington, D.C.: 13 miles
From I-495 (Capital Beltway): From Maryland, take exit 41 (Carderock/Great Falls, MD) and merge directly onto Clara Barton Parkway westbound. From Virginia, take exit 41 (Clara Barton Parkway/Glen Echo), and on the exit ramp veer left, following signs for Carderock and Clara Barton Parkway. Drive 0.9 mile on the Clara Barton Parkway and take the Carderock Recreation Area exit. Turn left at the top of the ramp, cross over the parkway, and follow the road as it sweeps right and downhill. Reach a stop sign in 0.3 mile from the parkway. Turn right (north) and drive 0.5 mile to the north parking area. The trailhead is adjacent to the bathrooms. Trailhead GPS: N38 58.570' / W77 12.344'

The Hike

In the woods above Great Falls, a small footpath called the Woodland Trail traverses a hillside. A few hundred feet below, walkers and bikers follow Berma Road between Old Angler's Inn parking area and Lock 16 on the C&O Canal. Here in the summertime woods, it's cool beneath a high canopy of oaks and yellow (tulip) poplars. All the signs of an active woodland community are present: hollowed-out logs, scurrying footsteps of chipmunks and squirrels on a dry, leafy forest floor. Wind rustles the leaves overhead, and there are myriad calls of songbirds.

Off to the left of the trail, there is a wide depression in the earth. Then another, then another. It looks as if someone started to dig a wide round hole, then gave up the effort, moved down the trail a bit, and started again.

▶ **KID APPEAL**

A stable of about six mules pull the C&O Canal boat rides, much like they did in the 1870s. The mules all have names and unique personalities. When not working the eight-month season on the canal, they relax at George Washington's Mount Vernon in Alexandria, Virginia. Mules— actually a cross between a horse and a donkey—were the "engines" of the C&O Canal boats, as explained by costumed park interpreters on board the boat rides. Children were usually the mule drivers, and the mules became their pets and companions.

These excavations—six in total spread over the first 0.1 mile of Woodland Trail after its junction with Angler Trail—are too obvious to be natural. Scattered about the edges of a few are piles of quartzite rock, milky in color and streaked with darker minerals. A healthy maple tree grows out of one depression, giving the impression that whenever these holes were made, it wasn't recently.

Legend has it that during the Civil War, a Union soldier was washing dishes in a stream nearby to these woods when a glint caught his eye. Thus was born Maryland's very own gold rush. The soldier, Private McCleary of Pennsylvania, returned after the war, bought several farms in the area, and began searching for gold. Rumors of his activity spread. The first mine shaft was sunk in 1867.

Out-fall at Great Falls Tavern

In all, some twenty-one mines operated in the Great Falls area in Maryland. The most successful mines were those that struck gold-bearing quartz veins. Exploratory trenches were dug to locate these veins, and horizontal tunnels, called adits, were drilled into hillsides. The largest mine, Maryland Mine, operated sporadically from 1900 to 1939, and evidence of its existence remains: vertical shafts as deep as 100

C&O CANAL HISTORY

Construction of the C&O Canal was spurred by a desire by East Coast merchants to tap into a growing Ohio River trade in farm goods and material. It was the third major water-based transportation system in America. The first, the Patowmack Canal, was a series of skirting canals around five significant falls on the Potomac between Harpers Ferry and Georgetown. It was bankrupt and out of business before the C&O ever broke ground. The second, and most successful, was New York's Erie Canal, completed in 1825. Construction of the C&O Canal was begun three years later, in 1828. It reached Cumberland, Maryland, in 1858 and went no farther. It operated until 1924, although for most of its career, the Baltimore & Ohio Railroad eclipsed it in terms of profitability.

Canal boat ride

feet in the hillside that hikers can explore via the Gold Mine Loop Trail. Maryland was also the most successful mine. It operated a mill for crushing extracted ore, a blacksmith shop, an assay office, and a water tower. Average yield, according to park interpretive material, was a half ounce of gold per ton of hard quartz.

Hikers can still see the Maryland Mine's old water tower (rebuilt by the park service) via a spur trail that links the Gold Mine Loop with Falls Road. The mine shafts are filled in and fenced off, leaving those small swales alongside the Woodland Trail as tantalizing clues to this era of speculation that ended in 1940. Official records of the U.S. Mint record some 5,000 ounces of gold from all of Maryland's mining activity, the majority coming from these hillsides.

Miles and Directions

0.0 START from the north parking area of the Carderock Recreation Area. Walk past the bathrooms on a concrete path that becomes a dirt path. Cross a boardwalk over low terrain that may be wet in the rainy seasons, and reach a T junction with blue-blazed Billy Goat Trail. (*FYI:* The rocks before you are the top of a 60-foot-high riverside bluff known to climbers as Jungle Cliff and Hades Heights. In the evening and on weekends, it is crawling with climbers setting up top rope anchors and testing their skills on well-worn routes.)

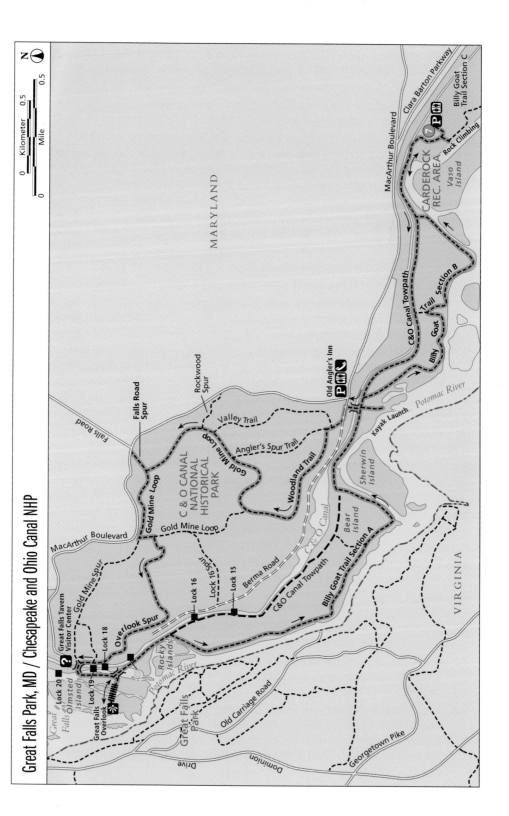

Great Falls Park, MD / Chesapeake and Ohio Canal NHP

N

Kilometer
0   0.5

Mile
0   0.5

MARYLAND

VIRGINIA

Potomac River

Clara Barton Parkway

MacArthur Boulevard

CARDEROCK REC. AREA

Billy Goat Trail Section C

Rock Climbing

Vaso Island

Section B

Billy Goat Trail

C&O Canal Towpath

Old Angler's Inn

Kayak Launch

Sherwin Island

Bear Island

Billy Goat Trail Section A

C&O Canal Towpath

C&O Canal

Berma Road

Lock 15

Lock 16 Spur

Lock 16

Overlook Spur

Lock 18

Gold Mine Spur

MacArthur Boulevard

Falls Road

Falls Road Spur

Rockwood Spur

Valley Trail

Angler's Spur Trail

Gold Mine Loop

C&O CANAL NATIONAL HISTORICAL PARK

Gold Mine Loop

Woodland Trail

Great Falls Tavern Visitor Center

Great Falls Lock 20

Falls Olmsted Island

Lock 19

Great Falls Overlook

Rocky Islands

Potomac River

Great Falls Park

Dominion Drive

Old Carriage Road

Georgetown Pike

0.05 Turn right (north) on Billy Goat Trail. As you walk through the woodland, watch for a double blue blaze, where you veer right to avoid a climber's path down to the base of the rocks.

0.1 Emerge from the woods onto the C&O Canal towpath. Turn left (north).

0.5 Pass a junction on the left for the Billy Goat Trail. Continue straight on the towpath. (*Note:* The trail left is the return portion of this route.)

1.5 Turn right and cross the C&O Canal on a footbridge that leads to the Old Angler's Inn parking area. Climb a set of rough-hewn steps to the lower parking lot. Look left and locate a set of wood stairs near the chemical toilets (the stairs have a track alongside them for pushing a bicycle uphill). Climb and, at the top, turn left onto Berma Road.

1.6 Reach a sewer facility surrounded by a chain link fence. Trace the fence around and behind the facility. Look for a dirt path that enters the woods and reaches the signed junction of Valley Trail and Angler's Spur Trail. Veer left at this forked junction and climb on the Angler's Spur Trail.

1.7 Turn left (north) onto the Woodland Trail, a single-track woods path.

2.4 Turn right (east) onto Gold Mine Loop Trail. At this point, it follows a wide roadbed.

2.7 Reach a junction on the right for Angler's Spur Trail. Continue straight on Gold Mine Loop. (*Bailout:* Turn right on Angler's Spur Trail; descend 0.7 mile to the C&O Canal towpath via Berma Road and the Old Angler's Inn parking area for a 4.9-mile loop.)

2.8 Pass a junction on the right for the Valley Trail. In a few feet, avoid a right turn for Rockwood Spur. Gold Mine Loop narrows and becomes a woodland path here. (*Bailout:* Turn right on Valley Trail; descend 0.8 mile to the C&O Canal towpath via Berma Road and the Old Angler's Inn parking area for a 5.1-mile loop.)

3.1 Gold Mine Loop makes a hard left (north) at the junction with a spur trail to MacArthur Boulevard at Falls Road. (*Side trip:* This short but worthwhile 0.1-mile spur takes you past ruins of an old gold-mining operation dating to the Civil War era.)

3.4 Double blue blazes herald a trail junction. Sweep left past an unmarked trail on the right that leads back to MacArthur Boulevard, and then, within 100 feet, turn right (north) to follow Gold Mine Loop toward Great Falls.

3.6 *Stay alert:* Veer left on an unmarked trail and follow it downhill along a small stream gully. (*Note:* This is a bushwhack on a well-trod trail that ultimately connects to the Overlook Trail.)

3.8 *Stay alert:* Reach a point where the stream you've followed drops precipitously off the hillside. Here, swing right and climb up and over a small knoll. You are now paralleling the canal on the Overlook Trail. Avoid an unmarked trail on the left that drops down into the stream gully and ultimately dumps you out onto Berma Road near Lock 16.

4.1 A spectacular view high above the C&O Canal and Great Falls. In late fall, winter, and early spring, you can see clear across the Potomac to Virginia's Great Falls Park.

4.2 Reach a junction with Lock 19 Loop and turn left. In less than 0.1 mile, emerge from the woods and walk north alongside the canal approaching Lock 19. A scenic spillway marks the lock.

4.3 Turn left on a hard-packed stone and dirt path, cross Lock 19 on a footbridge, and descend to the C&O Canal towpath. (*FYI:* To reach the park visitor center inside Great Falls Tavern, plus bathrooms, a snack bar, and the canal boat ride, turn right at this junction and follow the dirt and rock path north to the large two-story brick building that houses the visitor center.)

4.5 Turn right (west) and detour along the Olmsted Island bridges to an overlook of Great Falls. After exploring, return to the towpath and turn right (south). (*FYI:* The island is named for the famous landscape architect Frederick Law Olmsted, designer of Central Park and other metropolitan oases.)

5.2 Turn right (west) at a sign for blue-blazed Billy Goat Trail (Section A). (*Caution:* This 1.6-mile trail is periodically closed due to flooding and hazardous conditions. Young children are discouraged, and pets are not allowed. See Special considerations on page 56 for more information on the risks this trail poses for young and/or beginner hikers. If the trail is closed, follow the towpath south and resume mileage cues at mile 6.8.)

5.4 Emerge from pine woods to your first views of the Potomac River and Mather Gorge on the right. Upstream, the Potomac streams through the Rocky Islands in three channels.

5.6 Emerge from woods onto open rock.

5.8 Descend to river level, then climb back up to resume walking at cliff height, overlooking the river.

6.1 Pass Purplehorse Beach, a small cove and sandbar at the river's edge.

6.2 Bear left (southeast) as the trail splits around a steep rock formation. (*Note:* The right fork rejoins Billy Goat Trail after taking a more difficult route over the rock promontory.)

6.3 Sweep around a pond on your right and descend to cross a stream. (*Bailout:* After crossing the stream, look for an unmarked path that turns left [east]. Follow this back to the towpath if you've had enough of uneven terrain and difficult trekking over open rock.)

6.5 Reach a final overlook onto the Potomac. On the shore opposite, Difficult Run is visible. Follow the trail as it sweeps left (east). In the next 0.1 mile, descend steeply to cross a stream, climb the opposite bank, and skirt a channel that divides Bear Island from Sherwin Island to the south.

6.8 Reach a junction with the C&O Canal towpath. Turn right (south).

7.2 Stay straight past a bridge to the Old Angler's Inn parking area.

7.3 Turn right (south) on blue-blazed Billy Goat Trail (Section B). The trail is a narrow footpath that is less technical than Section A. (*FYI:* For views over the Potomac, follow any one of a number of unmarked footpaths that lead to rock outcrops.)

7.8 Turn right and descend to the river's edge. Climb steeply up and between large boulders. (*Caution:* The trail here is not self-evident, and it takes some scouting to locate the blue blazes. Watch your footing.)

8.0 Swing left into a stream gully. Cross on the large boulders, turn right, and follow the trail back to the river's edge.

8.6 Reach a junction with the C&O Canal towpath. Turn right (south) onto the towpath.

9.0 Turn right (west) onto Billy Goat Trail (Section C).

9.1 HIKE ENDS at the north parking area of the Carderock Recreation Area.

Hike Information

Local information: C&O Canal Trust, 1850 Dual Highway Suite 100, Hagerstown, MD 21740; (301) 714-2233; www.canaltrust.org/plan

Montgomery County Visitors Information Center, 12900 Middlebrook Road, Suite 1400, Germantown, MD; (301) 916-0698; www.cvbmontco.com

Good eats: Old Angler's Inn, 10801 MacArthur Blvd., Potomac, MD; (301) 365-2425; www.oldanglersinn.com. Serving canal travelers since 1860, located just off the trail for a casual post-hike lunch on the patio.

Irish Inn at Glen Echo, 6119 Tulane Ave., Glen Echo, MD; (301) 229-6600; www.irishinnglenecho.com. Located at the corner of Tulane Avenue and MacArthur Boulevard in Glen Echo.

Local outdoor stores: REI, 910 Rose Avenue, North Bethesda, MD; (301) 770-1751; www.rei.com

Dick's Sporting Goods, 2 Grand Corner Ave., Gaithersburg, MD; (301) 947-0200; www.dickssportinggoods.com

Hike tours: C&O Canal park rangers lead weekly hikes. Check with the Great Falls Tavern Visitors Center for schedules.

Organizations: C&O Canal Association, Glen Echo, MD; (301) 983-0825; www.candocanal.org

The Nature Conservancy, Maryland/D.C. Field Office, Bethesda, MD; (301) 897-8570; www.tnc.org

Potomac Conservancy, Silver Spring, MD; (301) 608-1188; www.potomac.org

GREEN TIP

When hiking with your dog, stay in the center of the path and keep Fido close by. Dogs that run loose can harm fragile soils and spread pesky plants by carrying their seeds.

8 Jug Bay Natural Area (Patuxent River Park)

At a wide spot on the Patuxent River, this 2,000-acre preserve is crisscrossed by 8 miles of trails. Our 4.5-mile loop, while not accessing every trail, manages to keep you in the woods the entire time while offering the best river views. Black Walnut Creek interpretive nature trail passes along boardwalks through a wetland, ending at an observation deck overlooking the serene bay. From here it is another 1-mile flat hike through sweetgum and yellow poplar to a quiet river bluff overlook. Trail blazes are hit-and-miss and trail signs nonexistent, but a free hand-drawn map supplied by the park's visitor center offers helpful mileage cues and routes.

Start: Dirt road opposite the visitor center, adjacent to the bathrooms
Distance: 4.5-mile loop
Approximate hiking time: 2 hours
Difficulty: Easy
Trail surface: Dirt footpaths, dirt forest roads, paved road
Seasons: April through Nov. Spring and fall bring migratory songbirds and waterfowl to the preserve.
Other trail users: Hikers, horseback riders, and mountain bikers
Handicapped accessibility: Handicapped-logo vehicles can drive a gravel road to the Patuxent Rural Life Museums, where several buildings are ADA compliant. Accommodations for groups on request, two weeks in advance.
Canine compatibility: Leashed dogs permitted, except on the boardwalk
Land status: County park
Fees and permits: None for hikers
Schedule: Open daily 8:00 a.m. to dusk. The park office and visitor center is open daily 8:00 a.m. to 4:00 p.m. The trails are for day use only, except for groups with prior arrangement.
Facilities/features: Restrooms, visitor center, fishing pier, canoe and kayak rentals, three public boat ramps, boat tours, and the Chesapeake Bay Critical Area Tour, a 4-mile driving/ bicycling tour. The Patuxent Rural Life Museums, a collection of late-nineteenth-century buildings, tell the story of farming life in southern Maryland. The American Indian Village replicates an Eastern Woodland Village.
Maps: DeLorme *Virginia Atlas & Gazetteer:* Page 38 A1. USGS 7.5 minute series: *Bristol, MD*. A trail map can be downloaded from www .pgparks.com
Trail contacts: Jug Bay Natural Area (headquarters for Patuxent River Park), 16000 Croom Airport Road, Upper Marlboro, MD 20772; (301) 627-6074; http://outdoors.pgparks .com/Sites/Jug_Bay_Natural_Area.htm
Special considerations: Bow hunters can use the park during white-tailed deer season (Sept through Jan). Waterfowl hunters lease duck blinds on the Patuxent River on a seasonal basis.

Finding the trailhead: Distance from Washington, D.C.: 23 miles
   From MD 4 East: Exit onto US 301 south and drive 1.7 miles. Turn left onto Croom Station Road. In 1.6 miles, turn left on Croom Road/Rt. 382. In 1.5 miles turn left on Croom Airport Road. The park entrance road is in 2 miles on the left. It leads 1.5 miles to the visitor center, parking area, and restrooms. Trailhead GPS: N38 46.407' / W76 42.662'

The Hike

The word *gem* means something prized, especially for great beauty. It's an apt description for Jug Bay, a 2,000-acre county park and nature preserve on the banks of the Patuxent River. Here is a true natural gem—a small, compact tidal freshwater marsh teeming with wildlife and natural significance.

This beauty is evident just minutes into Black Walnut Creek. As you descend through a valley created by a feeder stream, the world of highways and stores and all its associated noise, which is located within minutes of this urban preserve, slip away. You're immersed in a lush world of plants and water. Maple and sweetgum shade the hillside; ferns and mayapple blanket the forest floor. There's a high-pitched whistle of an osprey that floats in from high above Jug Bay. Near the mouth of Black Walnut Creek, bald cypress trees stand in thigh-deep water, fringed by arrow arum and pickerelweed. In spring, a gentle breeze off the water might rustle the papery tan leaves of American beech that have hung onto the branches so tenaciously all winter.

Birdwatching on Jug Bay

The bulk of Jug Bay Natural Area's 8 miles of trails passes through upland forest of sweetgum, tulip trees, oak, hickory, and elm. The best of these trails are those along the river, where views open up across Jug Bay in winter and spring. Winter is a time of seasonally low water. With Jug Bay's depth only a few feet deep outside the main channel, the embayment can appear to be one huge mudflat. With the warmer months come the freshwater marsh plants. By midsummer, the pickerelweed's blue blossoms are showing, intermixed with yellow pond lilies. A marsh that can appear so devoid of life in winter has a lush, green tropical look in summer.

Birdlife fluctuates seasonally as well. It is said that 25,000 waterfowl descend on the more than 4,000 protected acres around Jug Bay. (In addition to this nature preserve, there is a wildlife sanctuary to the south, and another across the river in Anne Arundel County.) Tundra swans, Canada geese, and green-winged teal winter over. In fall, tens of thousands of sora rails flock here during migration. They seek grains of northern wild rice, which is more abundant here than anywhere else in all of the Chesapeake Bay's freshwater estuarine reaches. It's this plant that so preoccupies scientists and researchers who use Jug Bay as a kind of outdoor laboratory to study marsh ecosystems, birds, and plant life. For while the sora loves the seed head, with its long black grains that congregate in a bushy head, ducks and Canada geese love the stems and roots. Researchers responded by fencing the biggest stands of wild rice and removed the offending geese, so to favor the sora.

Sora belong to the genus *Gruiforms*, and together the six species form a fascinating aspect of any marsh ecosystem. Their call is a harsh, repetitious series, with variety between the six species in pitch and tone. All of them, however, call in a series of five or six, with the last few calls tailing off to silence. One call can set off six, ten, or even twenty other rails in the vicinity, resulting in a cacophony. It is unforgettable, and a bit mysterious given that the bird is rarely seen, hunkered down in the thick vegetation.

Miles and Directions

0.0 START on a dirt road that heads downhill opposite the visitor center. Before reaching the bottom, veer left (south) onto Black Walnut Creek Nature Trail. Over the next 0.2 mile, this trail, marked by black arrows on white sticks, will descend to and cross Black Walnut Creek via a boardwalk.

0.2 Bear left at a fork in the boardwalk. (*Note:* The right fork leads to an observation platform overlooking Black Walnut Creek.) Within a few feet after this split, the boardwalk ends. Bear left again when a dirt footpath forks right.

0.3 Bear left (east) on a boardwalk leading to an observation blind overlooking Jug Bay. After visiting the blind, return to the Black Walnut Creek Nature Trail, turn left (south), and climb a short, steep hill. At the top, turn left (south) again and follow Green Trail, which is an old dirt forest road. (*Note:* This trail is multiuse for horseback riding.)

0.9 Stay straight (south) and merge onto Brown Trail at an intersection where Green Trail turns right.

1.3 Reach the end of the Brown Trail at an overlook of the Patuxent River shaded by a large oak tree. Return to Green Trail.

Jug Bay Natural Area (Patuxent River Park)

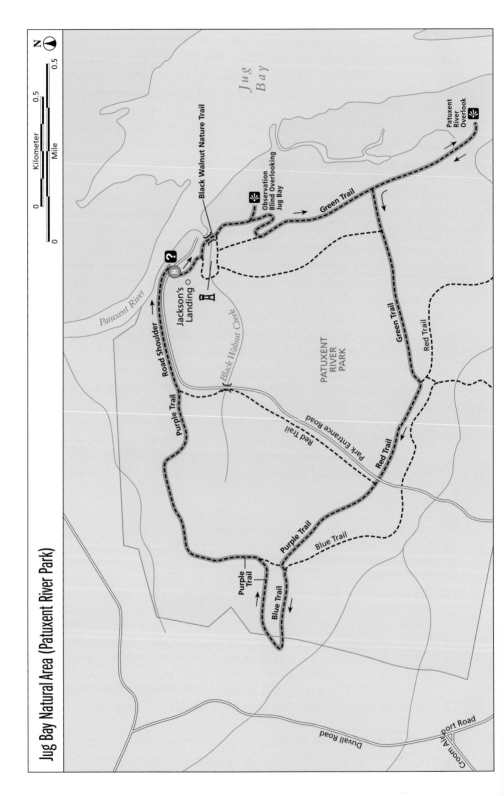

1.6 Turn left (west) on Green Trail.

2.2 Turn right (north) on Red Trail. (*Note:* A left on Red Trail leads to the park's southern trails, which can add as many as 4 miles to a day's hike.)

2.5 Cross Park Entrance Road. Two posts mark where the Red Trail reenters the woods.

3.1 Turn right (east) onto an unmarked, but clear, dirt trail. It swings south, parallels Red Trail for a few hundred yards, merges with Purple Trail, and swings east to follow the edge of a loblolly pine tree plantation.

3.5 As the trail passes through a forest of young maples and sweetgum, notice on the right the headwaters of Black Walnut Creek.

4.0 Turn right (east) and walk alongside the paved Park Entrance Road.

4.5 HIKE ENDS at the visitor center.

OPTIONS

The Chesapeake Bay Critical Area Tour links Jug Bay Natural Area and Merkle Wildlife Sanctuary, a 2,000-acre preserve south of Mattaponi Creek. The 4-mile-long one-way road is open to hikers and bikers daily 8 a.m. to dusk and to vehicles on Sunday, 10:00 a.m. to 3:00 p.m. The road can be used to extend a hike into Merkle lands by hiking for several miles on pavement.

Hike Information

Local information: Prince George's County Conference and Visitor's Bureau, 9200 Basil Court, Suite 101, Largo, MD; (301) 925-8300; www.visitprincegeorgescounty .com

Good eats: Rip's Country Inn, 3809 N. Crain Highway, Bowie, MD; (301) 805-5900; www.ripscountryinn.com. The former 1950s truck stop is frequented by local farmers and Washington politicians alike for the catch of the day and the free warm muffins (the flavor changes each day).

Hike tours: Guided nature and birding hikes and geocaching are offered in the park. Sign up online in advance at www.pgparks.com.

Organizations: Jug Bay Wetlands Sanctuary, 1361 Wrighton Rd., Lothian, MD 20711; (410) 741-9330; www.jugbay.org

Chesapeake Conservancy, Annapolis, MD; (443) 321-3610; www.chesapeake conservancy.org and www.findyourchesapeake.com

9 Patuxent National Wildlife Refuge

Patuxent Research Refuge offers a pleasant contrast to the sprawl of Washington, D.C., and Baltimore. Set in the metro corridor between these two cities, it protects almost 13,000 acres of woodlands within the watershed of the Little Patuxent and Patuxent Rivers. Its northern tract, where the featured trails are located, was a former military base. Army recruits trained in ordnance here, learning to shoot guns and detonate bombs, grenades, mortars, and tank shells. Hikers today enjoy other sights and sounds—birds, frogs, deer, and wildflowers—but the refuge's explosive past informs the first rule of hiking here: Always stay on the trail.

Start: From the North Tract Visitor Contact Station on Bald Eagle Drive

Distance: 3 miles of woodland trails and 9 miles of gravel road

Approximate hiking time: 2 to 6 hours depending on routes

Difficulty: Easy to Moderate

Trail surface: Forest paths, a boardwalk, gravel roads

Seasons: Best in spring and fall for observing migrating waterfowl and songbirds

Other trail users: Little Patuxent River Trail and Forest Habitats Nature Trail are for hikers only. Other trails are open to hiking, biking, horses, cross-country skiing, and hunters in season.

Handicapped accessibility: The first 150 feet of the Forest Habitats Nature Trail is an accessible boardwalk. All gravel roads in the North Tract are open to vehicles with disabled persons tags, available at the Visitor Contact Station. The Blue Heron Blind at the end of the Orange Trail is a fully accessible observation/hunting blind. The 0.5-mile Loop Trail from the National Wildlife Visitors Center (South Tract) is paved and fully accessible.

Canine compatibility: Leashed dogs permitted. Pets are not allowed in ponds or waterways.

Land status: National wildlife refuge

Fees and permits: No fees. Obtain parking and visitor pass at the Visitor Contact Station.

Schedule: Visitor Contact Station and grounds open daily 8:00 a.m. to 4:00 p.m. Closed on federal holidays. Last permit is given 1 hour before closing.

Facilities: Bathrooms, nature center, camping (for scouts only)

Maps: DeLorme *Maryland/Delaware Atlas & Gazetteer:* Page 47 A6. USGS 7.5 minute series: *Odenton, MD* and *Laurel, MD.*

Trail contacts: Patuxent Research Refuge, North Tract Contact Station, 230 Bald Eagle Drive, Laurel, MD 20724; (301) 497-5770; http://patuxent.fws.gov

Special considerations: The North Tract of Patuxent National Wildlife Refuge was once part of Fort George G. Meade, a U.S. Army training facility. Trails and areas around them have been cleared of all known unexploded ordnances (bullets, bombs), but some remain and are hidden just beneath the ground or in wetlands. *Do not venture off trail.* If you find what looks to be an unexploded ordnance or ammunition, report it to the Visitor Contact Station. There remains an active firing range on adjacent Fort Meade, so visitors must sign a waiver and agree to stay on marked trails and roads.

Finding the trailhead: Distance from Washington, D.C.: 28 miles

From I-495 (Capital Beltway): Exit onto the Baltimore-Washington Parkway North at Greenbelt. Drive 8.3 miles and take the exit for MD 198 East (Fort Meade Road). After 1.9 miles, turn right at the refuge sign onto Bald Eagle Drive. Go 1 mile to the North Tract Visitor Contact Station (road turns to dirt after 0.4 mile). Trailhead GPS: N39 04.669' / W76 46.305'

The Hike

A hike doesn't have to be long and winding or steep and rugged in order to transport you to imaginative places. Combined, the Little Patuxent River Trail and the Forest Habitats Nature Trail in the Northern Tract of the Patuxent Research Reserve total just over 3 miles' walking distance. Yet the few hours spent walking them is bound to bring forth renewed appreciation for the natural world.

Forest Habitats Nature Trail

On the 0.75-mile Little Patuxent River Trail, a gnawed tree trunk indicates recent beaver activity. Standing on the boardwalk overlook onto this tributary of the Patuxent River, you'll hear the grunts of Canada geese. Stream water sings as it riffles around a stony midstream island. In springtime, the deep green floor of this forested wetland bursts blue with bluebell wildflowers. Around a small man-made pond, there are deer hoofprints in the mud. Calls of bullfrogs and tree frogs silence as you walk the boardwalks spanning low, wet ground.

Leaving the Little Patuxent behind, you enter a mixed pine and hardwood forest on the 2.5-mile Forest Habitats Nature Trail. Here, there is a chance to delve deeper into the woodland environment. Elevation loss/gain is minimal, although the trail does a nice job of riding a small knoll before dropping down into a stream valley. A fox may leave its scat strategically in the middle of the dirt trail, a reminder that something other than humans lays stake to this ground. From somewhere deep into the pines, an unseen northern cardinal calls *tic-tic-tic* from its perch. If you're walking in springtime, linger beneath the canopy of mature American beech trees. You may feel a light brushing on your skin, like raindrops. It's the tiny scales from the beech's thornlike buds that have peeled away and fallen.

The American beech in many ways symbolizes woodland hikes in the Coastal Plain region of Maryland and Virginia. It is everywhere: as a skinny-trunked tree in the understory of larger sweetgums and tulip poplars or as a large, broad-trunked specimen in the forest canopy. Its tight gray bark splits as the tree grows larger; the tree is an oft-preferred canvas for young lovers with pen knives. Its light tan leaves linger on the branch throughout winter, only to be pushed off by new buds come spring. Where they grow in clusters, it's likely that the beech are of the same family; this tree sends out rhizomes, or undergrown stems, that send up sucker shoots that grow into full-blown trees. Each sucker is genetically a clone of the mother tree.

PATUXENT: NWR HEADQUARTERS

In the world of wildlife biology, Patuxent's name stands out for another reason. The refuge's Central Tract (off-limits to general public) is the administrative and research headquarters for our National Wildlife Refuge system—the nerve center for the 550 refuges in America. This is a clearinghouse for research data and administrative rulings, where hard science gathered in far-flung places like the Florida Everglades and the Alaskan arctic is stored. Bird-banding studies alone represent more than eight million records (and counting) dating back to the early twentieth century.

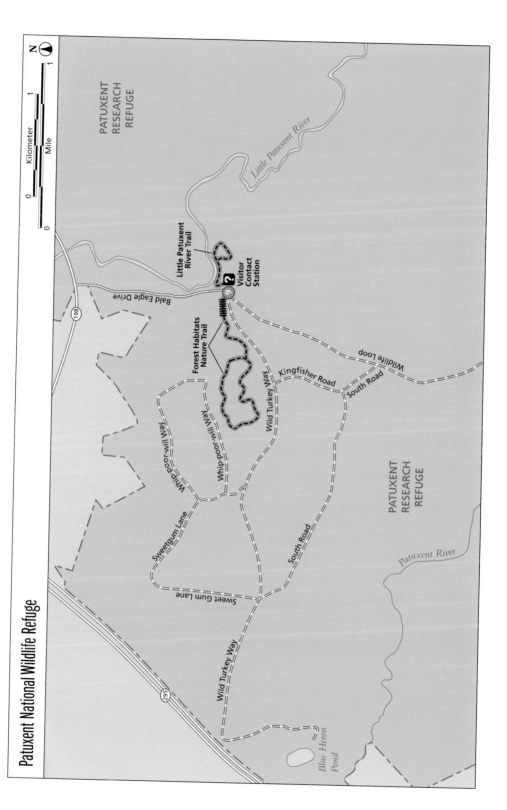

Patuxent National Wildlife Refuge

Volunteer Pamela Waterworth removes invasive Lesser Celandine.

Beech trees share a trait of one of the most inconspic-uous plants of a wet forest: the club moss. Ground pine, a type of club moss, is evident along the Forest Habitats Nature Trail after it descends off a hill and parallels a seasonal stream. At a glance, it looks like a dollhouse-size pine tree. It is a marker plant, in that it can tell you how old (or young) a forest is. Rarely do you find ground pine in a forest more than fifty years old. As tiny as they are, they share something in common with the beech trees upslope a few feet away: They replicate themselves via underground stems and suckers that rise up a few inches away. Biologists say that in prehistoric time, the small ground pine grew to more than 100 feet high. Its spores and decaying vegetation formed coal that we have mined for more than a century. Today, this inconspicuous ground cover is a chance to appreciate that in small things, there are big stories.

There are a dozen types of frogs, fourteen types of snakes, and dozens of species of dragonflies and damselflies in the refuge.

OPTIONS

The South Tract of the refuge is home to the National Wildlife Refuge Visitor Center and Cash Lake.

Hike Information

Local information: Prince George's County Conference and Visitor's Bureau, 9200 Basil Court, Largo, MD; (301) 925-8300; www.visitprincegeorgescounty.com

Local events/attractions: Patuxent Wildlife Festival, National Wildlife Visitor Center, 10901 Scarlet Tanager Loop, Laurel, MD; (301) 497-5763; http://patuxent.fws .gov. Annual autumn festival in early October marks National Wildlife Refuge Week. Live animals, kids' activities, tours of the USGS Patuxent Wildlife Research Center. The Wildlife Conservation & Recreation Day takes places in August and the Monarch Festival in September.

Good eats: Mango's Grill, 14605 Baltimore Ave., Laurel, MD; (301) 776-8834; www.mangosgrillrestaurant.com. Authentic, fresh, affordable Mexican fare. Great margaritas.

Local outdoor stores: Modell's Sporting Goods, Greenway Center, 7409 Greenbelt Rd., Greenbelt, MD; (301) 345-4401; www.modells.com

Hike tours: Wildlife Conservation Tram Tours depart from the National Wildlife Visitor Center (South Tract) spring through fall. In the North Tract of the refuge, volunteers and naturalists lead wildflower walks, bird tours, and wildlife-themed hikes. See http://patuxent.fws.gov for a month-by-month schedule of tours.

Organizations: Friends of Patuxent, 10901 Scarlet Tanager Court, Laurel, MD; (301) 497-5789; www.friendsofpatuxent.org

10 Rosaryville State Park

The Perimeter Trail was built with mountain bikers in mind, which explains its meandering route through the forests and fields of Rosaryville State Park, near Upper Marlborough. As it passes through a mature forest of American beech and oaks, the trail skirts large fields. Here, where fields meet forest, the "edge" habitat is thick with vines and fruit- and nut-bearing trees that offer a variety of shelter and food for songbirds. It happens to be one of the busiest places in the outdoors, making this route especially conducive to birding and wildlife-watching.

Start: From the Perimeter Trail parking lot at a trail map board and sign

Distance: 8-mile loop

Approximate hiking time: 3 to 4 hours

Difficulty: Moderate due to distance, but gently rolling topography, little elevation gain, and well-marked and well-maintained trails make going easy.

Trail surface: Perimeter Trail is a dirt woods path that merges with old dirt forest roads in several areas.

Seasons: Best in early spring and fall, when birding activity is at its peak

Other trail users: Mountain bikers, horseback riders, archery-only hunting

Handicapped accessibility: While trails are not accessible, there is reserved handicapped parking at picnic shelters. The shelters and nearby bathrooms are wheelchair accessible.

Canine compatibility: Leashed dogs permitted

Land status: State park

Fees and permits: Pay fee at an honor box at the park entrance. Annual pass is available by calling (301) 856-9656 or visiting www .mountairymansion.org.

Schedule: Open daily year-round, sunrise to sunset

Facilities: Historic Mount Airy Mansion (you can walk the grounds, but the house is open only for special event rentals); picnic shelters with nearby bathrooms, 0.5 mile into the park from the turnoff for trailhead parking.

Maps: DeLorme *Maryland/Delaware Atlas & Gazetteer:* Page 37 A6. USGS 7.5 minute series: *Upper Marlboro, MD.* See also National Geographic's TOPO! software, Mid-Atlantic Region, Disc 4: Washington, D.C. A trail map can be downloaded from the park's website.

Trail contacts: Rosaryville State Park, Fred Eskew Recreation Area, 7805 West Marlton Ave., Upper Marlboro, MD 20735; (301) 856-9656; www.dnr.maryland.gov/publiclands/ pages/southern/rosaryville.aspx

Special considerations: The state park is home to the Marlborough Horse Trials cross-country course, considered one of the finest in the country (www.marlboroughhorsetrials.org). The park pond is stocked with bass, bluegill, catfish, and sunfish. A Maryland Freshwater Sport Fishing license is required and may be obtained at www.dnr.state.md.us/fisheries. Archery-only deer hunting is allowed on select dates. A permit and reservation are required by calling (855) 855-3906 or visiting www.dnr .maryland.gov/huntersguide.

Finding the trailhead: Distance from Washington, D.C.: 17 miles

From US 301 and MD 4: Drive south on US 301. In 3.8 miles turn right onto Marlton Avenue West, a one-way road heading south. In 0.2 mile veer right to enter the state park at a self-serve pay station. In 0.2 mile from the pay station, turn right into a parking lot. Locate a map board and trail register. (*Note:* Continuing straight from the turnoff for trailhead parking leads to bathrooms and picnic shelters in 0.5 mile.) Trailhead GPS: N38 46.814' / W76 48.142'

The Hike

An autumn woods walk on the Perimeter Trail is a noisy affair: Your footsteps crunch dry leaves. Ankles roll as you step on the spiky "gumballs" that have dropped off the sweetgum trees. Overhead, the wind whistles through the bare tree branches.

Flash forward to spring. A streambed that was dry through late autumn and winter is awash with early spring runoff. Your footsteps scare up a pair of red-headed woodpeckers hacking at a downed log; they leave with a disgruntled chortlelike call. The

Old barn

Mushrooms on a nurse log

colossal-size buds of yellow (tulip) poplar litter the trail. Mayapple is past blossom, but the broad-lobed green leaves of this low plant are easily identified against the leaf litter of the forest floor. (Only mayapples with three leaves produce the red applelike fruit that gives this understory plant its name.)

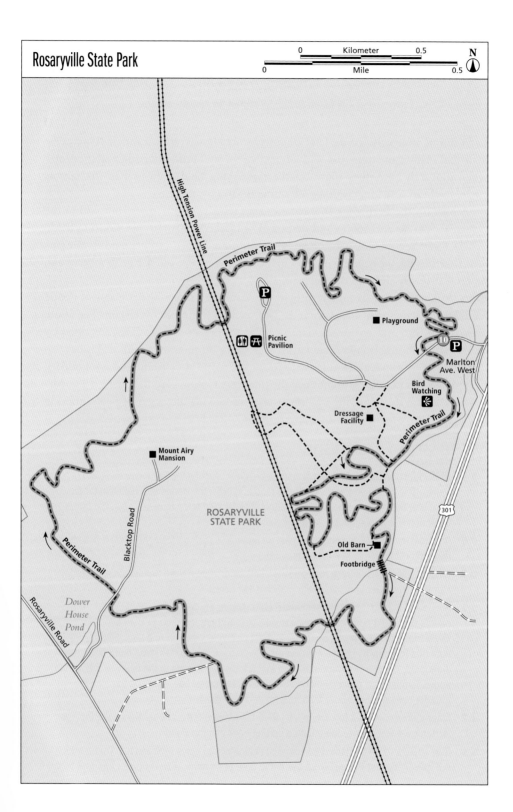

Rosaryville State Park

Kilometer
0   0.5

Mile
0   0.5

N

High Tension Power Line

Perimeter Trail

P

Picnic Pavilion

Playground

10

P

Marlton Ave. West

Bird Watching

Dressage Facility

Perimeter Trail

Mount Airy Mansion

ROSARYVILLE STATE PARK

Blacktop Road

301

Old Barn

Footbridge

Perimeter Trail

Dower House Pond

Rosaryville Road

Autumn and early spring lend themselves to a great walk through Rosaryville State Park. This is the time that warblers and vireos are found under the forest canopy; when monarch butterflies alight on the nourishing field plants; when the raptors circle overhead watching, waiting for a time to dive.

A hike on the Perimeter Trail by and large remains in the forest, but within the first mile, two detours follow old roads and unmarked trails into neighboring fields. Where forest segues into grassy field, birds and four-legged critters tend to congregate. Overhead, raptors swing in lazy circles, keeping an eye out for small rodents and moles that scurry through the tall grass.

A large power line easement through the state park serves as a convenient divide for hikers. West of this line, Perimeter Trail tackles more pitchy terrain. The route dives down into and crosses numerous gullies. Some stream crossings are aided by footbridges. On others, hikers are left to cross them on their own (although none are that difficult or impassable). Where it crosses the paved road leading to Mount Airy, the trail reaches its farthest point from the trailhead. Coming around, first via a northward track, and then east, the trail once again flirts with the edges of fields, offering more excellent wildlife-viewing opportunities.

Miles and Directions

0.0   START from the map board and sign in the trailhead parking lot. Exit the parking lot by walking toward the park road. Cross the road and enter the woods at a trailhead for the Perimeter Trail. A trailboard and a white trail stick labeled MILE 0 mark the spot. The trail is open to hikers, mountain bikers, and equestrians.

0.5   Continue straight on Perimeter Trail past an unmarked path on the right. (*Side trip:* Turn right and climb to a field ideal for bird-watching.)

0.7   Cross a gully. After climbing the opposite bank, swing right (north) and continue on Perimeter Trail. (*Note:* An unmarked path branches left here.)

1.1   Stay alert: Stay straight as an unmarked path crosses Perimeter Trail. (*Bailout:* Turn left on this unmarked path, double back to mile 0.7, and retrace steps to the parking lot.) (*Side trip:* Turn right [north] on this unmarked path and climb up to a large field [taking note of a four-way junction as you climb]). Bushwhack through tall grass north down the lower field, locate a two-track road, and follow it clockwise back to the four-way mentioned above. Turn left and descend thirty or so steps to Perimeter Trail. Combine this side trip with the bailout noted above for a neat figure-eight hike.)

1.2   Enter a power line easement, turn left (south), and reenter the woods. Ahead, the trail will skirt this easement once more before delving back into the woods.

1.9   Stay straight as an unmarked trail crosses Perimeter Trail going right and left. Over the next 0.2 mile, Perimeter Trail will cross this same path twice more. (*FYI:* Perimeter Trail was built and is maintained by MORE, a mountain bike club. Bike riders dig this ribbon-candy–like trail pattern, even if it sometimes drives hikers up a wall [or a tree]!)

2.2 Bear left (south) onto a road that merges from the right. In forty steps, split left (east) off the road back into the woods.

2.3 An old gray barn looms like a ghost through the trees off the right side of the trail. There's a rusted farm tractor on the trailside.

2.4 Make a hard left (south) as Perimeter Trail merges with a dirt road that enters from the right. Immediately, cross a footbridge over a stream, and begin a long climb on an old road.

2.7 After skirting a pine plantation—with sounds from US 301 audible on the left—Perimeter Trail reenters the canopy of woods and swings hard to the right (north).

2.9 Cross straight across a power line easement and reenter woods.

3.3 Stay straight (east) as an old overgrown road splits right (south) off Perimeter Trail. In 0.2 mile, this road intersects Perimeter Trail again.

3.9 Cross straight across a road and reenter the woods, descending on a narrow footpath.

4.4 Cross straight over a blacktop road and reenter the woods. (*FYI:* This blacktop road is the private drive to historic Mount Airy, which is closed to the general public but may be reserved for special events.)

4.7 Briefly, Perimeter Trail merges with a road that enters from the right. In about 50 feet, stay straight on the trail as the road splits left. Over the next 0.5 mile, the trail takes a northerly track as it winds through woodland with occasional views to fields on the left.

5.5 Pass through a clearing that looks like it might have been an old home site. A stream forms left of the trail as you descend.

5.6 Emerge from the woods and cut diagonally left through a field that sweeps uphill on your right. Briefly enter the woods, then reemerge to skirt the field at its woodland edge.

6.3 Cross straight over a power line easement and reenter woods. Immediately, turn left (north). (*Bailout:* In a gap in the trees, enter the field and cross to the bathrooms and picnic pavilion. Follow the park road to the trailhead parking lot in 0.8 mile.)

6.6 Cross a large footbridge across a ravine.

6.8 Emerge from the woods, skirt the edge of a field, and reenter the woods. Ahead, the trail winds between woodland gullies and the edge of the field. (*FYI:* The trail here displays more "ribbon-candy" trail routing courtesy of our mountain-biking brethren.)

8.0 HIKE ENDS at the trailhead parking lot.

Hike Information

Local information: Prince George's County Conference and Visitor's Bureau, 9200 Basil Court, Largo, MD; (301) 925-8300; www.visitprincegeorgescounty.com

Local events/attractions: The Rosaryville Half Marathon and 10K Trail Run takes place in late March.

Good eats: Rip's Country Inn, 3809 N. Crain Highway (intersection of Routes 197 and 301) Bowie, MD; (301) 805-5901; www.ripscountryinn.com

11 Seneca Creek Greenway Trail North (#1)

This 7-mile stretch is one leg of the 25-mile-long Seneca Creek Greenway Trail. It follows the serpentine path of Great Seneca Creek through rich forested river bottomland, up and over steep stream hillsides, and across wide grassy meadows valued for bird-watching. There is a surprising diversity of wildlife tucked into this narrow stream valley. You may hear a pileated woodpecker as you walk through the woods or encounter an eastern box turtle crossing the trail. Whatever nature moment you enjoy, you'll be surprised by how secluded this stream valley trail feels.

Start: From the trailhead parking lot on MD 355
Distance: 13.8-mile out-and-back
Approximate hiking time: 4 hours
Difficulty: Moderate, generally flat terrain, with only a few steep inclines
Trail surface: Forested trail, dirt path, meadow paths, sidewalks, paved roads
Seasons: Best in all seasons
Other trail users: Mountain bikers, equestrians, joggers
Canine compatibility: Leashed dogs permitted
Land status: Montgomery County park
Fees and permits: None
Schedule: Park access is daily from dawn to dusk
Facilities: There are no facilities associated with this trail. Hikers must pack out all waste. There are restrooms at nearby Seneca Creek State Park.
Maps: DeLorme *Maryland/Delaware Atlas & Gazetteer:* Page 56 D1. USGS 7.5 minute series: *Gaithersburg, MD.* A trail map can be downloaded from the trail website.
Trail contacts: Montgomery County Department of Parks, 9500 Brunett Ave., Silver Spring, MD 20901; (301) 528-3450; www .montgomeryparks.org/park-and-trails/ seneca-creek-greenway-trail

Seneca Creek Greenway Trail Coalition, www.senecatrail.info. This all-volunteer group maintains the trail in cooperation with Montgomery County, the Maryland–National Capital Parks and Planning Commission, and Seneca Creek State Park. Its Web site features brief trail descriptions and rudimentary maps.
Special considerations: This trail crosses busy state and county roads three times between the trailhead and Magruder Branch Trail. Use extreme caution at each crossing. Also, there are no freshwater sources on this trail (the stream water is not safe to drink).

Finding the trailhead: Distance from Washington, D.C.: 30 miles
Southern trailhead from I-270: Take exit 11 (Montgomery Village Road). The long exit ramp ends at a traffic light, where you merge onto MD 124 northbound. Move into the left-hand turn lanes, and in 0.4 mile, at the traffic light at MD 355 (North Frederick Road), turn left onto MD 355. Drive 1.3 miles. After crossing Seneca Creek, turn right into the trailhead parking lot. Trailhead GPS: N39 10.045' / W77 13.735'
Northern trailhead from I-270: Follow directions for the southern trailhead. At the southern trailhead parking lot, continue driving west on MD 355 for another 2.6 miles. At a four-way intersection, turn right onto Henderson Corner Road. This short road ends in 0.2 mile at a junction with MD 27/Ridge Road. Turn right onto Ridge Road. In 0.4 mile, turn right onto CR 420/Brinks Road. Follow Brink Road for 1.2 miles, where you'll keep a sharp eye out for Davis Mill Road on the left.

The Hike

Even though you'll be in close physical proximity to it, you're likely to soon forget the suburbia that crowds Great Seneca Creek. It only takes a few minutes, after stepping away from the trailhead parking lot, for your senses to kick in. A tulip poplar tree is host to a bright tiger-striped mushroom. Where the stream banks steepen, in spring the pink flame azalea hangs over the creek. Up the hillsides, mountain laurel blooms its white flowers in May and June. And in the quiet forest understory, white petals of the dogwood flower fall from the trees and carpet the trail.

Seneca Creek Greenway Trail is a well-cared-for trail, supported by volunteers who patrol the trail, keep it maintained, and advocate to keep its secluded quality unspoiled. It's also a well-plotted route that takes hikers through a variety of terrain and habitats.

The first is the stream bottom forest. While wooded with tulip poplars and beeches, it nonetheless feels open. Trees are widely spaced, and ankle-high grass gives the scenery a gladelike effect. This is an environment susceptible to quick, sudden change should flooding occur. The low herbs and grasses spread quickly, giving the appearance of a lush green carpet.

When the trail takes to the hills, the route can be steep, although rarely is it a long climb. Within the first 1.5 miles, an incline tops out at a rock outcrop that gives you long looks down onto a bend in the river. From there, you follow a path that winds up and down gentle grades, passing over small seasonal tributaries of Great Seneca Creek. The deep woods gives way to more meadow habitat on the central leg of this hike, but north of Huntmaster Road, the forest canopy closes in again. There are assemblages of jack-in-the-pulpit, wild onion, mustard garlic, and other herbs alongside the trail.

The trail moves through meadows at stream level through much of the middle section of this hike. It's a habitat ripe for birders. Just before the Brinks Road crossing, the trail exits the woods to pass through a grass field. A scan of the far tree line might bring sighting of a red-shouldered hawk. This raptor favors lightly wooded wetlands such as this. Its striking feather patterns—gold-speckled chest, banded tail-feathers, and gold legs—make for quick identification. Again, north of the Brink Road crossing, you cross Goshen Branch, a major tributary of Great Seneca Creek, and enter a field. By midsummer, the grass

▶ **KID APPEAL**

The first leg of this route, from MD 355 to Watkins Mill Road, is a short 2.8-mile end-to-end hike with two natural highlights: tall rock outcrops north of the Midcounty Highway, and a natural rock bridge over a small tributary stream just 0.2 mile before you reach Watkins Mill Road.

Rocky overlook

is waist high, and bird-watching is in high gear. Sightings include indigo bunting, red-eyed vireo, and scarlet tanager.

Great Seneca Creek's watershed lies entirely within Montgomery County, and the stream's health is intrinsically tied to the surrounding community. There are large communities—Montgomery Village and Gaithersburg—and adjoining farmland is being developed for homes. Three wastewater treatment plants discharge into tributaries of Great Seneca, yet in spite of all this, the stream is cited by the county as being well stocked with fish, from coldwater species near its headwaters to smallmouth bass farther south.

From the trail, the stream's character varies from a wide, broad waterway to a narrow and winding creek, especially north of Huntmaster Road. There are no waterfalls, but rather riffles and small rapids formed by stream rocks. At particularly sharp bends, the creek carves out the inside corner, leaving a sheer wall of sand. Tree roots

Historic gristmills were located on Seneca Creek from the colonial period to the early twentieth century. Watkins Mill was a gristmill and sawmill located on the south side of Watkins Mill Road. Ruins of Davis Mill can be seen upstream of the northern trailhead. A third mill, the Middleton Mill, was located near the MD 355 bridge.

uncovered by the erosion stick out from the bank, and where the cut is particularly fast and deep, a tree's foothold will weaken, and it leans over the stream.

The river bends offer another place to explore, on small bars where the moving water has deposited piles of sand. Here, the amateur tracker can scan the soft mud for clues of past visitors and their tracks. Canada geese tracks are webbed, while the great blue heron leaves a wide track showing three talonlike claws. There may be the dainty footprints of a raccoon or the deep imprint of a deer.

Miles and Directions

0.0 START from a trailboard in the parking lot on MD 355. Walk around the trailboard and down a grass slope. Follow a gravel path that veers left (north) into the woods. En route, you will pass a small brown trail sign that reads SENECA CREEK GT TO MIDCOUNTY HWY TRAIL PARKING. There are light blue blazes on the tree. Within 100 yards, the trail splits. Turn left and continue north on the Seneca Creek Greenway Trail (GT), which is now a dirt footpath.

0.5 After a brief climb, swing right (north) to stay on the Seneca Creek GT to avoid an unmarked trail that branches left.

0.9 Pass an outfall from a pond formed by a large earthen dam that is up the hill on your left. After rock-hopping across the outfall stream, veer right at a junction with a spur trail on the left that leads to the Midcounty Highway trailhead parking lot.

1.4 After a short but steep climb, linger for a moment at a rock outcrop that offers a wonderful perch and view down into the stream valley. The Seneca Creek GT continues north from this outcrop.

1.8 Continue straight on the Seneca Creek GT where another dirt footpath branches left, leading to the Midcounty Highway.

2.6 Cross Rock Bridge, a natural stone bridge over a tributary of Great Seneca Creek.

2.8 Emerge from the woods onto a paved road. Turn left (north) and climb the paved road to Watkins Mill Road. Turn right (east), walk cross Great Seneca Creek via the Watkins Mill Road highway bridge. On the other side, turn left and cross Watkins Road to its north side.

3.0 Pass through the Watkins Mill parking lot and continue north on the Seneca Creek GT. Here, a single-track dirt path sweeps to the right and passes an electrical substation on the left side of the trail.

3.3 Cross a small tributary stream on a footbridge and, in about 10 feet, swing left on the Seneca Creek GT to avoid an unmarked trail that goes straight and uphill. (*Note:* Over the next 0.4 mile, numerous foot trails intersect with Seneca Creek GT. None are blazed, while the Seneca Creek GT itself is clearly marked with blue blazes.)

3.6 As you descend back into the stream valley, stay straight on Seneca Creek GT at a junction with an unmarked trail on the left. (*Bailout:* Turn left [south] and follow the unmarked trail as it doubles back alongside the stream to rejoin Seneca Creek GT in 0.7 mile. It is another 3.3 miles back to the MD 355 trail parking lot, for a 7.6-mile round-trip.)

4.3 Reach a trailboard at the junction of Wightman and Brink Roads. Cross straight over Wightman, turn left, walk to the corner, and cross Brink Road. Follow the Seneca Creek GT as it skirts the edge of woods on your left and the lawn of a private residence visible on the right.

4.45 Reenter the woods on the Seneca Creek GT.

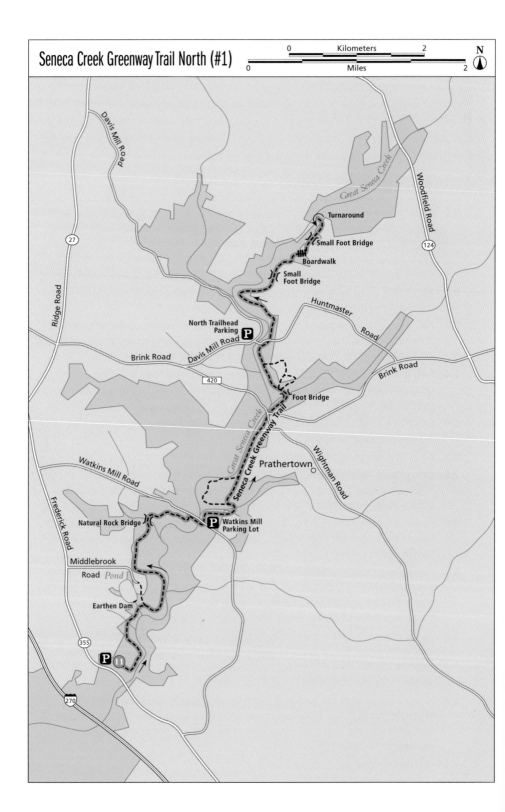

Seneca Creek Greenway Trail North (#1)

Kilometers
0 ... 2

Miles
0 ... 2

N

Davis Mill Road

Great Seneca Creek

Woodfield Road

Turnaround

Small Foot Bridge

Boardwalk

Small Foot Bridge

27

124

Huntmaster Road

North Trailhead Parking

Ridge Road

Brink Road

Davis Mill Road

420

Brink Road

Foot Bridge

Great Seneca Creek

Seneca Creek Greenway Trail

Prathertown

Wightman Road

Watkins Mill Road

Frederick Road

Natural Rock Bridge

Watkins Mill Parking Lot

Middlebrook Road

Pond

Earthen Dam

355

270

11

Stream crossing at the north end of Seneca Creek Greenway Trail

4.5 Cross a large footbridge over a tributary of Great Seneca Creek. Ahead, veer left (north) as the trail passes over flat terrain of a streamside field.

4.8 A mowed path splits right off Seneca Creek GT and heads for the hillside woods. Continue straight on blue-blazed Seneca Creek GT and enter the woods. (*Bailout:* Veer right on the mowed path and climb the wooded hillside. In 0.1 mile, turn right on a woodland path. This trail becomes a wide grassy road and swings left to descend to the Seneca Creek GT near the bridge you crossed at 4.5 miles. Follow the trail south and return to the MD 355 trailhead parking lot for a 10-mile round-trip.)

5.2 Cross straight over Huntmaster Road. From here north, Seneca Creek GT takes on deep-woods character as you cross hilly terrain overlooking Great Seneca Creek.

6.3 Seneca Creek GT merges with a utility easement marked by orange pipes sticking straight up. Follow the trail's narrow dirt footpath through tall grass. Ahead, stay alert as the Seneca Creek GT takes a hard right (east) to thread a thin buffer between the easement and private property on your right.

6.5 Seneca Creek GT takes a brief detour into the woods to cross a tributary stream of Great Seneca Creek. Reemerge onto the utility easement and cross straight over. The easement continues uphill off to the right, while the creek is far downhill on your left.

6.9 Reach Great Seneca Creek at a stream crossing with large stepping-stone rocks. This is the northern end of the Seneca Creek GT. Retrace the trail back to Huntmaster Road.

8.6 Return to Huntmaster Road. (*Options:* If you're hiking this as a point-to-point, turn right and follow the paved road 0.1 mile downhill to cross Great Seneca Creek on a road bridge. The parking area is immediately after the bridge, on the right, at the junction of Huntmaster and Davis Mill Roads. If you are hiking this route as an out-and-back, cross straight over Huntmaster Road and reenter the woods.)

13.8 HIKE ENDS at the MD 355 trailhead parking area.

OPTIONS

The Lower Magruder Trail links to the Seneca Creek GT at its northern end. By crossing the stream and continuing north, you'll follow first Great Seneca Creek, and then veer northwest to follow Magruder Branch. In 3.3 miles, the trail enters Damascus Recreational Park. There are future plans to link Seneca Creek GT to Patuxent State Park to the north, which will create a 25-mile-long stream valley trail from the Patuxent to the Potomac.

Hike Information

Local information: Visit Montgomery, 1801 Rockville Pike Suit 320, Rockville, MD; (240) 641-6750; www.visitmontgomery.com

Good eats: Dogfish Head Alehouse, 800 West Diamond Ave., Gaithersburg, MD; (301) 963-4847; www.dogfishalehouse.com

Local outdoor stores: REI, 910 Rose Ave., North Bethesda, MD; (301) 770-1751; www.rei.com

Dick's Sporting Goods, 2 Grand Corner Ave., Gaithersburg, MD; (301) 947-0200; www.dickssportinggoods.com

Organizations: Seneca Creek Greenway Trail Coalition, www.senecatrail.info. Offers volunteer opportunities for helping maintain and patrol trail sections.

12 Seneca Creek Greenway Trail South (#2)

This lower leg of the 25-mile Seneca Creek Greenway Trail, from River Road to Black Rock Mill, sees less foot traffic than either the middle or northern sections. Consequently, its gentle mix of woods and meadows offers hikers hours of walking time with few interruptions. Seneca Creek State Park manages a portion of this trail and its handiwork is noticeable as you pass through fields planted with row upon row of sycamore saplings. Bookending the nature walk are two relics of history, an old mill and a restored lock house on the C&O Canal.

Start: From a trail sign on Seneca Road
Distance: 6.5-mile point-to-point
Approximate hiking time: 2.5 hours
Difficulty: Moderate due to steep hill climbs where the stream valley narrows. Otherwise, the trails are well marked and maintained, and crossovers of state and county roads are easy to follow.
Trail surface: Paved road and sidewalks, dirt footpaths, fields and meadows
Seasons: Best in all seasons
Other trail users: Equestrians permitted on the trail between Berryville Road and MD 28
Canine compatibility: Leashed dogs permitted
Land status: State park
Fees and permits: None
Schedule: Open daily dawn to dusk. See *Options* for tours of Riley's Lockhouse in nearby C&O Canal National Historic Park.
Facilities: There are bathrooms at Seneca Creek State Park to the north, and to the south in Seneca Landing Park on Riley's Lock Road. To reach them from the southern trailhead, walk down Seneca Road to River Road, cross straight over, and follow Riley's Lock Road south. Bathrooms are on the left in a parking area within 0.5 mile. (*Note:* At the end of this 0.7-mile dead-end road is Riley's Lockhouse and the Seneca Aqueduct, both part of the C&O Canal Park. See *Options*.)
Maps: DeLorme *Maryland/Delaware Atlas & Gazetteer:* Page 54 (inset) D2. USGS 7.5-minute series: *Seneca, MD/VA* and *Germantown, MD.* A trail map can be downloaded from the Greenway's website. The Seneca Greenway Trail Coalition has a rudimentary map on its Web site, www.senecatrail.info.
Trail contacts: Montgomery County Department of Parks, 9500 Brunett Ave., Silver Spring, MD 20901; (301) 528-3450; www.montgomeryparks.org/park-and-trails/seneca-creek-greenway-trail
Seneca Creek State Park, 11950 Clopper Rd., Gaithersburg, MD 21561; (301) 924-2127. Park facilities are centered around Clopper Day Use Area, which is not part of this route. You can reach the main park entrance on MD 119/Great Seneca Highway.
Seneca Creek Trail Coalition, www.senecatrail.info. A volunteer group dedicated to maintaining, monitoring, and growing the trail.

Finding the trailhead: Distance from Washington, D.C.: 25 miles
  Southern trailhead from I-495 (Capital Beltway): Exit for MD 190 / River Road West. Follow this local highway west for 11.4 miles to a junction with MD 112 / Seneca Road. Turn left onto River Road West (the road loses its MD 190 designation), and then in 0.3 mile turn right back onto Seneca Road. The trailhead is on the right between 0.1 and 0.2 mile. Park along the roadside

shoulder. (*Note:* You've missed the trailhead if you reach a sharp left curve in Seneca Road and thereafter an intersection with River Road.) Trailhead GPS: N39 04.765' / W77 20.121'

Northern trailhead from I-495 (Capital Beltway): For a point-to-point hike, place a shuttle vehicle at this trailhead. Follow directions for the southern trailhead. At the junction of MD 190/River Road and MD 112/Seneca Road, turn right onto MD 112. After driving 0.2 mile, turn left on Berryville Road. Drive north on Berryville Road to a T intersection with MD 28. Here, turn left onto MD 28 West and, in 0.3 mile, turn right onto Black Rock Road. In 0.6 mile, turn left into a parking lot for Black Rock Mill, which sits on Great Seneca Creek. Trailhead GPS: N39 07.627' / W77 18.874'

The Hike

From hunting grounds for the Seneca Indians to powering of gristmills and sawmills, Seneca Creek has long served a variety of human activity. When this first leg of the 25-mile-long Seneca Creek Greenway Trail opened in 1995, it marked a new twist in the stream's narrative. Survival and industry may have driven past uses, but today it is the appetite for recreation and nature-viewing that is fulfilled by this long trail.

Seneca Creek Aqueduct

The name Seneca derives from the Native Americans who hunted and camped along this stream valley. Early charts show the name as "Sinegar Cr." Its translation from the Algonquin-speaking Senecas is likely "Stony Creek," an apt description for the quality red sandstone mined nearby.

Seneca red stone quarried near the mouth of Seneca Creek is the building blocks of not just the Seneca Creek Aqueduct and many C&O Canal locks, but the Washington Monument, U.S. Capitol, and in the famous red Smithsonian Castle as well.

Initially, Seneca Creek became well known to English settlers not for the stream itself, but for red sandstone found nearby. It was prized because it was a rock easy to mine; it came out of the ground "soft" and pliable, but the longer it was exposed to air, it would harden and form a sturdy, reliable foundation.

George Washington used blocks of Seneca sandstone to build locks on the Patow-mack Canal, which was built to skirt the Great Falls of the Potomac on the Virginia side of the river. The successor of the Patowmack was the C&O Canal from George-town to Cumberland, Maryland. The canal had to span the mouth of Seneca Creek, and it was done by building a stone aqueduct that still stands today.

As valued as the sandstone was, settlers found that the creek's constant and reliable source of water flow, even in dry seasons in summer and fall, could be tapped as a source of power. Seneca Creek and its tributaries drain more than 82,000 acres in Montgomery County; Great Seneca Creek, which the greenway trail follows north of MD 28, begins far to the north near Damascus and supplies water to the stream course all year long.

A written history of the trail counts the sites of nineteen mills located on either Seneca Creek or its tributaries. One of the oldest was Seneca Mill (also called Tschiffely Mill after its last owner, Wilson B. Tschiffely), recorded as being in existence in 1732. Today, there are no remains of the mill to be seen, after it was destroyed and then paved over during construction of River Road. Still visible, and visibly dramatic, are the tall stone walls of Black Rock Mill, where this hike ends. It opened in 1815 and operated as a sawmill and gristmill until the 1920s.

▶ **KID APPEAL**

Short length and easy terrain make this a perfect weekend day hike for the youngster. You can add a history lesson by spending time at the Black Rock Mill (northern trailhead) and Riley's Lockhouse on the C&O Canal (near the southern trailhead).

Black Rock Mill's imposing edifice is but one reminder of many of the human activity in the stream valley. There is a small farmer's pond downhill from the trail near its southern trailhead on Seneca Road. In spring, this small depression is teem-ing with frogs and toads. Close inspection finds wetland plants like skunk cabbage prominent near a small spring that trickles off the hillside. The jack-in-the-pulpit wildflower grows here, too, and is worth getting down on hands and knees for a closer look. The flower looks like it has a hood, but closer inspection shows that its floral

Trailhead for Seneca Creek Greenway Trail

spike, called a spadix, is wrapped in a sheath that then curves over the flower. The spadix is the "jack," and the sheath, also called a spathe, is the "pulpit."

"Indian turnip" is an old nickname for jack-in-the-pulpit, a reference to its tuber-like root used by Native Americans as a food source. The period when this plant was valued as a food source is gone, but like Seneca Creek and the greenway trail, its value now lies in its natural beauty and the pleasure it brings to those of us who like a few hours of quiet woodland walking.

Miles and Directions

0.0 START from the Seneca Creek Greenway Trail (GT) trailhead on Seneca Road. There is a trail sign that gives mileage to Berryville Road. Enter the woods on a blue-blazed dirt footpath that traces a hillside above an old farmer's pond—now a vibrant wetlands alive with frog and bird calls—downhill on the left.

0.4 Veer right (north) at a V junction in the Seneca Creek GT. (*Note:* The trail that merges from the left is also marked with blue blazes; it is a low-country route leading left [south] to Seneca Road via the streamside in 0.5 mile.)

1.0 After a long climb, the trail levels briefly, then descends toward Berryville Road.

Seneca Creek Greenway Trail South (#2)

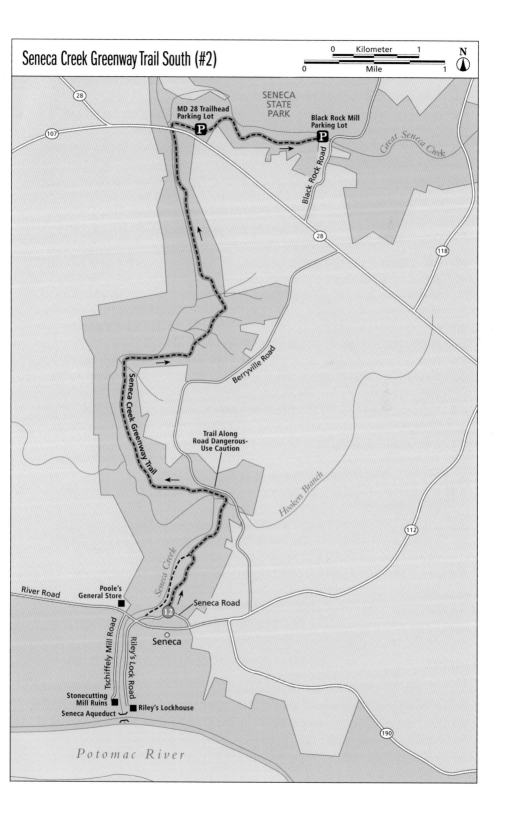

1.1 Cross Hookers Branch, a tributary of Seneca Creek, on large rocks and turn left to parallel Berryville Road. Within a few hundred yards, you will leave the woods to walk alongside the road shoulder. Look for blazes on the metal guardrail as the trail exits the woods. Walk along the road shoulder, following the guardrail.

1.2 Reenter the woods on the Seneca Creek GT. There are signs marking both the trail and Seneca Creek State Park. The trail here is a well-worn streamside path.

1.3 Pass from woods into a field by crossing over a low barbed-wire fence. Skirt the lower edge of the field as it winds north.

1.5 Briefly reenter woods to cross a narrow and deep tributary of Seneca Creek. Ahead, reenter another field. (*FYI:* There are rows upon rows of young oak and maple saplings, evidence of a reforestation project spearheaded by Seneca Creek State Park.)

2.3 Enter a long stretch of trail through a young pine forest, passing by a massive spreading oak tree.

2.8 After a stretch of walking along hillside woodlands, the Seneca Creek GT regains the river's edge. Cross a footbridge over a small tributary here. (*Note:* Over the next 2.3 miles, the trail undulates in and out of hillside stream gullies, crossing nine more tributaries of the Seneca Creek [some seasonal, others showing good flow all year long].)

3.1 Turn left on the Seneca Creek GT and avoid an old road on the right that is blocked by downed trees. The trail ahead is an old overgrown forest road.

4.6 Cross two streams in quick succession, aided by wooden footbridges. The trail past this leaves the woodland for the final time to walk along the river bottomland through a grass field.

5.0 Pass beneath the large MD 28 bridge. Enter a paved turnaround and turn left (east). Where the pavement ends, follow a gravel path uphill to the MD 28 trailhead parking lot.

5.1 Enter the MD 28 parking lot for the Seneca Creek GT. Pass straight through and continue walking north. The trail parallels MD 28 as it climbs through a field. When you reach the tree line, turn left and parallel the trees, keeping them to your right.

5.3 Pass through a line of trees and continue walking through the field. The trail crests atop a hill and descends.

5.5 Turn right and follow the Seneca Creek GT as it enters the woods. This turn is marked by a post with a blue blaze. (*FYI:* From the MD 28 trailhead, the trail switches from following Seneca Creek to following its major tributary, Great Seneca Creek.)

5.7 Descend the hillside and cross Great Seneca Creek. Over the next 0.3 mile, the hike regains elevation and undulates along the wooded bluffs overlooking the creek.

6.5 HIKE ENDS at the Black Rock Mill. (*Option:* You can do this hike as an out-and-back; just retrace your route south along the Seneca Creek GT to reach the southern trailhead for a 13-mile hike.)

OPTIONS

Walk 0.7 mile south of the southern trailhead to visit Riley's Lockhouse on the C&O Canal. From the trailhead, follow Seneca Road south to where it intersects with River Road. Cross straight over River Road and follow paved Riley's Lock Road through a county park to reach the lock house. Here, too, is the famous Seneca Aqueduct, one of eleven built along the canal to bridge the mouths of large streams.

Hike Information

Local information: Visit Montgomery, 1801 Rockville Pike Suit 320, Rockville, MD; (240) 641-6750; www.visitmontgomery.com

Local events/attractions: Volunteers in period costume offer guided tours of Riley's Lockhouse (see *Options*) most weekends in spring and fall. Call the C&O Canal National Historical Park for schedule: (301) 384-8584.

Calleva, 13015 Riley's Lock Road, Poolesville, MD; (301) 216-1248; www.calleva .org. An outdoor adventure company based on Seneca Creek near Riley's Lockhouse. Offers outdoor adventures for camps, school groups, and corporate outings.

Good eats: Rocklands Farm Winery, 14531 Montevideo Rd., Poolesville, MD; (301) 825-8075

Local outdoor stores: REI, 910 Rose Ave., North Bethesda, MD; (301) 770-1751; www.rei.com

Dick's Sporting Goods, 2 Grand Corner Ave., Gaithersburg, MD; (301) 947-0200; www.dickssportinggoods.com

Organizations: Friends of Seneca Creek State Park, Gaithersburg, MD; (301) 924-2127; www.dnr.maryland.gov/publiclands/central/senecafriendsof.html

Seneca Creek Greenway Trail Coalition, www.senecatrail.info

GREEN TIP

Be courteous of others. Many people visit natural areas
for quiet, peace, and solitude, so avoid making loud
noises and intruding on others' privacy.

13 Sugarloaf Mountain

A solitary mountain surrounded by flat Piedmont farmland, Sugarloaf Mountain stands out in more ways than one. It is a beacon for outdoors enthusiasts in the Greater Washington, D.C., area, drawing an estimated quarter of a million people annually who hike, horseback ride, and mountain bike. Its forests are flush with wildflowers in spring and songbirds throughout summer. Upon its heights, views stretch to the Blue Ridge, the Potomac River, and beyond. Miles of trails can be linked into outings as short as a few hours or as long as a full day. We designed this route to capture as many viewpoints as possible, starting with the peak and stretching to the park's remote northern ridges. The length is modest, but the rewards are ample.

Start: From the East View Overlook parking area

Distance: 5.9-mile loop

Approximate hiking time: 3 hours

Difficulty: Moderate due to several short, but very steep, climbs. There is some open rock terrain and some eroded sections of steep trail where footing may be difficult.

Trail surface: Forested trails, open rock face, and old forest roads

Seasons: May through Oct

Other trail users: Horses are permitted on the Yellow Trail only. Mountain bikes are permitted on the Yellow Trail only between Memorial Day and Labor Day, Mon through Fri.

Handicapped accessibility: Trails are not accessible, but the East View and West View Overlook parking areas offer panoramas across the surrounding countryside.

Canine compatibility: Leashed dogs permitted

Land status: Private land conservancy

Fees and permits: None

Schedule: Daily 8:00 a.m. to 1 hour before sunset

Facilities: Portable toilets, picnic tables, and drinking water at the main entrance gate. A historic mansion and formal gardens can be rented for special events.

Maps: DeLorme *Maryland/Delaware Atlas & Gazetteer:* Page 55 C6. USGS 7.5 minute series: *Buckeys-town, MD/VA.* You can download the park's own line-drawn trail map at www.sugarloafmd.com. That same map is available at the park entrance on Comus Road.

Trail contacts: Stronghold, Inc., 7901 Comus Rd., Dickerson, MD 20842; (301) 874-2024; www.sugarloafmd.com

Special considerations: Timber rattlesnakes and copperheads, both poisonous snakes, are found on Sugarloaf Mountain. They prefer open rock areas and small caves. Use caution when exploring around the peak, as well as at White Rocks on the Northern Peaks Trail.

Finding the trailhead: Distance from Washington, D.C.: 42 miles

From I-270: Take exit 22, the Barnesville and Hyattstown exit, which is also marked as the exit for Sugarloaf Mountain. At the bottom of the ramp, merge onto MD 109 South and follow it for 2.9 miles. In the crossroads community of Comus, turn right onto MD 95 (the turn is marked by the Comus Inn). Drive another 2.3 miles to Stronghold, a wide spot in the road at a four-way intersection. As you enter this intersection, veer right and pass through the gated boundary of Sugarloaf Mountain Preserve. Follow this paved road between two barns, and then uphill for 2 miles to the East View Overlook parking area. Trailhead GPS: N39 15.632' / W77 23.406'

The Hike

On the short, steep climb to Sugarloaf's summit from East View Overlook parking area, soil underfoot is thin and flinty, laced with small white stone chips. They're evidence of the mountain's distinctive quartzite bedrock. Mountain laurel adapts well by sinking its sinewy roots into the thin soil, and by doing so, this small understory tree with clusters of pink and white spring blossoms offers important erosion control.

At a particularly steep incline, a washout mars the hillside. Devoid of the stabilizing effects of the mountain laurel and other plants, the slope becomes a minichute that carries bucketloads of stone and dirt downhill after heavy rainstorms.

This washout and its related erosion is an apt metaphor for Sugarloaf as a whole. The mountain is a monadnock, a lump of resistant bedrock surrounded by relatively flat terrain. Textbooks say Sugarloaf's quartzite bedrock dates back 500 million years and the mountain formation itself resulted from the mountain-building activity of fourteen million years ago that created the Blue Ridge and the mountains to the north in Catoctin Mountain Park. To oversimplify, Sugarloaf's present condition is the culmination of fourteen million years of erosion.

Larger examples of the bedrock quartzite are on ample display on Sugarloaf's peak, where boulders and outcrops crown the top of the mountain. You can scramble atop them to catch views that span south and west across central Maryland farmland. The Potomac River is visible to the south, and South Mountain, which is part of the Blue Ridge chain of mountains, is the long dark ridge on the western horizon. Closer

Early Maryland settlers saw in this mountain's distinctive profile a resemblance to their tall conical-shaped mounds of sugar—also known as sugarloafs.

WHITE ROCKS FLORA AND FAUNA

White Rocks is one of four mountain knobs linked by the Northern Peaks Trail, a hikers-only path that leads away from West View Overlook parking area. As you traverse the western slope of Sugarloaf, the sound of cars drifts away. Where the route turns and begins its gradual descent to cross Mount Ephraim Road, there's a chance another jarring sound will fill your ears: the drum of a pileated woodpecker declaring its territory. Off the trailside, the broad leaves of false Solomon's seal serve as a reminder that this wildflower is part of the lily family. Its name is an unfortunate label—using the word *false* for what is truly a beautiful spring wildflower, with clusters of delicate white blossoms that remind you of a bursting star frozen in place. True Solomon's seal has demonstrated medicinal uses; its starchy root was used to treat ailments ranging from stomachaches to poor complexion. The so-called false variety, on the other hand, was better known as a source of food; its roots were cooked like asparagus.

in, the summertime canopy of green-leafed oak and hickory trees far below beckon you to explore the preserve's trails.

The story of Sugarloaf is typical for Maryland's Piedmont region. In prehistoric times, Indians camped around the base of the mountain. At one time, the mountain was owned by the brother of a Maryland governor, and it was clear-cut for a charcoal-making operation. As the highest point for miles, its peak was used as a lookout during the Civil War. Confederate scouts watched Union forces cross the Potomac in 1864 en route to the Battle of Monocacy. Union forces occupied the same perch as a scouting point as control of the mountain traded sides throughout the war.

In the twentieth century, Sugarloaf's narrative took a twist. Gordon Strong, a wealthy industrialist, found the views here so spectacular that he bought the mountain and land around it. In 1946, he created the private nonprofit group Stronghold, Inc., that to this day continues to own, protect, and promote the preserve. Local history tells the story of how President Franklin Delano Roosevelt developed an intense interest in Sugarloaf as a site for a presidential retreat. Strong, a card-carrying Republican, resisted the offers and instead pointed Roosevelt north to mountainous country around Thurmont, Maryland. Thus, the official presidential retreat at Camp David is located in the Catoctin Mountains, not Sugarloaf.

As a result of Strong's ownership, Sugarloaf is today a unique amalgamation of developed property and preserved woodlands. There are carved stone steps built by the park's first superintendent, Albert M. Thomas. Winding paved roads lead almost to the summit, and there are traffic circles and lookouts with benches. The man-made landscaping blends in well with more than 3,000 acres of untouched woodland. In summertime, you can enjoy vistas from popular West View Overlook and within the hour stand atop White Rocks and feel as if you're the last person left on earth.

Miles and Directions

0.0 START from a trailboard sign at the East View Overlook parking area. Follow orange-blazed Sunrise Trail north as it climbs steeply through an understory of mountain laurel and blueberries. The path is wide and dirt. (*Note:* The unblazed dirt footpath that leads east from this trail junction leads to White Trail and is the return portion of this hike.)

0.3 Turn left (west) on red-blazed Monadnock Trail. (*FYI:* The term *monadnock* is a technical description of the geologic formation that is Sugarloaf Mountain.)

0.4 Reach the 1,282-foot summit of Sugarloaf Mountain. Views span west to the Potomac River and northwest to South Mountain and Catoctin. Turn left (south) on the green-blazed A. M. Thomas Trail.

0.5 Descend a long stone staircase and continue hiking downhill.

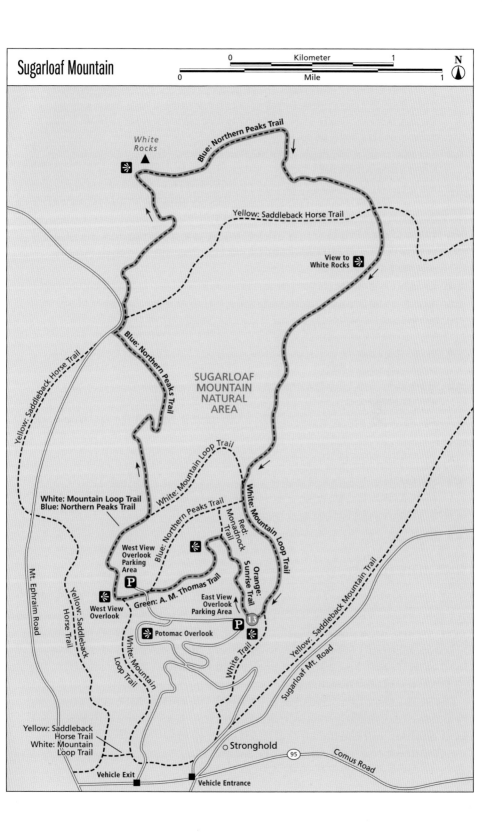

Sugarloaf Mountain

0 — Kilometer — 1

0 — Mile — 1

N

White Rocks

Blue: Northern Peaks Trail

Yellow: Saddleback Horse Trail

View to White Rocks

Blue: Northern Peaks Trail

SUGARLOAF MOUNTAIN NATURAL AREA

Yellow: Saddleback Horse Trail

White: Mountain Loop Trail

White: Mountain Loop Trail
Blue: Northern Peaks Trail

White: Mountain Loop Trail

Blue: Northern Peaks Trail

Red: Monadnock Trail

Orange: Sunrise Trail

West View Overlook Parking Area

P

West View Overlook

Green: A. M. Thomas Trail

East View Overlook Parking Area

P 13

Yellow: Saddleback Mountain Trail

Mt. Ephraim Road

Yellow: Saddleback Horse Trail

White: Mountain Loop Trail

Potomac Overlook

White Trail

Sugarloaf Mt. Road

Yellow: Saddleback Horse Trail
White: Mountain Loop Trail

Stronghold

95

Comus Road

Vehicle Exit

Vehicle Entrance

0.7 Reach the West View Overlook parking area. Stay left of a picnic pavilion and follow a stone path to an ornate stone staircase. Descend to a traffic circle with picnic tables in the middle. Turn right, begin to walk around the traffic circle counterclockwise, and locate a blue blaze on a chestnut oak. Enter the woods on the Northern Peaks Trail, a wide dirt footpath. (*FYI:* West View Overlook, a National Historic Landmark, is just to the left of this trailhead and is a worthy detour.)

0.8 Turn right (north) at a T junction where white-blazed Mountain Loop Trail merges with blue-blazed Northern Peaks Trail.

1.2 Turn left (north) and follow the blue-blazed Northern Peaks Trail. (*Bailout:* If you're pressed for time, follow the Mountain Loop Trail straight from this junction and return to East View Overlook in 2.5 miles. Resume below at mile 5.3.)

2.0 Exit the woods onto a paved road. Turn right (north), walk 300 feet downhill, and turn left to follow the road, which makes a hard left turn here. (*Note:* The Saddleback Horse Trail goes straight [north] from this hard left turn.)

2.1 Turn right (north) off the road and reenter the woods on a dirt path to begin a gradual climb.

2.9 Turn left (north) onto a spur trail to White Rocks. After enjoying the views, return to and turn left onto the Northern Peaks Trail. In quick succession, you will climb to two knobs in the ridgeline and pass through a clearing that boasts a 10-foot-high rock cairn.

4.0 Cross straight over the yellow-blazed Saddleback Horse Trail and reenter the woods on a single-track woods path.

4.4 After a short climb, top out onto the third knob in this ridgeline walk. Views span back north to White Rocks.

5.3 Turn left (south) and merge with the white-blazed Mountain Loop Trail. The trail for the next 0.1 mile is combined Mountain Loop Trail/Northern Peaks Trail. (*Note:* If you chose to shorten this circuit by following the Mountain Loop Trail where it split away from the Northern Peaks Trail [mile 1.2 above], resume directions from this point.)

5.4 Veer left (south) to remain on white-blazed Mountain Loop Trail. (*Note:* Blue-blazed Northern Peaks Trail forks right (west) to return to West View Overlook parking area.)

5.8 Turn right on a spur trail that leads uphill at a gradual slope.

5.9 HIKE ENDS at the East View Overlook parking area.

Hike Information

Local information: Visit Montgomery, 1801 Rockville Pike Suit 320, Rockville, MD; (240) 641-6750; www.visitmontgomery.com

Local events/attractions: Sugarloaf Mountain Vineyard, 18125 Comus Road, Dickerson, MD; (301) 605-0130; www.smvwinery.com. Live music on weekends.

Good eats: Bassett's Fine Food & Spirits, 19950 Fisher Ave., Poolesville, MD; (301) 972-7443; www.bassettsrestaurant.net

Denise Bakery & Deli, 25901 Frederick Road, Clarksburg, MD; (301) 607-4596; www.denisebakeryanddeli.com. Salvadorean fare. It is closer to the I-270 exit.

Local outdoor stores: Hudson Trail closed, need another

Organizations: Maryland Native Plant Society, Silver Spring, MD; www.mdflora.org

View of Sugarloaf Mountain from below

Other resources: The Nature Conservancy has a Sugarloaf Mountain visitors guide and audio tour on its website, www.nature.org.

Sugarloaf: The Mountain's History, Geology and Natural Lore and *An Illustrated Guide to Eastern Woodland Wildflowers and Trees: 350 Plants Observed at Sugarloaf Mountain, Maryland*, both by Melanie Choukas-Bradley and illustrated by Tina Thieme Brown.

GREEN TIP

When you just have to go, dig a hole 6–8 inches deep and at least 200 feet from water, camps, and trails. Carry a zip-lock bag to carry out toilet paper, or use a natural substitute such as leaves instead (but not poison ivy!!!). Fill in the hole with soil and other natural materials when you're done.

Blossom of a tulip poplar

Virginia

Northern Virginia is so much more than merely a bedroom community of Washington, D.C., especially for the outdoors explorer. The region encompasses the pastoral hills of Fauquier County, the ragged 90-foot cliffs at Great Falls, the calm estuaries around Mason Neck, and even the northern extent of Shenandoah National Park and the Blue Ridge Mountains.

There are streams that over the centuries have carved out channels through granite, schist, and metagraywacke. Healthy forests of hardwoods crown river bluffs. Microcosms of Appalachian cove forest—with its stunning array of flowers, trees, mosses, and animals—pop up along quiet, secluded streams. Virginia's fall line bisects the region, creating picturesque waterfalls and cascades that transport you hundreds of miles away.

American white dogwood, the Virginia state flower

Northern Virginians work hard for these special environments. Preserved tracts of land on the Potomac, below Washington, D.C., are recognized as top spots in the East for nesting and roosting bald eagles. Even land that has been logged, farmed, mined, and left to waste away—like Prince William Forest Park—has rebounded to a state of natural and scenic beauty. Years of preservation work have made possible just about every type of outdoor pursuit, from walking to rock climbing, bird-watching to hunting.

The history of the region makes exploration doubly rewarding. Civil War sites and presidential homes interpret the landscape. The paths of our history are today the paths of hikers, bird-watchers, and nature lovers. The stories behind place-names and old buildings are as much a part of the outdoors experience as the flowers, birds, and trees.

14 Arlington National Cemetery

Any number of ways exist to approach a hike in Arlington National Cemetery. Starting a hike at Theodore Roosevelt Island links a memorial to our great president/conservationist with memorials to other great Americans. The short stint on Mount Vernon Trail offers a view far removed from Washington's iconic skyline. Arlington National Cemetery, with its acres of tree-shaded lawn and rows of uniform white tombstones, is a refuge of calm and contemplation.

Start: From the Theodore Roosevelt Island parking area on the George Washington Memorial Parkway

Distance: 6.1-mile loop

Approximate hiking time: 3 hours

Difficulty: Easy due to graded paths and easy terrain

Seasons: Apr through Oct

Other trail users: Bikers and joggers on the Mount Vernon Trail

Handicapped accessibility: Roads and walking paths in the cemetery are all paved and handicapped accessible, as is the Mount Vernon Trail. Accessibility of trails on Theodore Roosevelt Island varies.

Canine compatibility: Only legitimate service animals and military service dogs are allowed in the cemetery. Leashed pets are allowed on Theodore Roosevelt Island.

Land status: National cemetery

Fees and permits: No entrance fees. Parking is free at Theodore Island, but be sure to park in a designated space and not on the grass or you may get a ticket. If you choose to start this hike at the cemetery, there is a parking fee.

Schedule: Theodore Roosevelt Island is open year-round, 6 a.m. to 10 p.m. The cemetery is open daily 8:00 a.m. to 7:00 p.m., Apr through Sept and daily 8:00 a.m. to 5:00 p.m. Oct through Mar

Facilities: Theodore Roosevelt Island has restrooms. The cemetery has a welcome center with restrooms, and a bookstore.

Maps: DeLorme *Virginia Atlas & Gazetteer:* Page 77 A5. USGS 7.5 minute series: *Washington West, DC, MD, VA.* See also the National Park Service–issued walking map available at the visitor center information desk.

Trail contacts: Theodore Roosevelt Island National Park; 700 George Washington Memorial Parkway, McLean, VA; (703) 289-2500; www.nps.gov/this. Arlington National Cemetery, 1 Memorial Ave., Arlington, VA; (877) 907-8585; www.arlingtoncemetery.mil

Special considerations: Please show respect and decorum in this solemn place. Joggers and bicyclists are not permitted inside the cemetery.

Finding the trailhead: Distance from Washington, D.C.: 3 miles

From I-66 West (Washington, DC): Take the U.S. 50 W/Arlington Boulevard W/George Washington Memorial Parkway exit. Keep right to merge onto George Washington Memorial Parkway North. In 0.4 mile, turn right into Theodore Roosevelt Island park.

Public transportation: Arlington National Cemetery is a stop on the Metro's Blue Line. Exit the station onto Memorial Drive South and pick up *Miles and Directions* below at mile 1.2, starting at the cemetery's visitor center. See www.mata.com for station details and train schedules.

Trailhead GPS: Theodore Roosevelt Island: N38 53.733' / W77 04.004'; Arlington National Cemetery Visitors Center: N38 52.991' / W77 03.943'

The Hike

It is hard to imagine Arlington National Cemetery looking any different than it does today: acres of green lawn; rows of white headstones; spectacular monuments to our country's greatest figures, both civilian and military. But, in fact, the property started not as a national cemetery, but as a memorial to our first president, George Washington.

As you walk Memorial Drive toward the white marble Memorial Entrance, your eyesight is drawn to a Greek Revival–style home, complete with white arches, that stands atop a hill. This is Arlington House, built by Washington's adopted son, George Washington Parke Custis, between 1802 and 1818. He stocked the home with memorabilia to Washington. In the surrounding fields, he rotated crops. Visitors were welcome to tour the building and listen as Custis retold stories of his famous father figure. In this home he raised his daughter, Mary Anna Randolph Custis, who would grow up to marry Robert E. Lee, future general of the Confederate Army during the Civil War.

After Custis's death, Lee and his wife lived in the home. When Lee took command of the Confederate Army, the house was abandoned, and later it was seized by the U.S. government. Over a circuitous route that saw it become a freedman's village for former black slaves, then a national cemetery, Arlington House and Lee were reunited—at least symbolically—when Arlington House was named a national memorial to Lee.

From high above the hill on which Arlington House sits, the view stretches north down Memorial Drive, across the Potomac to the Lincoln Memorial. The link between the two memorials is no accident. Architects designed the road as a link between two men who are forever linked in history.

While this book is about recreation, the walk in Arlington Cemetery is about something else. The Custis Walk, which hikers can merge onto just west of the Memorial Entrance, via Schley Drive, is pastoral and calm. On a clear afternoon, sunlight dapples the ground beneath tall oak trees. The headstones that adjoin this leg of Custis Walk date to World Wars I and II, and the Korean Conflict. Some bear names; others do not.

After a short detour outside the cemetery to see the iconic U.S. Marine Corps Memorial (also known as the Iwo Jima Memorial) and the Netherlands Carillon (the source of the hourly Westminster chimes that can be heard throughout the cemetery), this route follows Ord & Weitzel Drive past a section of graves reserved for residents of the freedman's village. This interesting chapter in the history of the cemetery land started as a village for blacks freed during the Civil War, but it lasted for thirty years. The actual site of the village is on the south end of the cemetery, but the gravestones you pass on

View of Washington Monument from Arlington National Cemetery

Ord & Weitzel Drive mark many of the freedmen's final resting spots. They occupy a thin strip on the right, hard against the brick cemetery wall, and many headstones bear a simple inscription: CITIZEN.

The draw for many people when they visit Arlington is what's termed "the big three"—the Kennedy memorials (to President John F. Kennedy and Senator Robert F. Kennedy), Arlington House, and the Tomb of the Unknowns. But it is worth veering off this course, as the route described in this chapter does, to find lesser-known, but historically significant, memorials. Every gravestone and memorial, whether a simple white marble stone marker or an elaborate sculpture, tells a story.

Miles and Directions

0.0 START from the south end of the Theodore Roosevelt Island parking area, at a junction of the Mount Vernon Trail and a footbridge across to the island. Walk south on the Mount Vernon Trail, which is a paved multiuse path shared with bike riders, joggers, and in-line skaters. Within 200 yards, the trail (now a boardwalk) forks. Bear left to continue south on the Mount Vernon Trail.

0.7 Veer right (southeast) off the paved trail onto a well-worn dirt footpath that rises to cross the northbound lane of George Washington Memorial Parkway, and a ramp road. Traffic on both roads approaches from the left (south).

0.9 Pass through a stand of pine trees and emerge at the west end of Arlington Memorial Bridge. Follow the traffic rotary counterclockwise to Memorial Drive.

1.2 Pass the cemetery's visitor center across Memorial Drive on your left. (*FYI:* The visitor center has bathrooms, and the information desk offers free walking maps of the cemetery.)

1.3 Turn right on Schley Drive at the Memorial Gate. Climb a small hill and bear right on the Custis Walk, a paved path through the northern sections of the cemetery.

1.4 Cross straight over Sherman Drive.

1.6 Cross straight over Ord & Weitzel Drive and exit the cemetery through the Ord & Weitzel Gate. Cross straight over Marshall Drive and walk along the roadside shoulder of the Iwo Jima Memorial Access Road.

1.8 Reach the U.S. Marine Corps War Memorial, popularly known as the Iwo Jima Memorial. Locate a paved path that leads south from the memorial, crosses the access road, and climbs a hill toward the Netherlands Carillon.

1.9 Turn right (west) at the Netherlands Carillon and continue downhill to the Ord & Weitzel Gate. (*FYI:* The carillon was a gift from the Netherlands in thanks for U.S. involvement in World War II. There are fifty bells in the tower; eighteen of them are programmed to play Westminster chimes and strike on the hour between 10:00 a.m. and 6:00 p.m. daily.)

2.0 Cross Marshall Drive diagonally left and reenter Arlington National Cemetery at the Ord & Weitzel Gate. Inside, turn right (west) and walk up Ord & Weitzel Drive. (*FYI:* Gravestones on the right, in Section 27, are those of black servicemen who served during the Civil War and residents of the freedman's village, a settlement for newly freed blacks during the war. Gravestones are simple, labeled with only a name and perhaps the designation Citizen.)

2.5 Continue straight past an intersection with Mitchell Drive on the left.

2.7 Climb the road to a junction with Lincoln Drive. Turn right and climb to a junction with Sherman Drive. Turn left on Sherman, and then immediately turn right onto Sheridan Drive.

2.8 Turn right (west) on Custis Walk and begin a climb up a long set of stairs. En route, pass the gravestone of Mary Randolph, the first person buried at Arlington.

3.0 Reach Arlington House, home of George Washington Parke Custis, adopted son of George Washington, and the national memorial to Custis's son-in-law, Gen. Robert E. Lee. After touring the home and Lee museum (located in a white building at the far end of the kitchen garden), find your way to the back of Arlington House. From the courtyard, shaded by a large pine tree, locate a crushed gravel path that borders a flower garden on your left. Follow the path to a small garden ringed by tall hedges where the Tomb of the Unknown Civil War Soldier is located. Pass straight through the garden, turn left on Lee Drive, and then immediately right onto Cook Walk, a paved footpath that descends through the cemetery.

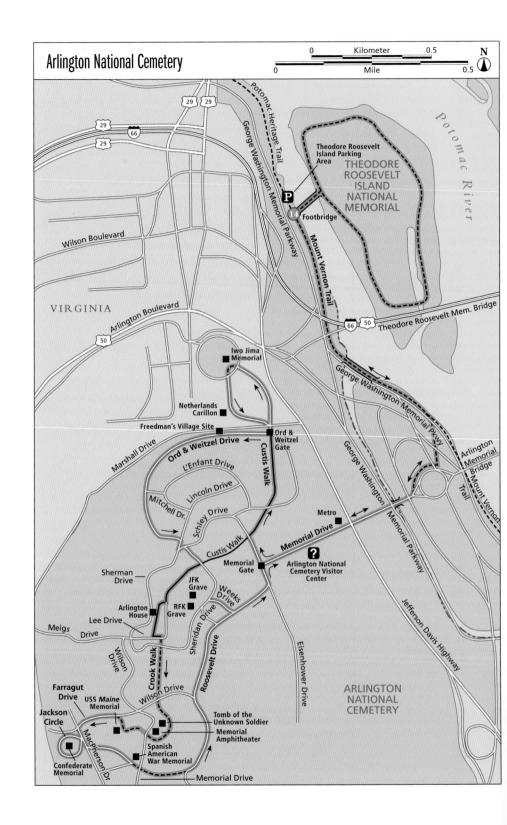

Arlington National Cemetery

0   Kilometer   0.5

0   Mile   0.5

N

29   29

29

66

29

Potomac Heritage Trail

George Washington Memorial Parkway

Theodore Roosevelt
Island Parking
Area

P

THEODORE
ROOSEVELT
ISLAND
NATIONAL
MEMORIAL

Footbridge

Potomac River

Wilson Boulevard

Mount Vernon Trail

VIRGINIA

Arlington Boulevard

50

66   50

Theodore Roosevelt Mem. Bridge

Iwo Jima
Memorial

George Washington Memorial Pkwy

Netherlands
Carillon

Freedman's Village Site

Ord & Weitzel Drive ←

Ord &
Weitzel
Gate

L'Enfant Drive

Marshall Drive

Custis Walk

George Washington Memorial Parkway

Arlington
Memorial
Bridge

Lincoln Drive

Mitchell Dr.

Schley Drive

Metro

Mount Vernon Trail

Custis Walk

Memorial Drive

Sherman
Drive

Memorial
Gate

?

Arlington National
Cemetery Visitor
Center

JFK
Grave

Weeks
Drive

Arlington
House

RFK
Grave

Lee Drive

Sheridan Drive

Meigs
Drive

Jefferson Davis Highway

Wilson
Drive

Crook Walk

Roosevelt Drive

Eisenhower Drive

Farragut
Drive

USS *Maine*
Memorial

Wilson Drive

ARLINGTON
NATIONAL
CEMETERY

Jackson
Circle

MacPherson Dr.

Tomb of the
Unknown Soldier

Memorial
Amphitheater

Confederate
Memorial

Spanish
American
War Memorial

Memorial Drive

3.2 Cross straight over Wilson Drive and climb a slate stone path toward the Tomb of the Unknown Soldier.

3.5 After touring the Tomb of the Unknown Soldier, walk around the Memorial Amphitheater. Cross straight over Memorial Drive and walk up a paved path to a memorial to the USS *Maine*. Here, turn right and walk away from the USS *Maine* Memorial on Sigsbee Drive, the memorial's access road. At a junction with Farragut Drive, turn left (west).

3.7 Turn left (south) on McPherson Drive. Take the first right on Jackson Circle to tour the Confederate Monument, which marks the burial section for Confederate soldiers. Return to McPherson Drive, cross diagonally left, and follow Lawton Drive. (*FYI:* Moses J. Ezekiel, buried at the base of the memorial, was a Confederate Civil War veteran who went on to an accomplished career as an artist. He sculpted the Confederate Memorial, which was dedicated on June 4, 1914.)

4.0 Reach the Spanish-American War Memorial at the bend in Lawton Drive. The memorial is a 50-foot-tall Corinthian column topped by a sphere and bronze eagle. Walk around the memorial and drop off the grass hillside marked by four large guns that date to this 1898 conflict. Cross Memorial Drive and enter cemetery Section 35. Walk between rows of tombstones as you head east to Roosevelt Drive.

4.1 Turn left (north) on Roosevelt Drive.

4.5 Turn left (west) on Weeks Drive to access the tombs of President John F. Kennedy and Senator Robert F. Kennedy. After touring the memorials, return to Roosevelt Drive via Weeks and turn left (north).

4.8 Bear left (west) onto Eisenhower Drive. Walk to the Memorial Gate and turn right (north) on Memorial Drive.

5.2 Bear left and follow the sidewalk around the traffic rotary in a clockwise direction. At the west end of Memorial Bridge, turn left and follow the dirt path through a grove of pines and descend to the Mount Vernon Trail.

5.5 Turn left (north) on the Mount Vernon Trail.

6.1 HIKE ENDS at the Theodore Roosevelt Island parking lot.

Hike Information

Local information: Arlington Convention and Visitors Services, Arlington, VA; (800) 296-7996; www.stayarlington.com

Local events/attractions: The guard at the Tomb of the Unknowns is changed in an elaborate ceremony every half hour, Apr through Sept, and every hour (on the hour) the rest of the year.

Local outdoor stores: REI, 3509 Carlin Springs Rd., Bailey's Crossroads, VA; (703) 379-9400; www.rei.com

Other resources: James Edward Peters's book, *Arlington National Cemetery: Shrine to America's Heroes,* makes a nice walking companion. It balances an overview of the history of the place with details about particular monuments and graves. Available at the visitor center bookstore.

15 Great Falls Park

For generations, Great Falls was simply an obstacle to the flow of goods from western farms to eastern seaports. To walk along cliffs that line the river and delve into the Piedmont forest and study the ruins of the Patowmack Canal—predecessor to both the C&O Canal and New York's Erie Canal—is to capture a bit of the essence of a place both naturally and historically significant.

Start: From the park visitor center
Distance: 5.1-mile loop
Approximate hiking time: 2 to 3 hours
Difficulty: Easy because of well-traveled trails with a few short, steep sections along the river. The bushwhack from Difficult Run north to Ridge Trail, while not physically difficult, demands a hiker stay alert.
Trail surface: The trail from the park visitor center is graded and gravel lined. River Trail is uneven, crosses open rock, and has some pitchy stretches. Ridge Trail follows old dirt roads and forest paths. Swamp Trail is a unique, narrow dirt footpath alongside marsh.
Seasons: Springtime for the wildflowers and Oct for the foliage
Other trail users: Joggers, cross-country skiers, equestrians, mountain bikers, and rock climbers
Handicapped accessibility: Falls Overlooks 2 and 3 are fully accessible, as is the Patowmack Canal Trail to the Holding Basin.

Canine compatibility: Leashed dogs permitted
Land status: National park
Fees and permits: Entrance fee (also valid for entry to Chesapeake & Ohio Canal National Historical Park in Maryland)
Schedule: Sunrise to sunset daily, except for Thanksgiving, Christmas, and New Year's Day. *Note:* During weekends and holidays in good weather, there can be long wait times to enter this popular park. Consider coming early or late.
Facilities: Interpretive museum, theater, restrooms, snack bar (summer months only), picnic tables, visitor center
Maps: DeLorme *Virginia Atlas & Gazetteer:* Page 76 A3. USGS 7.5 minute series: *Vienna, VA* and *Falls Church, VA*
Trail contacts: Great Falls Park, 9200 Old Dominion Drive, McLean, VA 22101; (703) 757-3101; www.nps.gov/grfa

Finding the trailhead: Distance from Washington, D.C.: 17 miles
From I-495 (Capital Beltway): Take exit 44 and turn left onto Georgetown Pike/VA 193. Go 4.4 miles and turn right onto Old Dominion Drive to enter the park. From the park boundary drive 1.2 miles to the visitor center parking lot. Trailhead GPS: N38 59.820' / W77 15.277'

The Hike

More than 15 miles between Riverbend Park and Theodore Roosevelt Island, the Potomac River descends 130 feet. Technically, the river's passage spans the "fall line," a boundary between the Piedmont region of Virginia to tidewaters of the Coastal Plain. Such technicalities are washed away as you witness this transition from Overlooks 1

Painter captures the Great Falls of the Potomac.

through 3 at Great Falls Park. The falls here are a roaring inferno of white water, an iconic image for most who visit the park.

After this grand watery tumult, the Potomac crams its daily average flow of 10,000 cubic feet per second into Mather Gorge. This mile-long chute averages a few hundred feet in width. Given that nearly 15,000 square miles of runoff drains into the Potomac from Virginia, Pennsylvania, and West Virginia, it comes as no surprise that during major storms, the 30- to 60-foot cliffs that form Mather Gorge on the Virginia side are washed over.

A section of River Trail traverses the cliff line of Mather Gorge. It's one of Great Falls Park's most popular foot routes. From the picnic area the pathway starts out wide and even, but soon it becomes winding and rocky underfoot. Dark gray angular rocks jut from the ground. This is stone—geologists call it schist and metagraywacke—that supports the gorge bedrock. Short paths branch off River Trail, and on these you can either head to the high cliff line or descend into fissures that lead to the water's edge. Rock climbers, view seekers, and fishermen keep the trails well worn.

The advantage a hiker enjoys—especially one without an agenda, set path, or time frame—is that small things start to occupy your attention. It might be the perfectly smooth round holes in the rocks. It takes a geologist's sense of time to comprehend that these were formed hundreds of millions of years ago, when the river flowed

> ▶ **KID APPEAL**

Check out the Falls Overlooks, then explore canal ruins in the vicinity of Matildaville. There are hands-on lessons to be learned (namely in how goods were shipped before FedEx and UPS). Trace the path of the canal from the holding basin past Locks 1 and 2, and end at an overlook of the Canal Cut, where three locks brought laden boats through a narrow passage in the solid cliff walls that form Mather Gorge.

at this level, and the potholes, as they're termed, were scoured by whirling sand and rock caught in a whirlpool effect.

A tree that appears, at first glance, to grow from solid rock has, on closer examination, actually found a toehold in a crevice filled with dirt. Grass sprouts from a pebble-and-sandbar along the river's edge. A pattern emerges as River Trail follows the shoreline. Here a rash of wildflowers, there a few bushes, and there a tree.

The rock and riverside habitats of the Potomac Gorge are increasingly drawing the attention of botanists, who have described bedrock terraces featuring Virginia pine and low shrubs. Down at river level are rocky bars and shores featuring a mix of hardwoods, like green ash and black willow, and grasses, like big bluestem. Whether they're 60 feet above the water on a cliff ledge or at the river's edge, they share one thing: They depend on the periodic disruption that comes with the flooding of the river.

River Trail eventually tails away from the Potomac River. Ridge Trail, Swamp Trail, and a variety of interconnecting dirt roads create a network of more than 12 miles covering more than 800 acres of preserved land. On a holiday weekend, a ranger at the contact station will process 125 cars an hour. Most flock to the Falls Overlooks, but others delve into the woodlands to walk under tall, thick-trunked tulip poplars. Young kids swarm the ruins of the old Patowmack Canal. Those who venture farther will find an unmarked route between Ridge Trail and Difficult Run. On Swamp Trail, a low wetland positively pops with the green of skunk cabbage in springtime and remains lush all summer while the forest around it dries out.

And out on the cliff, a pine clings to its precarious perch, a reminder that the Potomac Gorge is, in the words of the Nature Conservancy, "one of the most important natural areas in the Eastern U.S."

Miles and Directions

0.0 START from the park visitor center. Walk around the building on a wide, graded path of dirt and crushed rock. Where the path splits, bear right (southeast). Once past the visitor center, turn left (east) onto the Falls Overlook Trail, which leads past Overlooks 1, 2, and 3.

0.2 Bear left (southeast) onto blue-blazed River Trail. The route starts out as a wide dirt path, and then narrows into a rocky footpath. (*Note:* The trail straight from this junction is the Patowmack Canal Trail and marks the return portion of this hike.)

0.5 Turn left (east) at a four-way trail intersection and descend a set of stairs to the edge of the Potomac. When you're finished exploring, return to this junction and turn left (east) to resume hiking the River Trail.

Great Falls Park

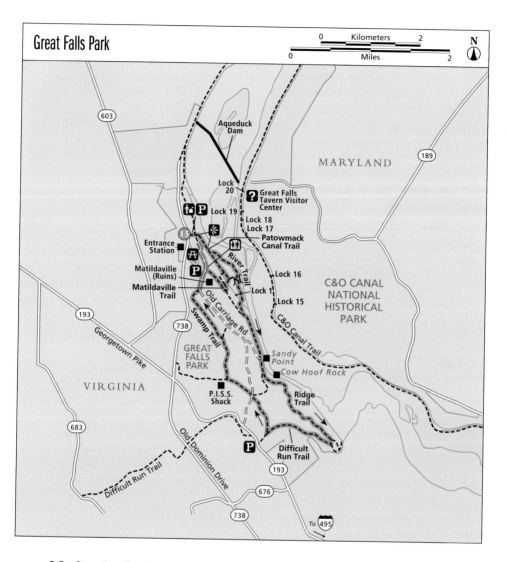

0 Kilometers 2
0 Miles 2

N

0.8 *Stay alert:* Turn right (west) on a dirt footpath for a detour around Canal Cut. Cross two boardwalks, and then turn left (south). Within 0.1 mile, the route returns to follow the cliffs high above Mather Gorge.

1.2 Cross straight over a paved service road and reenter woods opposite. Stay alert over the next 0.1 mile when River Trail runs close and parallel to the Matildaville Trail on the right.

1.4 Look for remains of a redbrick fireplace off the left side of the trail. A few hundred yards beyond this, look downhill to the left, where a sandy beach is visible. The trail here crosses exposed rock, and footing is tough and technical as you come to Cow Hoof Rock. (*FYI:* This promontory is your last chance to catch stellar views of the Potomac as it flows through Mather Gorge.)

1.6 A steep climb ends at a T junction with Ridge Trail. Turn left (south) onto Ridge, which is a wide dirt road.

2.1 Turn right (south) and descend to Difficult Run Trail. In 0.1 miles, reach Difficult Run Trail and turn right (north) on a wide road of hard-packed dirt and gravel. *Option:* Stay straight at this right turn in Ridge Trail. A steep footpath dives off the hillside to reach Difficult Run near its confluence with the Potomac. This short, steep descent is a bushwhack on an unmarked trail. If you chose this route, descend to Difficult Run at its confluence with the Potomac River and turn right

2.8 *Stay alert:* Turn right (north) on an unmarked footpath that climbs steeply uphill. (*Note:* This is a bushwhack on an established, but unmarked, trail. There are no trail signs or blazes at this junction. Prior to reaching it, look for a clearing on the right side of the trail that has the appearance of an old quarry—or a severely eroded hillside. If you reach Georgetown Pike, you've gone too far. Turn and retrace your steps.)

3.0 Veer left (north) onto Ridge Trail and descend in 0.1 mile to a junction with Old Carriage Road. Cross straight over the road and climb.

3.2 Turn right (north) onto the Swamp Trail Connector.

3.5 Turn left (northwest) onto Swamp Trail. (*Note:* This junction may not be marked, and the trail straight ahead [leading to Old Carriage Road] seems like the more obvious route. Swamp Trail is a single-track woodland path, while the spur is a wide, grassy path elevated above the low, wet ground on a berm.)

3.9 Turn left (north) onto Old Carriage Road.

4.1 Turn right (south) onto Matildaville Trail. (*FYI:* There is a bathroom a few feet north of this junction.)

4.3 Veer left and downhill where Matildaville Trail branches right and enters the woods as a narrow footpath. Descend to a T junction with Patowmack Canal Trail. Turn right and follow the old canal route to Lock 1. After exploring the ruins, return to this junction and continue straight (north) on the Patowmack Canal Trail. Look for side trails on the left that lead to ruins of the canal superintendent's home and other Matildaville homes.

4.6 Turn right at a fork in Patowmack Trail and cross the canal's holding basin. Within a few feet, a footbridge spans a small creek that was dug to control water levels in the holding basin. Beyond this footbridge, continue straight past a trail on the right that descends on a set of stairs to the River Trail.

4.7 Stay straight as a leg of the Patowmack Canal Trail merges on the left.

5.1 HIKE ENDS at the visitor center.

Hike Information

Local information: Fairfax County/Capital Region Visitors Center, Tysons Corner Shopping Center, 1961 Chain Bridge Rd., McLean, VA; (703) 752-9500; www .fxva.com

Local events/attractions: Wolf Trap National Park for the Performing Arts, Vienna, VA; (703) 255-1800; www.nps.org/wotr

Good eats: Deli Italiano Gourmet Pizza & Subs, 9911 Georgetown Pike, Great Falls, VA; (703) 759-6782; www.deliitaliano.com

The Old Brogue Irish Pub, 762 Walker Rd., Great Falls, VA; (703) 759-3309; www .oldbrogue.com

Ruins of the historic Patowmack Canal

Local outdoor store: Tysons REI, 8209 Watson St., McLean, VA; (703) 506-1938; www.rei.com

Hike tours: Ranger-led programs and tours on nature and history are given throughout the year.

Organizations: The Sierra Club Potomac Region Outings (PRO) (202-547-2326; www.sierrapotomac.org) sponsors hikes throughout the region, including Great Falls Park.

Other resources: Potomac Appalachian Trail Club (PATC), Vienna, VA; (703) 242-0315; www.patc.net. Contact for maps, book orders, cabin rentals, scheduled hikes, and membership. PATC Map D covers Great Falls and vicinity.

16 G. Richard Thompson Wildlife Management Area

The 4,000-acre area rises in a series of steep inclines to the crest of the Blue Ridge, with elevations ranging from 700 to 2,200 feet. The scenery is diverse, from fruit orchards surrounding old homesites to a serene trout pond to rocky outcrops. The network of trails includes a 7-mile section of the Appalachian Trail. There is an abundance of wildflowers—the area harbors one of the largest populations of large-flowered trillium in North America. Virginia's Native Plant Society lists the area on its register of important native plant sites.

Start: From parking area 7

Distance: 4.3-mile lollipop

Approximate hiking time: 2 hours

Difficulty: Easy

Trail surface: Dirt road, forest path

Seasons: In spring, when the large-flowered trillium are in bloom. Avoid the height of deer-hunting season, Nov through Jan.

Other trail users: Anglers, cyclists, equestrians, hunters (in season), and naturalists. Viewing wildflowers is very popular in the spring.

Handicapped accessibility: None

Canine compatibility: Dogs must be leashed at all times outside of open hunting, chase, or training seasons.

Land status: State wildlife management area

Fees and permits: No fees. Appropriate hunting and fishing licenses are required. A trout license is required in addition to a Virginia fishing license.

Schedule: Dawn to dusk, daily, year-round

Facilities: Parking

Maps: DeLorme *Virginia Atlas & Gazetteer:* Page 75 A5. USGS 7.5 minute series: *Linden, VA; Upperville, VA*

Trail contacts: Region 5 Office, Virginia Department of Game & Inland Fisheries, Fredericksburg, VA; (540) 899-4169; www.dgif.virginia .gov/wmas

Other: Swimming in Thompson Lake is prohibited. Primitive camping (no facilities) is allowed for up to 14 consecutive days.

Special considerations: Avoid the height of deer-hunting season, Nov through Jan.

Finding the trailhead: Distance from Washington D.C.: 71.5 miles

From I-66: Take exit 13; turn left and drive 0.2 mile south on VA 79. Turn left (east) onto VA 55 and drive 1.3 miles to Linden. Turn left (north) on Freezeland Road (VA 638). Drive 6 miles to where the road turns to gravel and becomes Fire Trail Road. Continue 0.1 mile to Parking Area 7 on the right. Trailhead GPS: N38 57.784' / W78 01.184'

The Hike

Virginia's Department of Game & Inland Fisheries oversees thirty wildlife management areas around the state with the hunter and angler in mind. Fields are kept clear to attract grazing animals, and seed plots are sown to keep them plump and healthy. Streams and man-made lakes are stocked with trout and other fish. As the state makes these areas hiker-friendly as well, they'd do well to model the G. Richard Thompson Wildlife Management Area in Fauquier County, where hikers and naturalists stake as much claim to the beautiful surroundings as outdoorsmen.

Who was George Richard Thompson? He was an avid hunter who bequeathed the land to the state for the enjoyment of future hunters.

Virginia's native plant lovers and wildflower aficionados can find respite here. Draped across the east side of the Blue Ridge Mountains, this small patch of land in far-western Fauquier County hosts an array of wildflowers. Most noticeable April through June are the large-flowered trillium that grow in large swatches on the slopes of the preserve.

The interaction between trillium and insects makes for a fascinating study of how various forms of life—plant, animal, and insect—rely on each other. The trillium's bright coloring attracts bees and butterflies, yet a nose-to-nose study of the flower proves it to have quite an offensive odor. That explains the presence of flies, which are the primary pollinators of trillium. In the matter of seed dispersal, plants generally rely heavily on birds ingesting then discharging seeds far afield. In the case of the trillium, its seeds excrete an oily substance that attracts ants, which come in droves and eat them.

The Stone Wall Loop is a wide grassy road from Parking Area 7 that takes you to Lake Thompson, a man-made impound upon which ducks float and anglers cast their lines. In summer, a plentitude of butterflies flutter around milkweed. There are plenty of distractions en route. You may see a snake crossing the path or even a box turtle.

Canada geese on Thompson Lake

Large-flowered trillium are common here. COURTESY U.S. FISH & WILDLIFE SERVICE

Left unmolested, this reptile could live more than sixty years. To tell its age, look at the shell. If it's 5 inches or smaller the turtle is probably ten years old or younger.

Miles and Directions

0.0   START from parking area 7. Hike down the chained-off road that drops off the left side of the parking lot. The road is gravel at first, then reverts to dirt and grass.

0.2   Walk straight past a junction with the Appalachian Trail (AT) on the Lake Trail. (*Side trip:* A right on the AT leads to Manassas Gap Shelter in 3 miles.)

0.5   A grass road veers off on the right. Continue straight downhill on the main grass road.

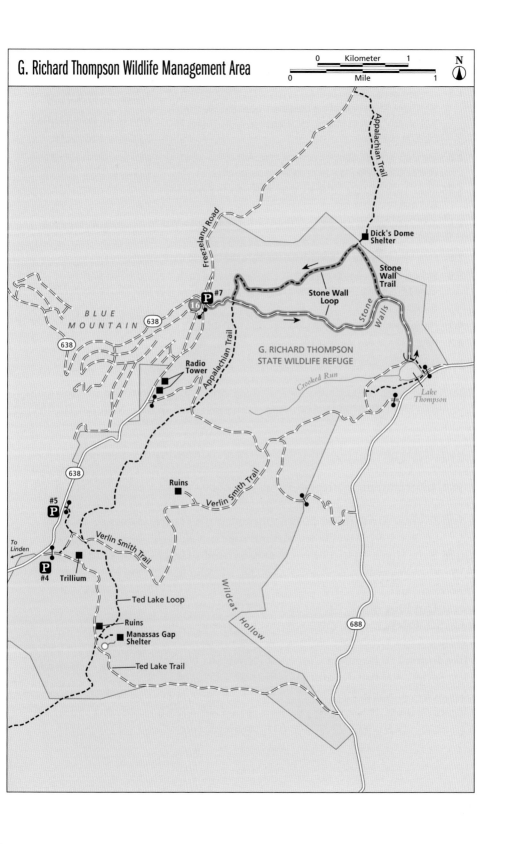

G. Richard Thompson Wildlife Management Area

0 Kilometer 1

0 Mile 1

N

Appalachian Trail

Freezeland Road

BLUE MOUNTAIN

638

638

638

16 P

#7 P

Dick's Dome Shelter

Stone Wall Trail

Stone Wall Loop

Stone Walls

G. RICHARD THOMPSON STATE WILDLIFE REFUGE

Radio Tower

Appalachian Trail

Crooked Run

Lake Thompson

Ruins

Verlin Smith Trail

#5 P

To Linden

Verlin Smith Trail

#4 P Trillium

Ted Lake Loop

Ruins

Manassas Gap Shelter

Ted Lake Trail

Wildcat Hollow

688

0.6 Continue straight downhill past another grass road that turns right into a clearing.

1.3 The trail levels, and on both sides, remnants of stone walls are visible. Make note of the overgrown, unblazed Stone Wall Trail branching off to the left. You'll return to it later. Curve to the right (south).

1.8 The road emerges from the cover of trees. Ahead is a nice view across a valley to a farm on the opposite hill.

1.95 Reach Lake Thompson. Retrace your steps back to Stone Wall Trail.

2.6 At the intersection with the Lake Trail, turn right onto Stone Wall Trail, crossing an old stone wall.

2.9 Pass by some large boulders in the woods to the left and climb steeply.

3.0 Emerge from the woods onto the AT. Continue walking straight ahead on the singletrack, white-blazed trail. (*Side trip:* The AT downhill to the right reaches Dick's Dome Shelter in 0.3 mile.)

4.1 The AT emerges onto a grass road. Turn right onto the Lake Trail and head uphill.

4.3 HIKE ENDS at Parking Area 7.

OPTIONS

The 2-mile Ted Lake Loop begins at Parking Area 4 and includes many interesting features including a trillium field, some homesite ruins, and the Manassas Gap AT Shelter.

Hike Information

Local Information: Warrenton–Fauquier County Visitor Center, Warrenton, VA; (800) 820-1021, www.visitfauquier.com

Local Events/Attractions: Linden Vineyards, 3708 Harrels Corner Road, Linden, VA; (540) 364-1997; www.lindenvineyards.com

Good Eats: Hunter's Head Tavern, 9048 John Mosby Hwy. (U.S. 50), Upperville, VA; (540) 592-9020; www.hunters headtavern.com.

Local Outdoor Store: Mountain Trails, 115 North Loudoun St., Winchester, VA; (540) 667-0030; www.mountain -trails.com

Hike Tours: The Piedmont Chapter of the Virginia Native Plant Society, 400 Blandy Farm Lane, Boyce, VA; (540) 837-1600; www.vnps.org

Organizations: Potomac Appalachian Trail Club (PATC), 118 Park Street SE, Vienna, VA 22180-4609; (703) 242-0315; www.patc.net

▶ **KID APPEAL**
The 10-acre Lake Thompson is stocked with trout, is frequented by ducks and geese, and is a pleasant, green space to have a picnic.

Since 2008 Thompson Lake has drained unexpectedly and inexplicably several times! Fortunately, water levels rise back to normal in the winter.

17 Harpers Ferry, VA/MD/WV

This "quadruple crown" of hikes touches on four high points in three different states: Split Rock in Virginia, Maryland Heights and Stone Fort in Maryland, and Jefferson Rocks in West Virginia. Front and center at each is the Potomac River and the picturesque town of Harpers Ferry, West Virginia, perched on a point at the confluence of the Shenandoah and Potomac Rivers. The Appalachian Trail weaves them together for a full day of climbing and a dash of history.

Start: From River Access parking area on Shenandoah St.
Distance: 12.1-mile loop
Approximate hiking time: 4 to 5 hours
Difficulty: Difficult due to the distance, several steep climbs, and the proximity to highways and traffic
Trail surface: The Appalachian Trail utilizes woodland footpaths, sidewalks, footbridges, town streets, and stone steps. The C&O Canal towpath is a level, graded dirt path. Old dirt roads and forest paths characterize trails through Maryland Heights.
Seasons: Best in all seasons
Other trail users: Joggers and bikers on paved sections; motorists on roadways
Handicapped accessibility: The *Accessible Route Map for Lower Town* is through the visitor center. There is also an accessible shuttle bus.
Canine compatibility: Leashed dogs permitted
Land status: National historical park

Fees and permits: Entrance fee
Schedule: Park is open daily year-round 9:00 a.m. to 5:00 p.m.; closed Thanksgiving, Christmas, and New Year's Day.
Facilities: Restrooms, picnic tables, visitor center, bookstore, historic buildings
Maps: DeLorme *West Virginia Atlas & Gazetteer:* Page 31 H7. USGS 7.5 minute series: *Harpers Ferry, WV, VA, MD.* PATC Map 7, AT in Northern Virginia (Potomac River to VA 7). Trail maps can be downloaded from www.nps.gov/hafe.
Trail contacts: Harpers Ferry National Historical Park, P.O. Box 65, Harpers Ferry, WV 25425; (304) 535-6029; www.nps.gov/hafe
Special considerations: Sections of this route involve hiking alongside busy US 340 and crossing an active railroad line. Use extra caution on a 0.4-mile section of this route along the US 340 road shoulder from the Loudoun Heights Trail to the Potomac River.

Finding the trailhead: Distance from Washington, D.C.: 66 miles
    From Washington, D.C.: From the Beltway, take I-495 to I-270 N. Follow I-270 to Frederick, MD and take the exit for Rt. 340 S toward Harpers Ferry. At the Harpers Ferry stoplight, turn left. Address for GPS is 171 Shoreline Dr., Harpers Ferry, WV.
    By Rail: MARC Commuter Rail and Amtrak run from Washington, D.C., to Harpers Ferry.
    Trailhead GPS: N39 19.302'/ W77 44.581'

The Hike

The advantage height offers is clear from the rocky promontory called Maryland Heights. The unobstructed view drops to the Potomac and Shenandoah Rivers and across to the small town of Harpers Ferry, West Virginia. "So long as Maryland

View of Harpers Ferry from Split Rocks on the Loudoun Heights Trail

Heights was occupied by the enemy, Harpers Ferry could never be occupied by us," wrote Maj. Gen. Lafayette McLaws of the Confederate Army.

Confederates won the battle by occupying three high points surrounding the town: Maryland Heights, Loudoun Heights, and Bolivar Heights. Captured were 12,500 Union troops, which is described as the largest single capture of Federal troops during the Civil War. With the exception of Bolivar Heights, these vistas are connected by a network of trails and roads. To reach these, and Jefferson Rock inside the town, is to achieve something few, if any, hikes can boast: Touching high points in three states in one day.

Harpers Ferry the town is as much defined by its geography as the people who settled here. Robert Harper founded the town in 1751; he had been running a ferry across the Potomac for several years prior to this. Its proximity to water foretold its rise as a mill town. John Hall ran Hall's Rifle Works here in the 1820s. George Washington, impressed with its strategic location, recommended the town as the site of an armory. Even the rock underfoot proved a resource. As you climb up the stone steps through town on the Appalachian Trail, you're walking over phylite, a type of slate, which was mined in town.

The rivers, however, were Harpers Ferry's most critical asset. In early America, the Blue Ridge was considered a formidable obstacle to westward travel. Passage was limited to "gaps"—a break or opening in the mountain ridge. The water gap at Harpers Ferry opened a major door to the Ohio Valley, where profitable farm goods were being shipped via the Mississippi River system to Gulf of Mexico ports. If East Coast ports like New York, Philadelphia, Baltimore, and Alexandria were to succeed, they needed access to the Ohio Valley. Thus, two of early America's major lines of transport—the Chesapeake and Ohio Canal, and the Baltimore and Ohio Railroad—pass through this gap. This hike passes along the canal's towpath, now a National Historic Trail, and it crosses the Potomac on a footbridge attached to the railroad bridge.

The town is, of course, the perceived halfway point on the Appalachian Trail—never mind that the true halfway point is north at Pine Grove Furnace in Pennsylvania—and headquarters for the Appalachian Trail Conference. The first miles of this trail were laid in Virginia, between Harpers Ferry and Chester Gap. It is a mile-long climb from US 340 to the Loudoun Heights Trail.

It is Thomas Jefferson who eloquently put into words the impression that many have as they hit the high points at Split Rocks, Maryland Heights, and the eponymous Jefferson Rocks. Standing on the red rock promontory, he took in "one of the most stupendous scenes in Nature": the confluence of the Potomac and Shenandoah Rivers. In his book *Notes of Virginia* he wrote: "On your right comes up the Shenandoah, having ranged along the foot of the mountain a hundred miles to seek a vent. On your left approaches the Patowmac in quest of a passage also. In the moment of their junction they rush together against the mountain, rend it asunder and pass off to the sea . . . This scene is worth a voyage across the Atlantic."

Enjoying a view that only these heights can afford, Jefferson's words resonate in any season.

Miles and Directions

0.0 START from a set of stairs in the River Access parking area on Virginius Island. Climb to Shenandoah Street, turn left (west), and walk to the intersection with US 340. Here, pick up the white Appalachian Trail (AT) blazes, turn left (south), and cross the Shenandoah River via a sidewalk, facing oncoming traffic.

0.3 Descend a set of stairs and pass beneath the US 340 bridge. Follow white blazes of the AT as the trail becomes a narrow dirt footpath.

0.7 Cross paved Chestnut Hill Road.

1.1 Junction with an orange-blazed trail on left. Veer right (south) and continue climbing uphill.

1.3 Turn left (north) on blue-blazed Loudoun Heights Trail.

1.9 Junction with orange-blazed trail on left. Stay straight on Loudoun Heights Trail.

2.2 A side trail on the left leads to a power line easement with views of the Potomac River.

2.8 Reach Split Rocks Overlook on the left, with views west back to the town of Harpers Ferry. (*FYI:* This view is a nice preview of the hike to come, with a clear view of Maryland Heights on the north side of the Potomac River.) After soaking in the views, continue downhill on the blue-blazed Loudoun Heights Trail.

3.2 *Stay alert:* After a switchback that takes you close to the private-property line (homes visible), watch on your right for a trail junction. Turn right and descend quickly and steeply on a set of rock steps.

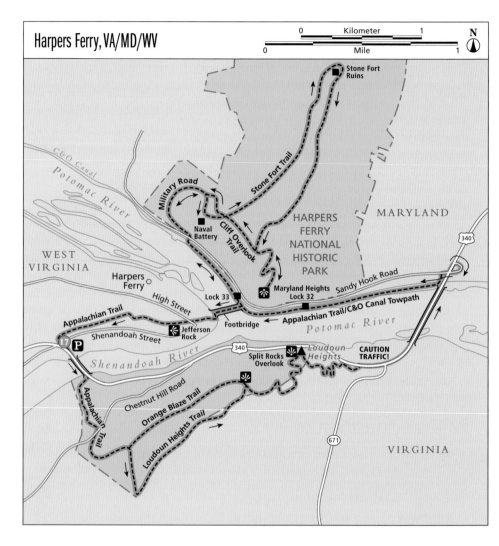

3.3 Exit the woods into a parking lot on the side of US 340. Walk east alongside the road (with traffic) and be sure to keep a guardrail between you and eastbound traffic. Walk through the parking lot of the Tri-State Exxon. Cross straight over VA 671 at its intersection with US 340. Thereafter, choose a safe time to cross US 340 and enter a River Access parking area.

3.7 Begin a long walk on a sidewalk across the US 340 bridge that spans the Potomac River, departing Virginia and entering Maryland.

4.1 Reach the north end of the US 340 bridge. Cross the highway and walk with traffic along the road shoulder to a blocked-off access road. Turn right and descend briefly on this abandoned road to Sandy Hook Road. Turn right (west) and pass beneath the US 340 bridge. Immediately past the bridge, turn left and cross the railroad tracks. Locate an earthen berm that crosses the old C&O Canal, and then descend to the towpath. (*FYI:* Sandy Hook Grocery is just west of the US 340 bridge.)

4.3 Turn right (west) on the C&O Canal towpath.

5.4 Pass Lock 33 and access to the AT footbridge that links Maryland Heights and Harpers Ferry. (*Bailout:* You will return to this junction after a 5.5-mile hike up Stone Fort and the Maryland Heights Overlook. To eliminate this section of the trip, climb the metal stairs and cross the footbridge to Harpers Ferry. Resume mileage cues at 10.9 miles.)

5.8 Turn right (north) and cross the old canal on a footbridge. Cross Sandy Hook Road diagonally left and climb a wide dirt path, passing a red metal gate en route.

6.3 Turn right (south) and descend to examine the ruins of an old naval battery situated some 300 feet above the Potomac. Beyond this, the trail swings back uphill and resumes its eastward course.

6.6 Turn left (north) on the blue-blazed Stone Fort Trail. Begin an unrelenting uphill climb that will extend for the next mile.

7.5 Reach Stone Fort. Turn right, cross a stone wall via steps, and enter what's termed the Exterior Fort. After exploring the ruins of this Civil War–era fortification, find your way to the crest of Maryland Heights, notable for the expansive views eastward. Follow the crest right (south) and begin to descend.

8.7 Turn left (east) on the red-blazed Cliff Overlook Trail and begin a series of switchbacks to the famous Maryland Heights overlook.

9.2 Reach a spectacular overlook off Maryland Heights onto the town of Harpers Ferry. After a rest, retrace your steps to the Stone Fort Trail.

9.7 Continue straight on Cliff Overlook Trail past a right turn, the east leg of the Stone Fort Trail.

9.8 Continue straight on Cliff Overlook Trail past a right turn, the west leg of the Stone Fort Trail. Within 200 feet or so, veer right and avoid a left turn that loops around the ruins of the naval battery.

10.5 Cross Sandy Hook Road diagonally right, cross a footbridge over the old C&O Canal, and turn left (east) to walk the towpath.

10.9 At Lock 33, climb a metal spiral staircase to reach the AT footbridge over the Potomac River, departing Maryland and entering West Virginia.

11.1 Come off the footbridge and enter a lot for a river overlook with views of the Shenandoah and Potomac confluence. Turn right, pass beneath a train trestle, and then turn left onto Shenandoah Street. Walk to the intersection of Shenandoah and High Streets, and turn right (north) on High Street. (*Note:* You are following the AT route through Lower Town, which is a district of the national historical park. Restrictions prohibit the trail's telltale white blazes inside the park.)

11.2 Turn left up a set of steps carved into the phylite bedrock. At the top, continue straight on a town street and walk past St. John's Episcopal Church.

11.3 At a right bend in the street, continue straight up a second set of stairs.

11.4 Reach Jefferson Rock, an overlook onto the Shenandoah just above its confluence with the Potomac. After soaking in the views, begin climbing a set of stairs uphill. After one flight, bear left (west) into the woods on the AT, here a dirt footpath. The AT's white blazes resume at this junction. (*Note:* If you miss this turnoff, the stairs continue a climb to a local cemetery. Retrace your steps to locate the junction.)

11.7 Continue straight past a junction on the right with a spur trail to the Appalachian Trail Conference headquarters.

Sarah Stevens, author's niece, hiking on the AT

12.0 Descend on the AT from the woods onto the shoulder of US 340. Follow it east (against traffic), staying to the inside of a guardrail. Cross straight over Shenandoah Street.

12.1 HIKE ENDS at the River Access parking lot at the junction of Shenandoah Street and US 340.

OPTIONS

Any one of the three overlooks featured in this hike can be done on its own. Make a loop from Split Rocks (Virginia) by utilizing the orange-blazed trail that intersects Loudoun Heights Trail at 1.1 and 1.9 miles above.

Hike Information

Local information: Jefferson County Convention & Visitors Bureau, 37 Washington Court, Harpers Ferry, WV; (866) HELLO-WV; www.discoveritallwv.com

Local events/attractions: The Park offers many programs throughout the year, including popular fall foliage walks. www.nps.gov/hafe

Good eats: The Cannonball Deli has lunch specials, take-out and a relaxed dining patio, 125-129 Potomac St., Harpers Ferry, WV; (304) 535-1762.

The Anvil Restaurant specializes in seafood in a cozy, family-style setting, 1290 W. Washington St., Harpers Ferry, WV; (304) 535-2582; www.anvilrestaurant.com.

For snacks, this route passes Tri-State Exxon, at US 340 and VA 617.

Local outdoor stores: Harpers Ferry Outfitters, 106 Potomac St., Harpers Ferry, WV; (304) 535-2087; www.theoutfitteratharpersferry.com

Hike tours: River & Trail Outfitters, 604 Valley Rd., Knoxville, MD; (301) 834-9950; www.rivertrail.com. Located across the river from Harpers Ferry.

Organizations: Potomac Appalachian Trail Club (PATC), 118 Park St. SE, Vienna, VA 22210; (703) 242-0315; www.patc.net

Appalachian Trail Conservancy, 799 Washington St., Harpers Ferry, WV; (304) 535-6331; www.appalachiantrail.org

Harpers Ferry Park Association & Bookshop, 723 Shenandoah St., Harpers Ferry, WV; (304) 535-6881; www.harpersferryhistory.org

18 Leesylvania State Park

Leesylvania State Park's trails are short, easy to hike, and fun. You'll find a virtual textbook worth of American history along the Lee's Woods Historic Trail. The bluff on Freestone Point was the site of a Civil War artillery. Colonial-era farmers rolled hogsheads of tobacco down to the water's edge for loading and shipment to England. Even up through the 1950s speculators looked to cash in on the beautiful Potomac waterfront with proposals for gambling boats and theme parks. There is a quiet side to the park as well, a place along Powell's Creek Nature Trail where you can learn the natural story of a small Potomac River tributary.

Start: Lee's Woods Historic Trail: From a trailboard sign and map near the Freestone Point Fishing Pier. Powell's Creek Nature Trail: From a trailboard sign and map in the Powell's Creek Nature Trail parking area.

Distance: Lee's Woods, 1.7-mile loop; Powell's Creek, 1.6-mile loop

Approximate hiking time: 1 hour for each loop

Difficulty: Easy due to level, graded paths; minimum elevation gain; and well-marked routes

Trail surface: Gravel and dirt paths, gravel and dirt roads, forested trail, stairs

Seasons: Best in late fall, winter, and early spring when the crowds thin out and bare trees allow for better views of the water

Other trail users: Hikers and joggers only

Handicapped accessibility: The 1-mile Bushy Point Trail and the Potomac Trail through the picnic area and along the waterfront

Canine compatibility: Leashed dogs permitted

Land status: State park

Fees and permits: Per-vehicle entrance fee

Schedule: 6 a.m. to a half-hour after sunset Mon through Fri. 5 a.m. to a half-hour after sunset on Sat and Sun.

Facilities: Restrooms, picnic shelters, visitor center, campground, camp store, boat ramp, marina

Maps: DeLorme *Virginia Atlas & Gazetteer:* Page 76 D4. USGS 7.5 minute series: *Quantico, VA, MD.* Line-drawn maps are available from the state park visitor center or ranger contact station at the park entrance.

Trail contacts: Leesylvania State Park, 2001 Daniel K. Ludwig Dr., Woodbridge, VA; (703) 730-8205; www.dcr.virginia.gov/state-parks/leesylvania

Finding the trailhead: Distance from Washington, D.C.: 29 miles

From I-95: Take exit 156 (Dale City/Rippon Landing) and follow signs for VA 784 eastbound. After driving 0.9 mile on VA 784, merge right onto US 1 South. Drive another 0.9 mile to Neabsco Hill Road, where you turn left onto Neabsco and drive 1.5 miles to Daniel K. Ludwig Drive. Turn right onto Ludwig Drive and in 2.2 miles reach the ranger contact station. Trailhead GPS: Lee's Woods Historic Trail: N38 35.454' / W77 14.876'; Powell's Creek Nature Trail: N38 35.567' / W77 15.680'

The Hike

A sharp scent of low tide drifts landward and over Freestone Point. Wind ruffles leaves on the small trees that cover the slope. It's 110 feet down to the sandy water's edge of Occoquan Bay. Atop this sandy bluff, the ground is pockmarked with sunken pits and earthen mounds. It was here that Confederate soldiers under the orders of Gen. Robert E. Lee placed cannon here to fire on Union gunships sailing up the Potomac toward Washington, D.C.

▶ **KID APPEAL**

Both Lee's Woods and Powell's Creek trails have fact-filled interpretive guides that are worth taking along on a hike with children. Every stop turns just another spot in the woods into a diorama of history and nature.

Lee knew of Freestone Point's strategic value firsthand. It and the land around it were his family's ancestral lands. It was his great-grandfather's home site and the birthplace of his father, Revolutionary War hero Light Horse Harry Lee. Its military value lay in its broad view of the Potomac. The

Site of historic fisheries on the Potomac River

THE LEES OF LEESYLVANIA

Leesylvania's name derives from Gen. Robert E. Lee's grandfather, who built a home here in 1747 and raised his family. The 100-plus acres bounded by Freestone Point and the Neabsco and Potomac Rivers had been in Lee's family for three generations. The Lee family home burned in 1792. In this short period of residency, the English colonies secured their independence, and Leesylvania produced one of the Revolution's leading military figures, "Light Horse Harry" Lee, father of the Confederate general Lee.

Confederacy had no navy to speak of, but they could—and did—harass Union navy sailing the Potomac to and from Washington, D.C. Freestone Point was one of several gun placements on Potomac bluffs stretching south to Chopawamsic Creek. In the fall of 1861, Union sloops fired on the position, and Confederate soldiers returned fire. It was the height of activity for this battery as the theater of war moved farther inland.

Brief as it was, this interlude with a Civil War moment is telling of Leesylvania State Park as a whole, and the 1.7-mile Lee's Woods Historic Trail in particular. Here, it is the breadth of history that characterizes the park. Where another park's value may lie in its size, old-growth forest, or rare plants, Leesylvania offers hikers a chance to tap into almost every era of American history up to, and including, the Great Depression of the 1920s and 1930s.

The long inventory of uses begins with Native Americans who fished here before English settlers set eyes upon the land. John Smith and his crew, on their exploration of the Chesapeake Bay in 1608, sailed past this point en route to Great Falls. English settlers mined sandstone from Freestone Point, and hikers can get up close by walking the small beachfront north of the park's fishing pier. Up through the end of the nineteenth century, fishermen hauled seine nets along the riverbank for herring and shad.

One of colonial America's most famous families, the Lees of Virginia, lived here. Their successor, the Fairfax family, farmed the land through the middle of the nineteenth century. The Alexandria Fredericksburg Railroad ran its line through this area. A private hunt club operated in the early twentieth century, and it was also a gambling resort and a public recreation area complete with Ferris wheel, miniature train, and a mile-long public beach.

In 1985, the park achieved its current status as a state park, and Lee's Woods Historic Trail and Powell's Creek Nature Trail are its two signature routes. If Lee's Woods is rich with history, Powell's Creek Nature Trail is equally rich, but in natural beauty.

Local students from the Freedom High School contributed the artistic renditions of plants and animals that decorate trailboards along Powell's Creek Nature Trail.

Powell's Creek is a small tributary that borders the southern side of the small neck on which Leesylvania State Park sits. Its entire route lies within Prince William County; when it passes beneath I-95, it enters the Coastal Plain. Soon after, the tidal regime of the Potomac River influences the creek. The tides fill the wide lower bays near the mouth of the creek, where purple flowers of the pickerelweed and bright yellow pond lily give the marsh a colorful hue in springtime. Farther upstream, the interior marsh supports healthy stands of wild rice, a critical food source for migrating sora rails and resident Canada geese.

For the first 0.5 mile along Powell's Creek Nature trail, you pass beneath a young forest dominated by sweetgum and maple. Sweetgum is especially abundant; in autumn, you can tell where this tree grows by the spiky balls spread about the forest floor (these dried seed pods give the ubiquitous tree its nickname, "gumball"). Beyond the junction for Bushy Point Trail, Powell's Creek Nature Trail takes on a different character. You cross over a small tributary and then turn to descend a finger of high land that ends at a heavily wooded bluff overlooking the lower reaches of Powell's Creek. The marsh is an active place, even if it's not readily apparent to the eye. There is a bald eagle's nest near the mouth of the creek, and the plants draw ducks, geese, and swans that eat the plants' roots and shoots.

Fairfax House ruins

"At the point of rock" is the translation of the American Indian word *neabsco*. It describes the high bluff of land more commonly known as Freestone Point. The location of Freestone Point is indicated on maps from the eighteenth century and was an important landmark for river pilots when navigating the Potomac.

What you can't see is the abundant aquatic life. A freshwater marsh like this is a nursery for spawning fish; studies have found abundant larvae of river herring, silverside, sunfish, and catfish. The shallow water, and the closed-in character of the marsh, with its numerous small water passages and small marsh islands, provide a safe environment for young fish like white perch, banded killifish, and alewife to feed and grow bigger. Their presence in turn draws in the wading birds—American egrets and great blue herons mostly—that hunt with stealthy and determined practice.

Powell's Creek has received a state-designated rating of "high" in terms of its natural heritage. A study by the Virginia Institute of Marine Science (VIMS) labeled it "one of the highest quality habitats of its kind in Northern Virginia." As you spend time soaking in the beautiful views from the Powell's Creek Nature Trail, both designations seem entirely appropriate.

Miles and Directions

Trail 1: Lee's Woods Historic Trail

0.0 START from a trailboard map and interpretive sign set between a traffic rotary and the Freestone Point fishing pier. Follow a wide gravel path into the woods. In less than 0.1 mile, turn right and climb on a wide dirt path. (*Side trip:* Before setting off on your woods hike, turn right from the trailboard and walk east to Freestone Point. A short beach extends north from the pier. When you're finished exploring, return to the trailhead and begin the hike.)

0.2 Top out on a 110-foot-high bluff overlooking Occoquan Bay and the Potomac River. Views from here are best in late fall and winter. The earthen breastworks date to the Civil War. Continue on the Lee's Woods Historic Trail by following red blazes as the trail heads into the woods and traces the bluff line.

0.3 In winter and spring, there are water views from a bench on the right side of the trail. Ahead, the trail swings to the left and descends a small hill. At the base of the hill, turn right (west) on a gravel road.

0.37 Reach a scenic overlook after a short climb on the gravel road. As you reach the top, stay left to avoid a path that branches right (north). (*Note:* The path on the right is the return portion of this hike.)

0.4 Pass the brick ruins of Fairfax House, downhill on the left. Beyond it, the trail enters a young deciduous forest of pawpaw, maple, yellow poplar, and sweetgum. The understory is thick with vines of the Virginia creeper. (*Side trip:* Between Fairfax House and an old barn, turn left and walk to the wood's edge, where a Bicentennial Oak, a white oak, grows. There's also an old brick-lined water well in this area.)

0.6 Continue straight (west) on the gravel road past a fire road that branches right.

Leesylvania State Park

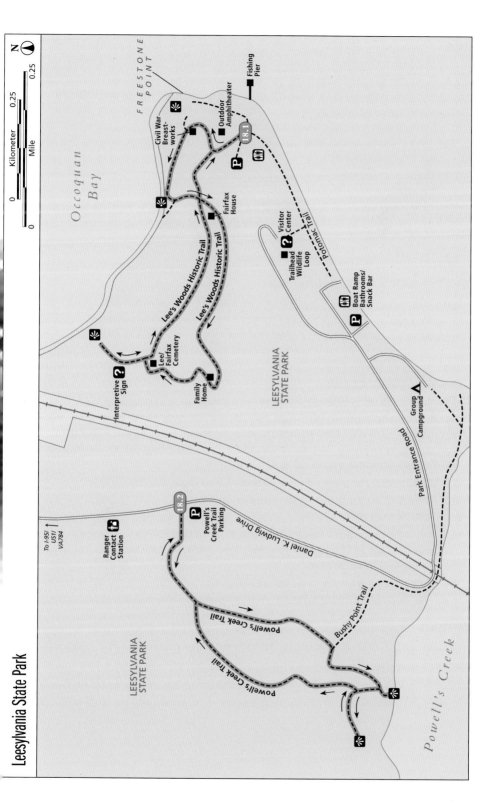

LEESYLVANIA STATE PARK

LEESYLVANIA STATE PARK

Occoquan Bay

FREESTONE POINT

Fishing Pier

Outdoor Amphitheater

Civil War Breastworks

Fairfax House

Lee's Woods Historic Trail

Lee's Woods Historic Trail

Lee/Fairfax Cemetery

Family Home

Interpretive Sign

Visitor Center

Trailhead Wildlife Loop

Potomac Trail

Boat Ramp Bathrooms/Snack Bar

Group Campground

Park Entrance Road

Daniel K. Ludwig Drive

Bushy Point Trail

Powell's Creek Trail

Powell's Creek Trail

Powell's Creek

Powell's Creek Trail Parking

Ranger Contact Station

To I-95/ US1/ VA784

18.1

18.2

N

Kilometer
0   0.25   0.25

Mile
0   0.25

0.8 Enter a clearing and turn right (north) on a woods path that leads to the ancestral home of the Lee family. A spur trail leads left (west) from this clearing to a family cemetery.

1.0 Reach the Lee and Fairfax family cemetery, surrounded by a wrought-iron fence. (*Side trip:* Behind the cemetery, follow the red-blazed footpath left into the woods for fifty steps to an observation point overlooking a historic railroad gap. Past here, the trail covers a short, but pitchy, route that ends on a knoll with stellar spring and winter views of Occoquan Bay. After exploring, return to the Lee and Fairfax cemetery and follow the red blazes east.)

1.2 Continue straight (east) on the Lee's Woods Historic Trail at a junction with a fire road on the right.

1.4 Emerge from the woods trail to views of the historic Fairfax home. Turn left and descend on a gravel road. Ahead, pass by the trail on the left that climbs to river overlooks and the Civil War battery.

1.7 HIKE ENDS at the Lee's Woods trailboard and sign.

Trail 2: Powell's Creek Nature Trail

0.0 START from a trailboard sign and map in the Powell's Creek Nature Trail parking area. Follow a rock-lined path into the woods behind the sign. Pass a newly constructed section of the Potomac Heritage National Scenic Trail that merges with Powell's Creek Nature trail on the right. Continue to follow blue blazes of the Powell's Creek trail.

0.2 Bear left (south) at another fork in the trail. (*Note:* The trail right from this junction is the return portion of this hike.)

0.5 Turn right (west) to continue on Powell's Creek Nature Trail at a junction with Bushy Point Trail. Descend steps dug into the dirt footpath, and then cross a seeping wetland on a footbridge. The trail arches left (west) to follow the stream. (*Note:* If you're following the route described under *Options*, turn left here to follow Bushy Point Trail and the Potomac Trail to Lee's Woods Historic Trail in 1.25 miles.)

0.6 Climb a set of stairs, and then turn left to reach an overlook onto Powell's Creek.

0.7 Veer left off the nature trail onto an unmarked path that descends to the river. Where it splits, veer left again.

0.8 Reach the bottom and a split rail fence. Take in the views of Powell's Creek and the railroad bridge, and then retrace your steps uphill. When you reach the nature trail, turn left (north) to continue the loop.

1.4 Bear left at a V junction with the first leg of the loop.

1.6 HIKE ENDS at the parking area.

OPTIONS

You can connect the Powell's Creek Nature Trail and Lee's Woods Historic Trail by using the park's Potomac Trail and Bushy Point Trail. This option adds 1.25 miles and makes the hike an end-to-end trip requiring a shuttle. Also, a segment of the Potomac Heritage National Scenic Trail connects Powell's Creek Nature Trail to Neabsco Hill Road.

Hike Information

Local information: Prince William County Tourism, 14420 Bristow Road, Manassas, VA; (703) 792-7060; www.discoverpwm.com

Local events/attractions: Monthly evening musical performances take place at the park's marina June through mid-Sept.

Good eats: Tim's Rivershore Restaurant & Crabhouse, 1510 Cherryhill Rd., Dumfries, VA; (703) 441-1375; www.timsrivershore.com. Enjoy fresh seafood and views of the Potomac River.

Local outdoor stores: Modell's Sporting Goods, 2700 Potomac Mills Circle, Woodbridge, VA; (703) 499-9696; www.modells.com

Hike tours: Park staff offer history and nature hikes and canoe trips.

Organizations: Friends of Leesylvania State Park, Woodbridge, VA; (703) 730-8205; www.virginiaparks.org/friends-le

Prince William Conservation Alliance advocates for conservation of Prince William County's fast-disappearing woodlands.; www.pwconserve.org.

Other resources: *A Potomac Legacy: Lee's Woods Historical Interpretive Trail* and *Powell's Creek Nature Trail*, booklets produced by the Department of Conservation & Recreation, are available in the park visitor center.

GREEN TIP
Observe wildlife from a distance. Don't interfere in their lives—
both of you will be better for it. If an animal interrupts its activity
and looks at you, chances are you've gotten too close.

19 Manassas National Battlefield Park

The grasslands and forests of Manassas National Battlefield Park offer a bucolic setting for a day hike that is steeped in Civil War history. The Battle of First Manassas in the summer of 1862 was a victory for the South. Historians point to it as the first sign the War Between the States would be a longer, more protracted fight than many believed or hoped. The Battle of Second Manassas opened the door for the South's first invasion of the North. In places like Deep Cut, Chinn Ridge, and the Unfinished Railroad, this battlefield's rich history is as palpable as the fields and pastures, woods and wetlands are beautiful.

Start: From the park visitor center

Distance: 8.6-mile loop

Approximate hiking time: 4 hours

Difficulty: Moderate due to length, but with gently rolling terrain and only a few steep climbs

Trail surface: Dirt footpaths, gravel paths, mowed grass paths, old farm roads, and paved roads

Seasons: Spring and fall

Other trail users: Mountain bikers, horseback riders

Handicapped accessibility: Stone Bridge Trail is paved and fully accessible. At Chinn Ridge, number 9 on the battlefield driving tour, a 0.3-mile paved path leads past historic markers. The Second Manassas Battlefield driving tour is 16 miles and covers 11 sites of interest from both the First and Second Manassas battles.

Canine compatibility: Leashed dogs permitted

Land status: National battlefield park

Fees and permits: Free entrance

Schedule: Open daily dawn until dusk. The visitor center is open daily 8:30 a.m. to 5:00 p.m. except Thanksgiving and Christmas.

Facilities: The visitor center features restrooms, interpretive displays,, and a bookstore. There are picnic tables in a grove of trees adjacent to the parking area.

Maps: DeLorme *Virginia Atlas & Gazetteer:* Page 76 B1. USGS 7.5 minute series: *Gainesville, VA.* See also National Geographic's TOPO! software, Mid-Atlantic Region, Disc 4. The park visitor center provides free maps upon request. History buffs can follow this hiking route using *The Manassas Battlefields* map, part of Cleverish Map Co.'s Civil War Watercolor Map Series (available in the park service bookstore).

Trail contacts: Manassas National Battlefield Park, 6511 Sudley Road, Manassas, VA; (703) 361-1339; www.nps.gov/mana

Other: Possession and/or use of metal detectors in the battlefield park is prohibited. Hikers should be on alert for ticks during summer months.

Finding the trailhead: Distance from Washington, D.C.: 35 miles

From I-66: Take exit 47B for VA 234 North. Drive 0.7 mile north and turn right into Manassas National Battlefield Park, following signs for the visitor center. In 0.1 mile, park in the lot at the top of Henry Hill. Trailhead GPS: N38 48.776' / W77 31.290'

The Hike

More so than the open fields that characterize much of Manassas National Battlefield Park, the Unfinished Railroad has an air of solemnity about it. This old earthen berm was built prior to the Civil War, intended to support a railroad between Manassas Gap Railroad and the port city of Alexandria.

During the Second Battle of Manassas, Gen. Thomas "Stonewall" Jackson used 2 miles of the railroad bed as his line of defense. Jackson had earned his nickname during the First Battle of Manassas in July 1861, when a fellow general is purported to have rallied his troops with the cry: "There is Jackson standing like a stone wall." Along with it, Jackson had a well-earned reputation as a brilliant military strategist. Selection of the Unfinished Railroad, a natural line of defense, was but one indicator of this.

Hiking past replica cannon

During the war, the North generally named a battle after the closest river, stream, or creek, and the South tended to name battles after towns or railroad junctions. Hence, the Confederates named the battle Manassas after Manassas Junction, and the Union named the battle Bull Run for the stream of the same name.

The woodlands that surround the Unfinished Railroad heighten the atmosphere, which makes the scenery around Deep Cut all the more striking. Climbing from the woods to the top of the old railroad bed on a wooden staircase, a wide vista unfolds. Just a decade ago, a forest of cedar and dense understory of brush stood here, but was removed as part of a large restoration project.

In an effort to bring historical accuracy back to the landscape, the Deep Cut Landscape Restoration project restored 140 acres of battlefield land into grasslands. By doing so, the National Park Service accomplishes two goals: to restore this area as closely as possible to how it was during the Civil War (generations of farming and tree planting in the last 150 years have altered the battlefield) and restore native grasslands, a habitat type that is fast shrinking in Virginia. The park service estimates that the state has lost more than half of its grasslands since 1945. With it goes habitat for songbirds, owls, raptors, and small mammals like field mice.

Miles and Directions

0.0 START at the east end of the visitor center parking lot, at a sign that reads: FIRST MANASSAS TRAIL/HENRY HILL LOOP TRAIL. Follow the mowed path through an open field. Beyond a line of replica cannons, a blue-blazed trail stick marks where the meadow path enters the woods. (*FYI:* The cannons approximate where Confederate soldiers held a line of defense against an advancing Union Army during the First Battle of Manassas, July 21, 1861.)

0.6 Turn left (north) onto a wide, graded road, First Manassas Trail, lined with crushed rock. (*Note:* A horse trail parallels the hiking trail for the next 0.3 mile.)

0.9 *Stay alert:* A blue-blazed trail stick marks a rerouting of the First Manassas Trail. Veer left off the gravel road, cross the bridle path, and skirt the edge of a field. After a few feet, veer right and descend to cross Young's Branch via a bridge. The hiking trail rejoins the gravel road on the other side of Young's Branch. (*Side trip:* Instead of crossing the bridge, follow horse trail markers uphill along a dirt road; as you climb, Young's Branch parallels the road on the right. Watch for a footpath that veers left off the road, passes through field and woodlands, and then loops back to intersect with the dirt road. Turn right and follow the road back to the footbridge over Young's Branch, cross, and resume the hike. This side trip adds 0.5 mile to the hike.)

1.2 Stay straight as the gravel road splits right. Walk down a wide path lined with wood chips to US 29/Lee Highway. Cross the highway and resume a northward track along a gravel road.

1.4 A brief climb ends at a sign pointing right to Van Pelt, a historic home site. Turn right (east), walk through the home site, and turn right again (southeast) on a mowed path. (*FYI:* Just before this mowed path trail descends off the hill, an interpretive sign marks the spot where the first musket volleys were fired in the First Battle of Manassas.) (*Note:*

Manassas National Battlefield Park

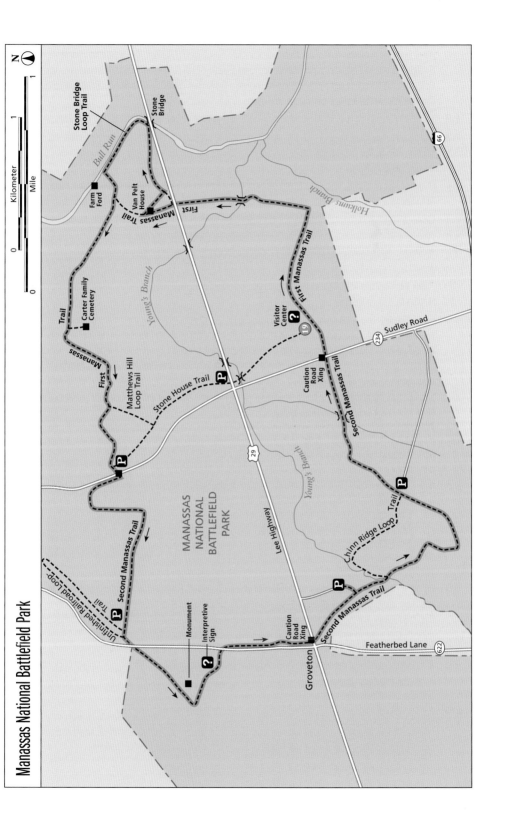

After heavy rains, the trail past this marker may be closed. *Option:* If the trail to Stone Bridge from Van Pelt is closed, follow a mowed path north from the Van Pelt home site for 0.1 mile, to where it rejoins the First Manassas Trail. This detour skips Stone Bridge and a streamside walk along Bull Run, and shaves 1 mile off this route.)

1.9 Turn left (north) at the Stone Bridge and follow a gravel streamside path along Bull Run.

2.2 Swing left (west) at Farm Ford, the spot where Union general William T. Sherman crossed on the attack the morning of July 21. (*Note:* An unmarked fisherman's path continues alongside Bull Run.)

2.4 Climb a set of stairs, and at a T junction on the edge of a field, turn right (north) on First Manassas Trail.

2.8 Cross a road and reenter woods on the opposite side.

3.0 Pass a spur trail on the left for the Carter Family Cemetery.

3.6 Continue straight past Matthews Hill Loop Trail on the left. In 0.2 mile, turn right (south) at a four-way junction and descend 0.1 mile to the Matthews Hill Loop parking lot. (*Bailout:* A left turn on the Matthews Hill Loop leads back to the park visitor center via the Stone House in 1.5 miles.)

3.9 Pass through the Matthews Hill Loop parking lot. As a handrail, use the historic marker for the New York national guard unit that drove Confederates off Matthews Hill during the Battle of First Manassas. Pass a trailhead for the red-blazed Stone House Trail, which leads south 1.2 miles to the park visitor center. Cross VA 234/Sudley Road, turn right (north), and follow a path lined with wood chips.

4.5 After tracing the edge of a field, turn right (west) as the Second Manassas Trail becomes a wide dirt lane shaded by cedar trees.

5.0 Enter the parking area for the Unfinished Railroad Loop Trail. Cross VA 622/Feather-bed Lane and look for a sign that reads SECOND MANASSAS TRAIL / BRAWNER FARM 1.0 MILE. This trailhead is marked by fence stiles intended to block mountain bikes and horses. Climb a short set of stairs and enter the woods, heading southwest. (*Note:* Avoid the horse trail that heads west into the woods from this spot. It is the wider and more graded of the two trails.) (*Side trip:* The Unfinished Railroad Loop is a worthwhile 1.1-mile trip along cuts and fills of what was, in the 1850s, intended as a railroad line linking the Manassas Gap Railroad with the port city of Alexandria. The earthen berms formed a natural line of defense used by Gen. Thomas J. "Stonewall" Jackson during the Second Battle of Manassas in 1862.)

5.3 Climb a set of wooden stairs to the top of the Unfinished Railroad embankment. Enter a cut-over area, the result of a park-sponsored habitat restoration project. (*FYI:* The Deep Cut / Brawner Farm habitat restoration project involves cutting down 140 acres of trees to restore the area to grassland habitat the park says more accurately reflects conditions at the time of the Civil War.)

5.5 Turn left (east) at a tall brick historic marker. Keep the marker on your right as you pick your way through tree and limb debris. Walk downhill on a mowed grass path to a small stream.

5.8 Cross VA 622/Featherbed Lane, turn right (south), and walk across a driveway apron of crushed rock, keeping on your left a metal gate that blocks the driveway. Walk south on an open path bordered by a split rail fence on your left and the road on your right.

Handicapped trail along the Fight at the Fences

6.3 Cross US 29/Lee Highway at a four-corners intersection. Walk south alongside VA 622/ Featherbed Lane for about 100 feet, then veer left (southeast) to pass through a gap in the split rail fence. The trail is now a mowed grass path heading southeast through a wide meadow.

6.6 Enter a clearing with three large monuments dedicated to the New York 5th and 10th Regiments. Here, the trail is a dirt path that skirts the paved rotary. Reenter the woods, heading south at a blue-blazed trail stick. The trail through the woods is wide and graded, lined with crushed stone.

6.8 Cross Young's Branch on a wooden footbridge, then turn right (south), following blue-blazed trail sticks. (*Note:* The dirt trail that goes straight uphill from this junction is the return leg of the Chinn Ridge Loop Trail.)

7.6 Walk straight (north) past a trail on the left (the return leg of the Chinn Ridge Loop Trail). Keep a parking lot to your right as you follow a mowed grass path. Past the parking lot, the trail joins a paved path.

7.9 Turn right at a marker detailing the death of Fletcher Webster, son of famed American statesman Daniel Webster. Climb a small hill and look for a blue-blazed trail stick in the northwest corner of the clearing. (*Note:* Stay alert for this historic marker. There is no trail marker indicating the turn off the paved path.)

8.1 At a junction with a paved road, turn left (north) and walk along the road shoulder.

8.4 Cross VA 234/Sudley Road and climb the paved driveway for the park visitor center.

8.6 HIKE ENDS at the park visitor center.

Hike Information

Local information: Historic Manassas, Inc., 9431 West St., Manassas, VA; (703) 361-6599; www.visitmanassas.org. The visitor center in Old Town Manassas is located in the restored 1914 train depot.

Local events/attractions: The Manassas Farmers' Market (703-361-6599; www.visitmanassas.org) takes place Thurs and Sat, Apr through mid-Nov, in Old Town. Get great local produce and baked goods.

Local outdoor stores: Dick's Sporting Goods, Bull Run Plaza, 10800 Sudly Manor Dr., Manassas, VA; (703) 257-4300; www.dickssportinggoods.com

Hike tours: The park service offers daily walking tours of the battlefield.

Other resources: National Park Civil War Series books: *The First Battle of Manassas* and *The Second Battle of Manassas*

20 Mason Neck State Park

Bordered by Mason Neck National Wildlife Refuge, Pohick Bay Regional Park, and Gunston Hall historic plantation, 1,856-acre Mason Neck State Park is part of 5,600 acres of remarkably undisturbed wildlife habitat on this peninsula, just minutes from Northern Virginia's urban sprawl. Gazing on views like these, George Mason framed the Virginia Declaration of Rights at his nearby home. Listen to the sounds of the marsh and forest, and reflect on the blue expanse of Belmont Bay. When you're done hiking the trails, you can head to the adjacent refuge, created to protect vital habitat for nesting bald eagles.

Start: From the visitor center

Distance: 5.6-mile loop

Approximate hiking time: 3 hours

Difficulty: Easy due to its short length, level terrain, and wide, well-marked, and graded trails

Trail surface: Gravel, stairs, boardwalk, forested trail, footbridge, paved

Seasons: In winter both resident and migrant bald eagle activity is high

Other trail users: Hikers only, except for the paved High Point Multi-Use Trail, which can accommodate joggers, strollers, wheelchairs, and bikes

Handicapped accessibility: The nearly 3-mile High Point Multi-Use Trail is paved, as is the .26-mile Marsh View Trail to a water view. Dogue Trail is gravel.

Canine compatibility: Leashed dogs permitted

Land status: State park

Fees and permits: Per-vehicle entrance fee

Schedule: Open daily 8:00 a.m. to dusk (gate locked at 8:00 p.m.)

Facilities: Restrooms, visitor center, environmental center, boat ramp, playground, picnic area

Maps: DeLorme *Virginia Atlas & Gazetteer:* Page 77 C4. USGS 7.5 minute series: *Ft. Belvoir, VA, MD.* A printable map can be downloaded from the park website.

Trail contacts: Mason Neck State Park, 7301 High Point Rd., Lorton, VA 22079; (703) 339-2385; www.dcr.virginia.gov/state-parks/mason-neck

Special considerations: Swimming is not allowed from the park shoreline.

Finding the trailhead: Distance from Washington, D.C.: 26 miles

From I-95: Take exit 163 for Lorton/VA 642. Turn left onto VA 642 East and drive 0.8 mile to Armistead Road. Turn right onto Armistead, following signs for Pohick Bay Regional Park and Gunston Hall. In 0.2 mile, turn right onto US 1 South (also called Richmond Highway). In 0.8 mile, turn left onto VA 242/Gunston Road. (*Note:* After passing Pohick Bay Regional Park, Gunston Road becomes VA 600.) In 4.5 miles, Gunston Road forks. Here, bear right onto High Point Road, following the sign for Mason Neck State Park and Mason Neck Wildlife Refuge. In 0.8 mile, enter the state park. The ranger station is 0.2 mile from the park boundary, and the visitor center is 1.7 miles from the park boundary. Trailhead GPS: N38 38.644' / W77 11.947'

The Hike

With every footstep along the Bay View Trail, nature springs into action. A turtle pokes its head above water; frogs sense our approach and hit the water with a *kerplunk*. A log rolls slightly as a painted turtle cuts short its sunning and slips into the water. Then the sight that freezes us in our tracks: A writhing conga line of tent caterpillars stretching along the boardwalk for 10 feet or so.

The first reaction—"Gross!"—lasts a minute or two, but the longer we watch, the more this parade fascinates. The first question—where are they going?—is answered when we follow their procession to a nearby tree. The inch-long, orange-and-black caterpillars form lanes of two-way traffic up and down the trunk. At one point, they amass in a dinner-plate-size whorl that moves like a psychedelic pinwheel.

How they all knew where to go, and why they followed each other, underscores why one entomologist has described these eastern tent caterpillars as standing "at the pinnacle of sociality." The moth larvae strike out from their tent three times a day

Canoe and kayak rentals on Belmont Bay

in search of food. On these solo forays, they lay down a pheromone called an "exploratory trail." Once a food source is found, the caterpillar eats and returns to the tent, leaving a "recruitment trail." This second trail is like a clarion call for other caterpillars, who follow the trail one after another until a line forms much like what we witnessed.

While considered a nuisance because they can defoliate entire trees, tent caterpillars are more a threat to orchards than the mature woodlands of Mason Neck. In the forests along Eagle Spur Trail, there are signs of a more serious caterpillar threat. Here, biologists have wrapped tree trunks with burlap, meant to trap and kill the gypsy moth caterpillar. An outbreak of this exotic, a native to Europe and Asia, can lead to millions of acres of deforestation. The caterpillar sees the burlap as cover from predators; the rangers use it to trap and capture them.

There is a lot of woodland to protect on the entire Mason Neck peninsula. Of the roughly 10,000 acres that make up the Neck, more than 6,000 acres are protected by public parks and refuges. Mason Neck State Park is one piece of that web, covering 1,813 acres. This includes 2 miles of shoreline on Belmont and Occoquan Bays, which empty into the Potomac River.

As you walk through the state park's oak forests, there are subtle signs of the historical use of this peninsula. Peninsulas like Mason Neck mark the Potomac River shoreline from Alexandria south. They were settled in the colonial period by wealthy planters, whose landholdings formed the basis of the colonial tobacco empire. Signs of tree-clearing for fields is seen with the tulip poplars, of which so many fork into two large trunks about knee-high. After felling, the trees re-sprouted and turned into mature trees over decades of undisturbed growth.

Mason Neck's hiking trails are short. Not counting the paved High Point Multi-Use Trail, none of the park's six trails is more than 1.25 miles long. For a diversity of plant and animal life, the Bay View and Wilson Spring Trails are tops. These paths follow the shoreline of Belmont Bay, through a freshwater marsh, and into dry upland woods. Where it descends to the wet bottomland along seep that forms from Wilson

▶ **KID APPEAL**

Rent bikes at the visitor center and ride the easy, 3-mile High Point Multi-Use Trail (6-mile round-trip). Stop for a picnic lunch and play in the playground. Canoes and kayaks are available for rent, or bring your own to launch into Belmont Bay.

There are more than 6,000 acres of protected land on Mason Neck out of a total land mass of 10,000 acres. State parks, wildlife refuges, regional parks, and historic plantations work cooperatively to create optimum conditions for nesting, mating, and roosting bald eagles.

Mason Neck National Wildlife Refuge was the first in the country established for the protection of bald eagles. It was formed in 1969 out of 845 acres and now totals more than 2,200 acres.

Boardwalk crosses a pond on the Bay View Trail.

Spring, the forest canopy closes in overhead. There's a musky scent, from skunk cabbage and other plants that love to get their feet wet.

Dogue Trail, a wide gravel path, features some of the park's largest trees. The American beech are especially impressive. This is the kind of tree that feels at home in any kind of forest, either as a tree that forms a canopy or as an understory tree in an oak/hickory forest. You can distinguish a beech while hiking in the winter and early spring. Their leaves, light, papery, and tan, stay on the tree throughout the winter, only to fall off when the new leaf buds push them off. Failing this, you might identify this tree by its tight gray bark (which is a perennial favorite of the initial-carving set).

If length is what you're after, Kanes Creek and Eagle Spur Trails combined offer the best option. Kanes Creek is a flat loop prone to washouts after a heavy rain. Eagle Spur is more varied, starting in dry oak and hickory woodland, passing into and out of small drainages marked by mountain laurel on the slopes, and finally ending at an overlook of Kanes Creek.

Mason Neck State Park

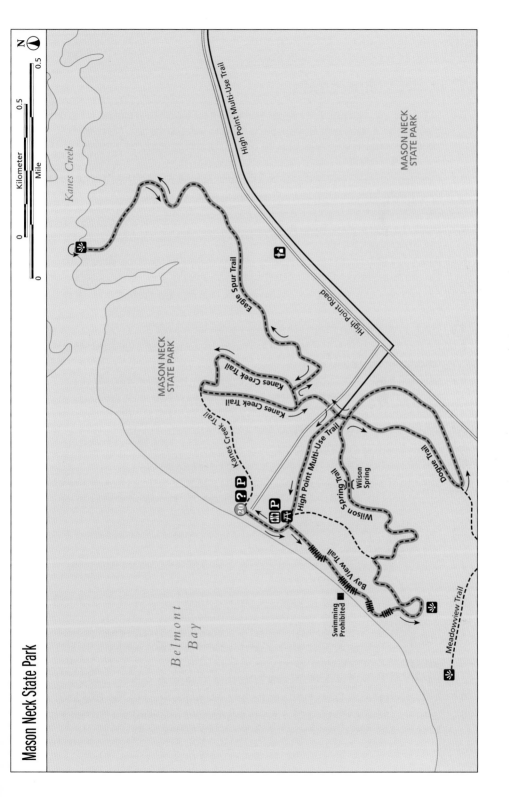

N

Kilometer
0   0.5

Mile
0   0.5

Kanes Creek

High Point Multi-Use Trail

MASON NECK
STATE PARK

High Point Road

Eagle Spur Trail

Kanes Creek Trail

Kanes Creek Trail

MASON NECK
STATE PARK

Kanes Creek Trail

20

High Point Multi-Use Trail

Wilson Spring Trail

Wilson
Spring

Dogue Trail

*Belmont
Bay*

Bay View Trail

Swimming
Prohibited

Meadowview Trail

Or you can do them all together, as we did, and get a fair sampling of what a coastal forest looks, feels, and sounds like.

Miles and Directions

0.0 START from the state park visitor center. Walk around the building and turn left (west) on Bay View Trail, a gravel path. Belmont Bay is the open water on the right. After seventy steps, descend a flight of stairs, pass the cartop boat launch, and follow a boardwalk around a small pond.

0.1 Climb a set of stairs uphill and away from the pond. At the top, walk across a picnic area, using a wood fence as a handrail, and reenter the woods on the Bay View Trail. The graded path, lined with wood chips, is red blazed.

0.3 Descend a flight of stairs. Follow a boardwalk that spans an eroded shoreline on the right and an estuary on the left.

0.45 Detour right and descend to the shoreline of Belmont Bay. After exploring, return to the trail and follow a second boardwalk that spans the estuary.

0.55 Turn right on a spur trail that loops to an overlook. Bear right again when this spur trail forks.

0.6 Reach an overlook with limited summer views across the estuary.

0.65 Reach a blind with all-season views up into the freshwater reaches of the marsh. After a rest, resume walking the loop.

0.7 Bear right (north) at the junction with steps leading down to the boardwalk and begin a stretch of walking through dry upland forest. A profusion of blueberries and mountain laurel show strong rebound from a subcanopy fire in these woods in 1986.

0.8 Turn right on the yellow-blazed Wilson Spring Trail.

1.2 Cross a footbridge over Wilson Spring.

1.3 Turn right on Dogue Trail, a gravel-lined, handicapped-accessible trail.

2.1 Turn right on Wilson Spring Trail. Cross straight over High Point Trail, pass through a parking lot, and cross straight over the park road. On the other side, follow a boardwalk into the woods.

2.3 Two benches mark the Y junction with Kanes Creek Trail. Turn right on Kanes Creek, then take the next right onto Eagle Spur at a fork in the trail.

3.4 Reach an observation blind overlooking Kanes Creek. After a rest, retrace steps to the junction of Kanes Creek Trail.

4.5 Turn right onto Kanes Creek Trail. (*Bailout:* Veer left on Kanes Creek Trail, walk to the park road, and return to the park visitor center via High Point Trail.)

4.7 Pass an old trail on the right that is blocked by downed trees and marked with sensitive habitat warning signs. Kanes Creek Trail swings left. (*FYI:* The now-closed trail is the old access to Kanes Creek, which still appears on many maps and in guides. State conservation officials closed it to protect nesting bald eagles at the mouth of Kanes Creek.)

5.0 Turn right onto Wilson Spring Trail. Cross the park road and turn right on High Point Trail.

5.3 High Point junctions with the access road to the picnic and playground area. Turn left and follow the road. Pass bathrooms on the left, and then a trailboard sign.

5.4 At the edge of the bluff overlooking Belmont Bay, turn right and follow the trail back to the visitor center.

5.6 HIKE ENDS at the state park visitor center.

OPTIONS

Make this route an all-day trek by adding 6.6 miles via the High Point Multi-Use Trail and the neighboring refuge's Woodmarsh Trail. Where Wilson Spring Trail crosses High Point Road, turn right (east) and follow the paved multiuse trail 1.8 miles to the parking area and trailhead for Woodmarsh Trail. The refuge trail descends from hardwood forest to a marsh and includes an observation deck. If a bald eagle nest visible from the trail is active, portions of the route may be closed in late winter and early spring.

Hike Information

Local information: Fairfax County/Capital Region Visitors Center, Tysons Corner Center, 1961 Chain Bridge Rd., McLean, VA; (703) 752-9500; www.fxva.com

Local events/attractions: Elizabeth Hartwell Mason Neck National Wildlife Refuge, 7301 High Point Rd., Lorton, VA; (703) 490-4979; www.fw.gov/refuge/mason_neck

Good eats: Dixie Bones, down-to-earth Southern BBQ, 13440 Occoquan Rd., Woodbridge, VA; (703) 492-2205; www.dixiebones.com

Local outdoor stores: Modell's Sporting Goods, 6701 Frontier Drive, Springfield, VA; (703) 971-8303; www.modells.com

Hike tours: Park staff offer eagle watches and paddling trips in season.

Organizations: Friends of Mason Neck, Lorton, VA; www.masonneckstatepark friends.org. Holds an Eagle Festival in mid-May.

21 Overall Run, Shenandoah National Park

Peaks and waterfalls surely rank as prime motivators—and rewards—for a day spent hiking, and doubly so if you work hard to get there. There are no shortages of waterfalls in Shenandoah National Park, from the wildly popular Whiteoak Canyon to the Rose River Falls, where multiple cascades flow off bare-faced rock after heavy rains. But there's only one "tallest": 93 feet to be exact, and it's found on the western slope of the Blue Ridge at Overall Run. From the staggering falls, the mountainous panorama unfolds westward over Massanutten's double ridges, and farther off on the hazy horizon looms Great North Mountain.

Start: From the Thompson Hollow Trail parking area on VA 630, 2.5 miles south of Bentonville, Virginia

Distance: 6 miles out-and-back, with an option for an 11.5-mile loop

Approximate hiking time: 4 hours

Difficulty: Moderate due to unaided stream crossings and a vigorous climb to the top of the Overall Run headwall

Trail surface: A brief stint on paved and gravel road leads to the park boundary. From there on it's single-track woodland paths interrupted by three stream crossings and an opportunity to rock-scramble near the lip of the Overall Run falls.

Seasons: Best in autumn, winter, and spring for color and views—and fewer humans

Other trail users: Hikers only

Canine compatibility: Leashed dogs permitted

Land status: National park

Fees and permits: None since this trailhead is located outside the park

Schedule: Park is open 24 hours

Facilities: None at this access point

Maps: DeLorme *Virginia Atlas & Gazetteer:* Page 74 B2. USGS 7.5 minute series: *Bentonville, VA.* See also the Potomac Appalachian Trail Club (PATC) Map #9 (*Shenandoah National Park: Northern District*).

Trail contacts: Shenandoah National Park, 3655 US 211 E., Luray, VA 22835; (540) 999-3500; www.nps.gov/shen

Special considerations: Winter is a spectacular time to visit, with huge ice sheets forming on the cliff. During the coldest snaps the falls may even be frozen solid. But be extremely careful on slippery rocks and keep your distance from the edge: It's 93 feet straight down. HEADS UP: Camping is prohibited on the Overall Run Trail from the top of the falls downhill for a half-mile. This is part of a project by SNP to protect sensitive plant communities on rocky outcrops. Educate yourself about these *rock outcrop communities* at www.nps.gov/shen, and keep in mind that while striving to leave only footprints, we always leave a trace.

Finding the trailhead: Distance from Washington, D.C.: 80 miles
   From Front Royal: Drive south on US 340 for 9 miles. In Bentonville, turn left (east) onto VA 340. After 0.5 mile, turn right (south) on VA 630 and drive 2 miles to the Thompson Hollow Trail parking area, a widened shoulder on the right side of the road. Trailhead GPS: N38 48.105' / W7818.888'

The Hike

On the western slope of the Blue Ridge, downhill from Hogback Mountain, in a crease where Beecher Ridge and Mathews Arm meet, a small spring gives rise to a stream. Its course for about a mile is that of a merry brook bouncing over river rocks, dropping a foot or so off small ledges, slipping under logs.

Then, with drama befitting a western panorama, comes the free fall.

Overall Run's 93-foot drop into a steep-sided box canyon ranks as the highest in Shenandoah National Park. Views from the lip of the falls stretch west to Massanutten Mountain and Great North Mountain beyond.

It's not the size of the river that impresses; it's the drop into a canyon that has few rivals in the park. Archaeological research has found evidence of prehistoric Indians who used the canyon as a place to herd and slaughter mastodons.

Highest waterfall in Shenandoah

April and May is the time to catch the drama of Overall Run unfold. By summer, Overall Run's flow is a trickle, and it has all but gone into hiding come September. Winter brings hints of a new flow as ice and snow form small ledges over the stream.

This hike starts outside the park boundaries, leading into Shenandoah through one of its many "back doors." As you drop down off Thompson Hollow Trail, Overall Run itself is audible long before you reach it. The landscape north of the trail is gently sloping, betraying none of the drama that will unfold a mile or so up the trail.

As you hike toward the falls, the river's bottomland forest spreads out. In summertime, the grass can be as high as your waist in some places, lending the trail a remote feel. Piles of small stones are visible off the trail, possible indications of field-clearing activity from the eighteenth- and nineteenth-century residents. A stream on the left side leads to a springhouse some distance off the trail, where there is evidence of a building foundation as well.

The last 0.75 mile of the trail scales Mathews Arm as it rises to the headwall of the canyon. It's easy to imagine a band of Paleo-Indians pressing their prey into the canyon's narrow confines. It is only 5 miles north, near Limeton, where archaeologists in the 1970s unearthed one of the East Coast's most influential prehistoric Indian settlements. Thunderbird, as its known, dates back to 10,000 B.C., with evidence in the form of points, tools, and weapons that indicate sites of a quarry, a base camp, and a bog where animals were driven for the kill.

Author and Shenandoah Mountain Guide Andy Nichols

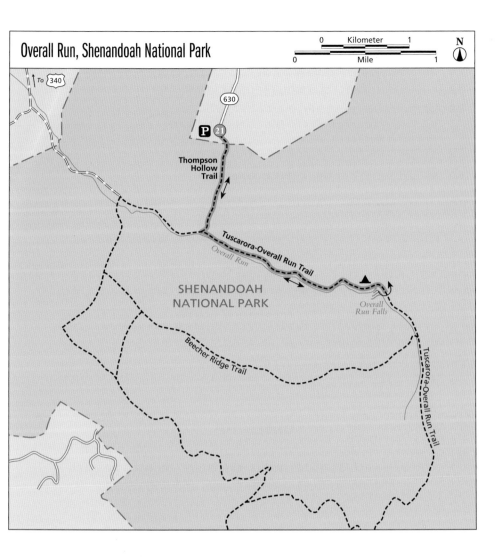

0   Kilometer   1

0   Mile   1

N

SHENANDOAH
NATIONAL PARK

Thompson
Hollow
Trail

Tuscarora-Overall Run Trail

Overall Run

Beecher Ridge Trail

*Overall
Run Falls*

Tuscarora-Overall Run Trail

To 340

630

P 21

Miles and Directions

0.0 START from the Thompson Hollow Trail parking area on VA 630. Walk south along the paved road past a gated road on the right. The road dips into and out of a streambed. After this, bear right onto a dirt path through the grass.

0.3 Enter Shenandoah National Park on Thompson Hollow Trail at a trailhead marked by a concrete post.

0.7 Stay straight as the blue-blazed Tuscarora Trail merges with Thompson Hollow Trail from the right.

1.0 The sound of rushing water cues you to the approach of Overall Run Trail. Descend to the T junction and turn left on a single track dirt trail that follows the streams bottomland forest.

1.5 Cross Overall Run.

2.0 Cross Overall Run again.

2.3 Begin a steep, 1-mile climb up the headwall of Overall Run.

2.5 Take a break at a small campsite that overlooks the falls and canyon.

2.8 A steady climb relents. Follow the trail right to the lip of the falls.

3.0 Top of Overall Run waterfall. Return to the trailhead by retracing steps down Overall Run Trail. (*Option:* Continue beyond the falls on Overall Run Trail for a strenuous 11.5-mile loop via Beecher Ridge Trail.)

5.0 Turn right onto Thompson Hollow Trail.

6.0 HIKE ENDS at the Thompson Hollow Trail parking area.

Hike Information

Local information: Front Royal Visitor's Center, 414 E. Main St., Front Royal, VA; (800) 338-2576; www.frontroyalva.com

Good eats: Melting Pot Pizza, 138 W. 14th St., Front Royal, VA; (540) 636-6146; www.meltingpotpizza.com. Locals and visitors alike get their pizza fix at the place that's been serving it since 1972.

Local outdoor stores: Front Royal Canoe, 8567 Stonewall Jackson Hwy., Front Royal, VA; (800) 270-8808; frontroyalcanoe.com.

Hike tours: Shenandoah Mountain Guides, (301) 695-1814; www.teamlinkinc.com Potomac Appalachian Trail Club (PATC), Vienna, VA; (703) 242-0315; www.patc.net

GREEN TIP
Don't take souvenirs home with you. This means natural materials such as plants, rocks, shells, and driftwood as well as historic artifacts such as fossils and arrowheads.

22 Piney River, Shenandoah National Park

Heavily settled prior to Shenandoah National Park's formation, the woods tucked between Piney River and Keyser Run today hold clues of past inhabitants, both obvious and obscure, from family cemeteries to low stone field walls long overgrown by a resurgent forest. Above all, this place is a sanctuary of rushing water and steep cliffs. Those who like to save the best for last will appreciate our twist on conventional wisdom: Most people like to climb up Little Devil Stairs, but we save this knee-knocking route along Keyser Run for a finishing act.

Start: From a parking area and park registration booth on VA 614/Keyser Run Road

Distance: 7.4-mile loop

Approximate hiking time: 5 hours

Difficulty: Moderate due to several unaided stream crossings and moderate elevation, with one strenuous segment through Little Devil Stairs due to steep, rough terrain and numerous unaided stream crossings

Trail surface: A gravel forest fire road gives way to centuries-old roads that have reverted to single-track paths. A majority of this hike is along streams, and in sections exposed rocks and roots make for uneven terrain. The last segment of this route is over exposed rocks, some as big as cars, and steep drop-downs. In spring, this section of trail may be washed out.

Seasons: Spring, when the streams run fast and fresh with runoff

Other trail users: Equestrian use is permitted on Hull School Trail between the Bolen family cemetery and Piney Branch Trail.

Canine compatibility: Leashed dogs permitted

Land status: National park

Fees and permits: Pay fee at a self-serve station at the trailhead. If camping, obtain a free backcountry permit at a park ranger station. A Virginia fishing license is required.

Schedule: Open year-round

Facilities: None

Maps: DeLorme *Virginia Atlas & Gazetteer:* Page 74 C2. USGS 7.5 minute series: *Thornton Gap, VA.* PATC Map #9 *(Shenandoah National Park: Northern District)*

Trail contacts: Shenandoah National Park, 3655 US 211 E., Luray, VA 22835; (540) 999-3500; www.nps.gov/shen

The Potomac Appalachian Trail Club (PATC), 118 Park St. SE, Vienna, VA 22210; www .potomacappalachian.org

Special considerations: Conventional wisdom says hiking *up* Little Devil Stairs is preferable to hiking down. The difficult terrain, some say, is easier to scramble up than lurch down. It's your choice; just flip this hike and do it backward.

Finding the trailhead: Distance from Washington, D.C.: 83 miles

From Sperryville: Follow the combined US 211/522 east. In 2.1 miles, turn left (north) on VA 622 / Gid Brown Hollow Road. Drive 2 miles and turn left onto VA 614 / Keyser Run Road. Stay straight on Keyser Run Road as first VA 672, then VA 623 branch off left and right, respectively. In 5 miles from the highway, enter a trailhead parking area with room for 10 or more cars. Trailhead GPS: N38 43.831' / W78 15.517'

The Hike

The woods that descend to Piney River are a beautiful place on a sunny morning, especially so after a strong spring rainstorm. Birdsong floats down from the tree canopy. Sunlight dapples the leaves and ground. Dry streambeds are flush with runoff. Deer poke about the forest understory, chewing on twigs. On the trailside, lush green plants grow in a seep from the rocks. Lettuce saxifrage and Solomon's seal are telltale plants that mark the spot of many natural springs.

Ephemeral streams emerge after a heavy rain. As you descend Hull School Trail toward Piney River, a run of small plate-size rocks may be visible off the left side of the trail. First instinct is to call it a boulder-strewn spring or streambed, but further exploration shows it's more likely a stone stream; while water runs down it after heavy rain, it is dry other times. Skinny-trunked maples grow from the rock bed, indicating soil stability not found in a consistently running stream. Crusty lichen, another indication of stability, appears on rocks near the edges of the stone stream.

Piney River, reached at the junction of Hull School and Piney Branch Trails, gushes downstream with force. Stream crossings without the aid of a footbridge force a search up- and downstream for a fallen log or rocks suitable for hopping. In the forest near the stream's edge, small rivulets form on both sides of the Piney Branch Trail, marking points of minor flooding.

Where Piney River passes through a steep gorge, the trail steepens as well, climbing the hillside on switchbacks. Where it briefly levels, the river can be heard but not seen. A small window through the forest canopy does offer a glimpse of the solid cliff wall on the opposite side. Just the spot, perhaps, a denning bear or a mountain lion might prefer.

BOLEN FAMILY CEMETERY

The Bolen family cemetery occupies the clearing called Jinny Gray Flats at the 90-degree bend in Keyser Run Fire Road, at the junction with Hull School Trail. A stone fence surrounds it. Upkeep of the cemetery is good, inviting passersby to swing open the wrought-iron gate and step inside. Some headstones are engraved, while others appear to be random stones from the woods—place markers as much as anything else. In total, there are fifty or more burials, according to a list of cemeteries compiled by Darwin Lambert in his book *The Undying Past of Shenandoah National Park*. Burials date to the late 1800s and early 1900s, with 1935 being the most recent.

Author at stream

The presence of mountain lions—also referred to as cougars, pumas, panthers, and catamounts—is subject to debate. Officially, the last eastern subspecies of mountain lion, *Felis concolor cougar*, was documented in Virginia in 1882. But sightings, if not actual documentation, are commonplace. A national park resource management newsletter in 1997 stated that reliable reports of mountain lion sightings had been made in the park since 1932. Whether the population is a resurgence of the native eastern cougar, a wanderer from another region (Florida currently has the only population of cougars in the East, the highly endangered Florida panther, *Felis concolor cory*), or an escaped or released pet, is unknown.

Any thought of a lurking predator is dispelled as you climb away from the Piney River gorge along Pole Bridge Link Trail. In spring, the grassy fringes of this trail are a spectacle of wildflowers, whether the ephemeral spring beauty, the white petals of giant chickweed, delicate purple wild geranium, or common violet and buttercup. Dry, grassy spots host a profusion of common lousewort, a red-and-yellow blossom that seems more at home in a cow pasture than these woodlands.

The descent through Little Devil Stairs offers what Piney Branch Trail only hinted at: up-close interaction with rugged nature. There are at least eight stream crossings, and, after a heavy rain, probably more. At one point, the cliffs on either side close in so tightly, you're forced to walk down a small island that conveniently emerges from the stream.

RETHINKING THE BLUE RIDGE IMAGE

The story of the people who lived in the Blue Ridge prior to creation of Shenandoah National Park is under constant revision. In the 1930s, they were depicted as isolated, primitive, and uncouth—ripe for "civilizing," and their farming practices were held up as destructive to the landscape. In the last decade, archaeological work has led to a reevaluation.

The work of the Survey of Mountain Settlement, which concentrated its studies in three hollows on the eastern slope of the Blue Ridge—Nicholson, Corbin, and Weakley—unearthed products from Sears, Roebuck & Co., such as toy ray guns that invoked memories of the Buck Rogers craze during the Depression, phonographic records, imported ceramic plates, and brass beds, which indicate there was plenty of interaction with the world outside their mountain hollows.

Reinterpreting the image of the people who settled the hollows of the Blue Ridge is an ongoing process. Created as a "natural" park, Shenandoah is now coming full circle to embrace and exhibit the livelihoods of the very people it displaced.

A rock talus marking the halfway point of the descent through Little Devil Stairs highlights the geologic dynamism of the park. A "river" of its own sort, the talus covers the hillside with rocks and boulders, most of them the size of tires or smaller. *Talus creep* describes the slow downward movement of this rock slope toward the valley bottom. In a geologic time frame, this slope is considered dynamic and moving. The slope and the quartzite rock itself show no signs of the stability (lichen or vegetation) that was evident on the stone stream alongside Hull School Trail.

Miles and Directions

0.0 START from the Little Devil Stairs parking lot. Follow a gravel road uphill from the west end of the parking lot.

0.2 Swing right (north) on the fire road and walk past signs marking the boundary of Shenandoah National Park.

1.1 After a steady climb, enter a clearing that is the junction of Keyser Run Fire Road and Hull School Trail. The Bolen family cemetery is off to the right. After exploring, depart the clearing on the left, following the yellow-blazed Hull School Trail, which descends as a narrow woodland footpath.

1.7 A small stream cuts across the trail. Ahead, in 0.2 mile, cross another stream, and then swing left as the trail continues a gradual descent to Piney River.

1.8 Turn right on Piney Branch Trail at a T junction and hike upstream on the blue-blazed trail. (*FYI:* Just before reaching this junction, study the woods off-trail on the right. Rock piles amid a young forest indicate possible field-clearing activity dating from when this park was settled. Careful exploration of the rock piles yields the presence of a freshwater spring at the base of a pile of rocks.)

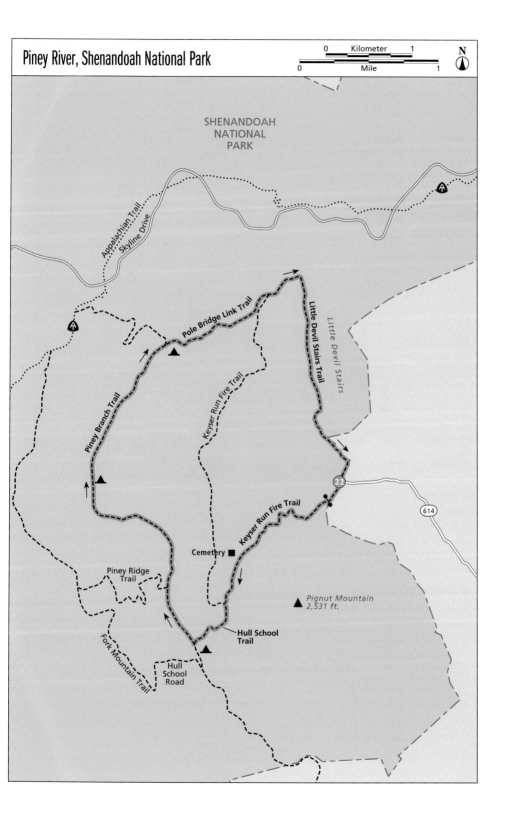

Piney River, Shenandoah National Park

SHENANDOAH
NATIONAL
PARK

Appalachian Trail

Skyline Drive

Pole Bridge Link Trail

Little Devil Stairs Trail

Little Devil Stairs

Piney Branch Trail

Keyser Run Fire Trail

22

614

Keyser Run Fire Trail

Cemetery

Pignut Mountain
2,531 ft.

Piney Ridge
Trail

Hull School
Trail

Fork Mountain Trail

Hull
School
Road

Trail worker

1.9 Pass a primitive campsite off the trail on the left. Soon after, cross Piney River. (*Note:* After a heavy rain, you may have to explore up- or downstream for a suitable place to cross.)

2.3 Continue straight (north) on Piney Branch Trail past a junction with Piney Ridge Trail on the left.

2.5 After a short stretch of trail that runs close to the stream, begin a climb from river-bottom forest up the side of a river gorge.

3.0 A vigorous climb levels briefly, and the forest canopy opens to views of the imposing cliff face on the opposite stream bank. In the next 0.1 mile of trail, look for unmarked paths leading off the trail right to the river's edge.

3.3 Cross Piney River on stream rocks and start a steady uphill climb on Piney Branch Trail. The stream is now on your left side.

3.5 The trail levels briefly, and off the trail to the left is a primitive campsite.

4.2 Detour off the trail to the left to explore the cliff line that gives visual proof of the elevation you've gained in the last 1.2 miles.

4.6 Turn right (east) on Pole Bridge Link Trail. Level terrain off both sides indicates you are traversing across the flat top of a ridge.

4.7 Pass a primitive campsite off the trail to the right.

4.9 Stay straight on Pole Bridge Link Trail at a junction with Sugarloaf Trail on the left.

5.4 Reach Fourway, a junction with Keyser Run Fire Road and Little Devil Stairs. Cross the fire road diagonally left and reenter woods on Little Devil Stairs Trail. The trailhead is marked by a concrete trail marker.

5.7 Begin a series of five switchbacks that carry you down a steep slope into the Little Devil Stairs Canyon.

5.8 Cross Keyser Run, the first of four unaided stream crossings over the next 0.3 mile. (*Caution:* The next 1.1 miles descend *extremely* technical terrain as you scurry across, squeeze through, drop down off, and hop across rocks and boulders that litter this stream gorge.)

6.0 Cross Keyser Run for the fourth time and pass beneath a twenty-story-high cliff line that forms the right stream bank of the canyon. A talus in this area is littered with tire-size rocks, and the trail footbed is loose rubble.

6.1 Two quick stream crossings put you back on the right stream bank. Ahead, Keyser Run is squeezed by cliffs, and the trail takes a middle course down an island formed by a split in the stream. Watch for blue blazes on trees for guidance. (*Caution:* In spring or after heavy rainfall, this section may be washed out and require you to ford downstream as you follow the blue trail blazes.)

6.3 Cross Keyser Run from the right to the left stream bank. This is the first of four stream crossings as the trail emerges from the gorge into a wider stream valley.

6.7 Cross from the left to the right stream bank, the last in this dizzying descent. Ahead, the trail separates from the streamside and crosses a small knoll.

7.2 Begin a long flat stretch of hiking across flat bottomland forest. Just before reaching the trailhead parking lot, cross a stream.

7.4 HIKE ENDS at the Little Devil Stairs parking lot at the end of VA 614/Keyser Run Road.

Hike Information

Local information: Rappahannock County Office of Tourism, Washington, VA; (540) 675-3153; www.rappahannock.com

Local events/attractions: Wilderness Weekend is held each Sept at the park's Byrd Visitor Center, mile 51 on Skyline Drive, near Big Meadows.

Quievremont Winery, Gid Brown Hollow Road, (540) 987-3192, www.quievremont.com

Good eats: Thornton River Grille, Corner Store and Pizza Kitchen all under one roof, 3710 Sperryville Pike, Sperryville, VA; (540) 987-8790; www.thorntonrivergrille.com

Local outdoor stores: Happy Camper Equipment Co. (opening spring 2018), 15 Main Street, Sperryville, VA; (540) 987-5088, www.happycamperequipment.com

Hike tours: Park rangers lead a variety of nature, wildflower, and geology hikes. www.nps.gov/shen

Organizations: Potomac Appalachian Trail Club (PATC), Vienna, VA; (703) 242-0693; www.potomacappalachian.org

23 Prince William Forest Park

Prince William Forest Park was one of forty-six recreation demonstration projects dating to the Great Depression of the 1930s that restored land considered unprofitable for farming. Civilian Conservation Corps workers planted trees and stabilized stream banks, built camps, and laid out roads. The CCC's "make-work" purpose reaped a practical result: It demonstrated that land considered to be largely worthless could be reclaimed for public recreation and enjoyment. Today, the park is one of Northern Virginia's largest woodlands, with 37 miles of hiking trails and 12 miles of roads for biking. As you walk stream valley trails, pass by beaver-created wetlands, and listen to wood thrushes sing in the forest, you can chalk up this Depression-era experiment as a success.

Start: From the Laurel Loop Trail map board behind Pine Grove picnic pavilion

Distance: 14.6-mile loop with three shorter options

Approximate hiking time: 5 to 6 hours

Difficulty: Difficult due to length. Trails are well graded, clearly marked, and have only moderate elevation change.

Trail surface: Combination of dirt path, dirt road, forested trail, gravel road, boardwalk, and footbridges

Seasons: May and June, when mountain laurel blooms in profusion

Other trail users: Joggers, cross-country skiers. Bicycles are allowed on paved roads and fire roads.

Handicapped accessibility: The 0.2-mile Piedmont Forest Trail is a paved loop with footbridges, boardwalks, and benches. A section of Scenic Drive between Parking Area D and Oak Ridge Camp is one way, with one paved lane suitable for wheelchairs.

Canine compatibility: Leashed dogs permitted

Land status: National park

Fees and permits: Entrance fee (good for 7 days, when paid per vehicle). Free backcountry camping permit required.

Schedule: Park is open daily dawn to dusk, year-round. The visitor center is open daily 9:00 a.m. to 5:00 p.m.

Facilities: Restrooms at the visitor center and picnic areas. Visitor center, historic cabins, and seasonal 100-site campground for tents and RVs (no hookups). Campground reservations: www.recreation.gov. Cabins must be reserved through the park at www.nps.gov/prwi. Chopawamsic Backcountry Area is a 1,500-acre area with 8 primitive campsites accessible from the 2-mile loop trail. There is no fee, but campers must obtain a permit at the park visitor center.

Maps: DeLorme *Virginia Atlas & Gazetteer:* Page 76 D3. USGS 7.5 minute series: *Quantico, VA* and *Joplin, VA.* The park gives out free brochures with park maps and roads depicted. Also, a binder in the visitor center has pages of hiking options, and rangers are nearby to give advice.

Trail contacts: Prince William Forest Park, 18100 Park Headquarters Rd., Triangle, VA 22172-1644; (703) 221-7181; www.nps.gov/prwi

Other: This is a "trash-free" national park: There are no garbage cans, so all trash must be packed out. The visitor center can supply garbage bags if needed.

Finding the trailhead: Distance from Washington, D.C.: 34 miles

From I-95: Take exit 150 (Joplin Road/VA 619). At the bottom of the exit ramp, turn west on VA 619. Drive 0.4 mile and turn right into Prince William Forest Park. In 0.5 mile, turn left at a sign for Pine Grove Picnic Area. Immediately turn right into the long-term parking area. Walk up the small knoll and locate the Laurel Loop Trail map board at the edge of the woods between the Pine Grove Picnic Area and the visitor center. Trailhead GPS: N38 33.644' / W77 20.943'

The Hike

Themes of disturbance and renewal crop up seemingly at every turn as you explore Prince William Forest Park. First, there is the park itself, 15,000 acres that protect nearly the entire watershed of Quantico Creek. It was considered unprofitable land for farming when the federal government removed 150 families from the area to create the park's predecessor, the Chopawamsic Recreational Demonstration Area. Since the 1930s, natural succession has taken hold and returned the park to a prized example of Piedmont forest.

South Fork Quantico Creek

Mountain laurel blooms are prolific in May.

In this state, other types of disturbances now occur, natural ones like wildfires and floods, each a reminder that in nature's balancing act, renewal nearly always follows catastrophe.

Perched as it is on the fall line—a natural boundary between the Piedmont and Coastal Plain—the park straddles two natural worlds. A mile-long stretch of the North Valley Trail along Quantico Creek nicely sums up the transition: Where you descend off the Quantico Falls Trail and turn downstream to walk the North Valley Trail, a granite rock shelf extends out into the stream. Several low-grade falls and rapids form downstream. Where the stream narrows and the banks become sheer, the trail is forced high up onto the hillsides, a wonderful opportunity to walk through thick groves of mountain laurel, which blooms here in May and June.

Soon the stream valley opens up, and the trail passes through a wide area of river bottomland. The terrain is flat, and the birch, tulip poplar, and sycamore trees are younger. The biggest change, however, is beneath your feet, where the earth is now the sandy soil typical of the Coastal Plain.

Of the forty-six recreation demonstration projects created by the Department of the Interior and the Civilian Conservation Corps, many have become state parks. Others, however, include some of our most recognizable national parks, including Acadia in Maine, Badlands in South Dakota, and, of note to metro D.C. residents, Catoctin Mountain Park in Maryland.

CABIN BRANCH PYRITE MINE

The woods of Prince William Forest Park are quiet save for bird calls and the wind rustling leaves, but from 1889 to 1920 the Cabin Branch pyrite mine was in full swing. Sometimes called fool's gold for its luster, pyrite was a cost-efficient source of sulfur that was used to make paper, rubber, medicine, and explosives. During this time, which included World War I, when pyrite miners were exempt from military conscription, Cabin Branch produced more than 224,000 tons for U.S. industry. Bringing the pyrite to the surface was dangerous business, and many men died in the process. Children worked for 50 cents a day sorting the pyrite rocks by size. When miners went on strike for higher wages, the owner closed the mine instead.

In recent years, signs of natural disturbance are dramatic along the North Valley and South Valley Trails. Effects of flooding mar the stream's bottomland forest. In particular, a period of heavy rainfall in spring 2008 left its mark. Floodwaters swept dead branches, leaves, and other forest debris downstream. Small footbridges for hikers were uprooted. Tree logs taller and thicker than telephone poles were moved hundreds of yards to land at odd angles far from the stream. Wherever this accumulated mass of debris hit an obstacle, like a fallen tree that spanned the creek from one bank to the other, the damming created a dramatic rise in water that spilled over into the creek's floodplain.

Another natural disturbance is found near Oak Ridge Campground, where the South Valley Trail rises away from verdant wetlands formed by beaver dams into drier forest where trunks of the oak and pine trees are charred and blackened. Wide swaths of felled trees have formed clearings, and there are cut logs stacked and piled. This was the site of a wildfire in March and April of 2006, when a camper's error led to burning of 318 acres of the park's forestland.

In the years since the floods and fires, renewal has followed. The stream bottomland that flooded has, on closer inspection, the look of a recently plowed-over field. Plants and tree saplings are bent in half, resembling images of the aftermath of a hurricane. The accumulation of debris around their trunks further enhances their frozen-in-time illusion. The loose crumbly topsoil of the floodplain is fertile ground for new trees and plants.

Biologists at Prince William Forest Park are paying close attention to the white pines in the burnt forest. This conifer's cones are serotinous, which means they remain closed on the tree until a stressor—in this case, intense heat from fire—causes them to open and drop their seedlings.

▶ **KID APPEAL**

The 1.4-mile Laurel Loop Trail is easily reached from the Pine Grove picnic area, where there is also a playground. The forested path gets you down to the stream quickly for some water play.

While the floods and fires are the most dramatic, there are countless other small disturbances where hikers can see the process of renewals. When a storm knocks down a few trees to create a small forest clearing, grass quickly takes root in the patch of sunshine. Small beetles and spiders begin the long process of decomposing fallen deadwood. Their activity attracts birds, including pileated and red-headed woodpeckers as well as songbirds, looking to feast on the small insect life. A shrub layer of spicebush will give way to young tree saplings—maybe maple or ironwood.

In these clearings, it is possible to imagine how Prince William Forest Park started its long road toward becoming the mature woodland it is today.

Miles and Directions

0.0 START from the Laurel Loop Trail map board behind the Pine Grove picnic pavilion. Do not enter the woods here, but rather turn left (north) and follow a narrow well-worn dirt path through a grassy area. You'll pass a playground and then enter a field at the far end of a paved parking lot. Walk down the right side of the field, keeping the woods hard to your right. In the far northeast corner of the field, locate the yellow blazes for the alternate Laurel Loop trailhead. The trail here is a wide, graded dirt path. The trailhead is marked by a yellow blaze on a tulip poplar and a concrete trail post with a metal band that gives the trail's name and mileage to the next junction.

0.4 Continue straight ahead on the Laurel Loop Trail at a junction with a short spur trail on the left that descends left to South Orenda Road.

0.5 Turn left (west) and cross the South Fork Quantico Creek on a cable-supported bridge. On the opposite side, turn left (west) on a dirt road that is the combined South Valley Trail and North Orenda Road. (*Bailout:* Don't cross the bridge; instead, bear right and follow a combination of Laurel Loop and Birch Bluff Trail to return to the Pine Grove picnic area for a quick 2-mile loop.)

0.7 Turn left (south) on South Valley Trail as it splits off North Orenda Road.

1.4 Stay straight at a T junction with Turkey Run Ridge Trail. Ahead, South Valley Trail winds through bottomland forest formed by a bend in the stream, and then turns north.

1.5 Bear left on South Valley Trail. (*Note:* The trail straight ahead becomes Turkey Run Ridge Trail where the cutoff from 1.4 miles merges on the right.) (*Bailout:* For a 6.15-mile loop, follow Turkey Run Ridge Trail [dark blue blazes] uphill to the Turkey Run Education Center, and return to Pine Grove via Mary Bird Branch, Quantico Falls, and North Valley Trails.)

1.6 Cross over Scenic Drive. (*Note:* This is a reroute of South Valley Trail built to replace a washout-prone route.)

2.1 Cross a footbridge over a small stream. After a strong rainfall, this tributary of the South Fork is a bubbling, cascading treat. Ahead, South Valley Trail climbs a hillside on switchbacks.

2.6 Cross beneath Scenic Drive via a boardwalk that hugs the concrete bridge abutment.

2.8 Stay straight on South Valley Trail at a junction with Taylor Farm Road on the right. (*Bailout:* For an 8.8-mile loop, turn right on Taylor Farm Road and use the High Meadow Trail to return to Turkey Run Education Center, and then back to Pine Grove picnic area via Mary Bird Branch, Quantico Falls, and North Valley Trails.)

2.9 Cross over Scenic Drive and continue west on the South Valley Trail.

Prince William Forest Park

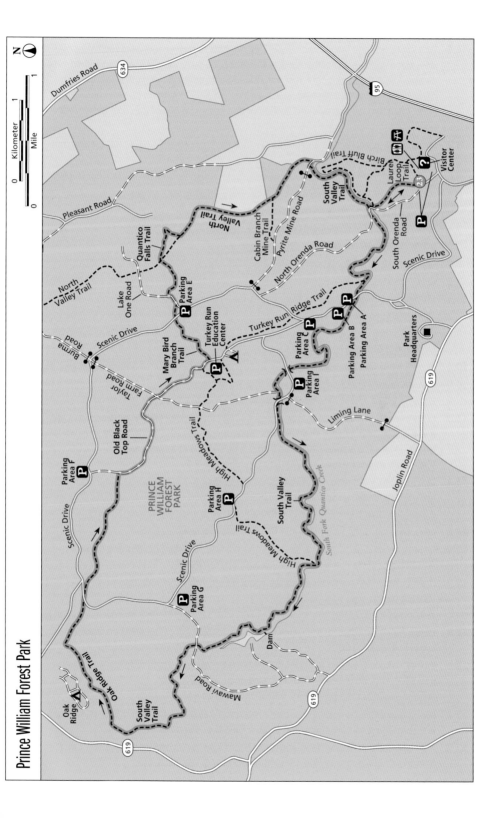

4.4 Turn left (west) and follow South Valley Trail downhill at this junction with High Meadow Trail, which continues straight uphill. In the next 0.75 mile, you will make three short, steep climbs from the river-bottom forest to hillside forests as the South Fork Quantico Creek narrows and twists through tight, steep terrain. (*Note:* In May, when its white blossoms show, mountain laurel crowd this section of trail, making it one of the most scenic in the park.)

5.2 Pass a dam across the South Fork. Above this, the creek spreads out to form a long, narrow lake.

6.0 Cross over gravel Mawavi Road and walk north on South Valley Trail up the stream valley.

6.4 Enter wetlands where, for the next 0.7 mile, the trail skirts an area of heavy beaver activity. This wet, wide open ecosystem attracts waterfowl, songbirds, deer, raccoon, and fox.

7.1 Begin a climb from the stream valley into dry upland forest of chestnut oak, yellow (tulip) poplar, and white oak that is in recovery from a 2006 wildfire that consumed 318 acres.

8.0 Turn right (east) on the yellow-blazed Oak Ridge Trail.

8.5 Cross straight over Scenic Drive.

9.2 After a level stretch of hiking through a young upland forest, descend into a small stream valley with a moist forest understory of fern and skunk cabbage.

9.5 Oak Ridge Trail ends at a T junction with Old Black Top Road. Turn right (south) and walk along the gravel road.

10.4 At a four-way junction with Taylor Farm Road, continue straight on Old Black Top Road.

10.9 Turn left (north) onto Mary Bird Branch Trail. There is a concrete trail post and a triple red blaze on a tree. Ahead, descend and cross Mary Bird Branch, a stream.

11.3 Cross straight over Scenic Drive and pass through the parking and picnic area E. Locate a white signboard for Quantico Falls Trail. Enter the woods on a footpath following yellow blazes. (*Note:* You'll periodically see brown trail blazes and trailside signs for the Geology Trail, which shares the trail from here to Quantico Creek.)

11.4 Turn left onto a dirt road. Stay alert when, in less than 0.1 mile, Quantico Falls Trail branches right off the dirt road. Turn right here and follow the yellow-blazed trail through an upland deciduous forest of oak and hickory with an understory of beech, maple, and elm.

11.8 Cross over the North Valley Trail at a four-way trail junction.

12.0 A sharp descent ends at the edge of Quantico Creek. Turn right (south) and follow the stream valley. There is a scenic set of waterfalls off to the left.

12.2 Cross a footbridge over a small tributary and merge with the blue-blazed North Valley Trail. Veer left (south) and walk downstream. (*FYI:* In summer and fall, the trail south of this junction offers good opportunities to rest and relax on exposed rock shelves in the river.)

12.9 Pass interpretive signs for the Cabin Branch pyrite mine, which operated on Quantico Creek in the early 1900s.

13.0 Cross Quantico Creek on a bridge. On the opposite side, turn right to follow a footpath through river-bottom forest. (*Side trip:* Before crossing the creek, walk straight ahead to another section of the pyrite mine in less than 0.1 mile.)

13.2 A long boardwalk carries the trail over a wetland. Ahead, look for an overlook on the right that gives you a vantage point of the Cabin Branch mine across the stream.

13.5 After walking a short stretch on gravel road, turn right (west) and cross Quantico Creek on a bridge. On the opposite side, turn left (west) onto South Valley Trail.

14.1 Turn left (south) and cross South Fork Quantico Creek on a cable-supported bridge. After crossing, turn right on red blazed Laurel Loop Trail and ascend.

14.6 Arrive back at the Pine Grove picnic area.

OPTIONS

Our goal was to plot a route through Prince William Forest Park that maximized its 37 miles of trails as well as its diverse natural habitats. The 14.6-mile hike described above provides three bailout options that reduce the length and difficulty. Laurel Loop (1.4 miles) is the shortest and easiest, and it can be done in an hour or less. The Turkey Run Ridge option (6.15 miles) is moderate due to length. An 8.8-mile route using Taylor Farm Road and the High Meadow Trail offers an interesting walk through meadows that are reverting to woodland. The full hike of 15.6 miles takes you to the farthest reaches of the park.

Hike Information

Local information: Prince William County Tourism, 14420 Bristow Road, Manassas, VA; (703) 792-7060; www.discoverpwm.com

Local events/attractions: The Prince William Forest Park Heritage Festival takes place in mid-Sept in the park.

Good eats: Tim's Rivershore Restaurant & Crabhouse, 1510 Cherry Hill Rd., Dumfries, VA; (703) 441-1375; www.timsrivershore.com. Enjoy fresh seafood and a view of the Potomac River.

Local outdoor stores: Modell's Sporting Goods, Potomac Mills, Woodbridge, VA; (703) 499-9696; www.modells.com

Hike tours: Park staff offer nature programs and orienteering classes.

Organizations: Potomac Appalachian Trail Club (PATC), Vienna, VA; (703) 242-0315; www.patc.net

24 Riverbend Park

This small, compact Fairfax County park sits on a deep bend in the Potomac River north of Great Falls and protects some of the globally rare natural communities that have in recent years made the Potomac Gorge a hot spot for naturalists. Terrain is diverse, ranging from riverside floodplain to upland forests. There is a trail through hilltop meadows excellent for bird-watching. Only the Potomac Heritage Trail along the river is longer than 2 miles, but several of the park's shorter trails can be strung together for a walk that, while lacking in distance and endurance, exceeds in natural beauty.

Start: From the park nature center

Distance: There are 10 miles of trails in the park, with options to link with Great Falls Park to the south

Approximate hiking time: 1 to 3 hours

Difficulty: Easy due to gentle terrain and short, well-marked trails

Trail surface: Forested trails, dirt riverside paths, paved roads, gravel paths

Seasons: Best in winter and spring. Many species of wildflowers thrive along the riverbank from Mar to June, and Virginia bluebell is especially prolific along the wooded trails.

Other trail users: Mountain bikers, equestrians, anglers

Handicapped accessibility: The Duff 'N' Stuff Trail is a 0.25-mile-long paved trail near the nature center. Paved roads and sidewalks descend from the visitor center to the river's edge.

Canine compatibility: Leashed dogs permitted

Land status: County park

Fees and permits: None

Schedule: Daily 7:00 a.m. to dusk. Visitor Center open weekdays, 9:00 a.m. to 5:00 p.m. (closed Tues), weekends noon to 5:00 p.m.

Facilities: Restrooms, picnic shelter and picnic area, visitor center, nature center, gift shop, snack bar

Maps: DeLorme *Virginia Atlas & Gazetteer:* Page 80 D3. USGS 7.5 minute series: *Rockland, MD/VA.*

Trail contacts: Riverbend Park, 8700 Potomac Hills St., Great Falls, VA 22066; (703) 759-9018; www.fairfaxcounty.gov/parks/riverbend-Special considerations: As Riverbend is part of a Globally Rare Environment, it is illegal to pick or otherwise harm plant life in the park.

Finding the trailhead: Distance from Washington, D.C.: 19 miles

From I-495 (Capital Beltway): Take exit 44 (Georgetown Pike/VA 193). Drive west on Georgetown Pike, and in 4.5 miles turn right onto Riverbend Road. In 2.1 miles, turn right onto Jeffery Road, following signs for Riverbend Park Nature Center. (*Note:* A right turn onto Potomac Hills Street leads to the park's visitor center.) Bear hard right as Jeffery Road bends east, avoiding River Birch Drive, which goes straight. In 1.3 miles from Riverbend Road, Jeffery Road ends at a parking lot for the nature center. Trailhead GPS: N39 01.330' / W77 15.002'

The Hike

The Potomac River's watershed drains nearly 15,000 square miles of land, from the Allegheny Highlands of western Pennsylvania all the way to the Chesapeake Bay. Its highest elevations are rugged peaks in West Virginia. The rivers and streams that drain eastward off the Allegheny Plateau originate in boreal bogs more typical of alpine Canadian climates. At Harpers Ferry, the Potomac cuts through the Blue Ridge Mountains and, after receiving the Shenandoah River, settles into a wide course through Piedmont farmlands. The southern bank marks the boundary between Maryland and Virginia. Great Falls marks the river's drop into flat land of the Coastal Plain, where the river is influenced by Chesapeake Bay tides. From there on, for more than 110 miles, the Potomac follows a serpentine course to its confluence with the Chesapeake Bay.

From time preceding English settlement of Virginia up until today, the Potomac River has influenced travel and settlement, trade and commerce, culture and recreation. Its role as a thread through different geographic regions and different eras

Potomac River View

Stroller-appropriate trails include the 0.25-mile asphalt Duff 'N' Stuff Trail that loops from the nature center into quiet, shady woods. There are also paved walks around the visitor center and down to the river. In summer, tractor-drawn wagon rides are offered to a remote area of the park.

helped inspire the Potomac Heritage National Scenic Trail (NST). Conceived in the 1970s, the trail is a route that strives to link not just the river's natural highlights, but the shared history of people and events along the river.

Small and compact, Riverbend's 402 acres preserve wooded bluffs whose forests are reminiscent of Appalachian cove forests. The hilltop meadows attract both birds and the people that watch them in all seasons. And along the floodplain of the Potomac River, the park's longstanding River Trail offers hikers an easy, rambling route with views onto the Potomac River and its many islands. In 2007, this 2.5-mile route officially joined the Potomac Heritage NST network, making Riverbend Park part of the still-unfolding story of the Potomac's natural and cultural history.

The riverside trail is short and easy on the legs. There are plenty of opportunities to explore side routes that climb up into the hillside forests. Tall, thick-trunked sycamore trees line the river's edge, noticeable by their blotchy white and gray bark. The ephemeral wildflowers bloodroot and spring beauty emerge for a day or two in spring, their white petals an uplifting sign of warmer weather. After a heavy spring rain, the trail is waterlogged at its low points. Spring peepers, a type of tree frog, raise a raucous chorus that quiets as your footsteps approach. Its call is a short, high-pitched whistle. A chorus of spring peepers sounds like a thousand jingle bells ringing, and on a quiet evening, it can be heard up to a mile away. These tiny frogs—their size is equivalent to your thumbnail—find shelter on the low branches of shrubs around a bog or wetland. Its telltale marking resembles a Christian cross, which inspired the frog's Latin name, *Pseudacris crucifer.*

Flooding is a fact of life along the Potomac River, and even more so at Riverbend Park. Water may rise higher and quicker at certain downstream locations, where the Potomac is squeezed into narrow Mather Gorge, but at Riverbend, a low-elevation, relatively flat, wide floodplain results in flooding five or six times a year. This in turn has given rise to peculiar landforms and plant communities. Hiking north from the

Capt. John Smith's 1608 exploration of the Chesapeake Bay and its tributaries brought him to the Great Falls of the Potomac. He and his crew hiked overland past the falls and encountered a tribe of Native Americans laden with bear, beaver, deer, and other meat. A crew member later wrote in his diary that they saw bison grazing. Archaeologists have documented over 11,000 years of Native American life at today's Riverbend Park, the most recent a tribe documented by Smith called the Nacotchtanks. The park's annual Virginia Indian Festival held each fall celebrates this Native American heritage.

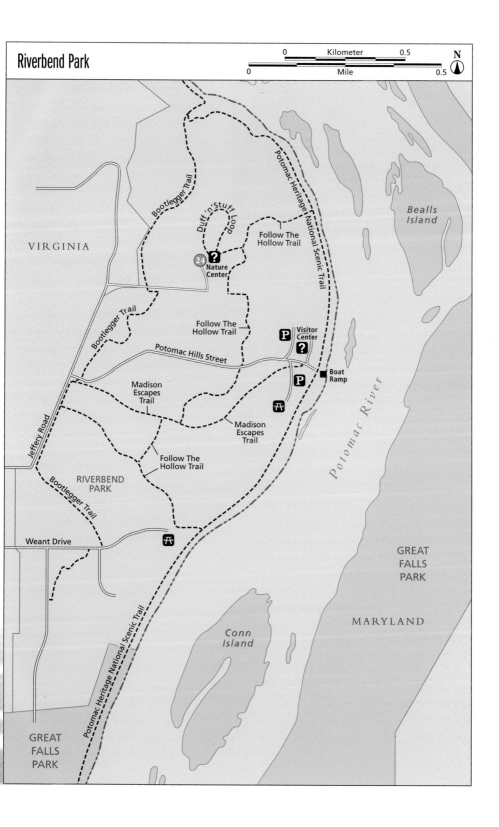

Riverbend Park

0 | Kilometer | 0.5
0 | Mile | 0.5

N

Bealls
Island

VIRGINIA

Bootlegger Trail

Duff 'n' Stuff Loop

Potomac Heritage National Scenic Trail

Follow The
Hollow Trail

24

Nature
Center

Bootlegger Trail

Follow The
Hollow Trail

Potomac Hills Street

Visitor
Center

P

Boat
Ramp

Madison
Escapes
Trail

P

Madison
Escapes
Trail

Potomac River

Follow The
Hollow Trail

Jeffery Road

Bootlegger Trail

RIVERBEND
PARK

Weant Drive

GREAT
FALLS
PARK

MARYLAND

Potomac Heritage National Scenic Trail

Conn
Island

GREAT
FALLS
PARK

Paw Paw blossoms

visitor center, you'll pass Black Pond, a seemingly benign backswamp. In flood conditions, however, Black Pond becomes a chute—literally a troughlike shortcut for river water that has spilled over the bank and seeks the short route across the river bend.

At the north end of Black Pond, a rerouting of the Potomac Heritage NST diverts you away from a globally rare, environmentally sensitive plant community. The Nature Conservancy helped document the site as part of their ongoing research in what they've termed the Potomac Gorge region. The gorge is presently defined as a 15-mile stretch of the Potomac starting at Riverbend Park and ending at Theodore Roosevelt Island. The assemblage of terrain from Riverbend's expansive floodplain to the 140-foot cliffs of Mathers Gorge hosts a diversity of plant, animal, and insect life that is still being documented and interpreted. At Riverbend, biologists identified one particular kind of rare plant community north of Black Pond, an area of exposed rocks and woodland called a woodland scour. After a particularly violent flood, or if the land has been raked over by ice flows, this may look more like a scrubland scour. Willow and sycamore trees are dominant, with smaller green ash, river birch, and silver maple present as well. While characterized as a highly disturbed environment, it is the disturbance of flooding that makes it unique.

To accommodate this plant community, volunteers rerouted the Potomac Heritage NST just north of Black Pond. Where you once followed the riverside, hikers now veer left, cross a dry section of the Black Pond chute and then a small tributary stream, and climb to the top of a knoll. It is a nice, short diversion from the river's edge and provides winter and spring views out over the mighty Potomac. There is something comforting about watching the mass of water moving downriver. So, too, is the thought that for as long as the Potomac has been flowing, we are still learning about just what makes this such a special river.

Hike Information

Local information: Fairfax County/Capital Region Visitors Center, Tysons Corner Center, 1961 Chain Bridge Rd., McLean, VA; (703) 752-9500; www.fxva.com

Local events/attractions: Wolf Trap National Park for the Performing Arts, Vienna, VA; (703) 255-1800; www.nps.org/wotr

Good eats: Deli Italiano Gourmet Pizza & Subs, 9911 Georgetown Pike, Great Falls, VA; (703) 759-6782; www.deliitaliano.com

The Old Brogue Irish Pub, 762 Walker Rd., Great Falls, VA; (703) 759-3309; www
.oldbrogue.com

Local outdoor stores: Tysons REI, 8209 Watson St., McLean, VA; (703) 506-1938;
www.rei.com

Dick's Sporting Goods, 12501 Fair Lakes Circle, Fairfax, VA; (703) 803-0300;
www.dickssportinggoods.com

Hike tours: The park conducts wildflower walks in spring, particularly in mid-Apr
when the Virginia bluebell blooms. In summer, there are tractor-drawn wagon rides to a
remote area of the park. Fishing guides and canoe tours are available May through Oct.

Organizations: Friends of Riverbend Park, www.forb.wildapricot.org. A volunteer
group that advocates for the park, holds a Native Plant Sale in the spring and Fall
Barbecue.

Potomac Appalachian Trail Club (PATC), Vienna, VA; (703) 242-0315; www.patc
.net

Other resources: Potomac Heritage National Scenic Trail, Harpers Ferry, WV; (304)
535-4014; www.nps.gov/pohe

THE THREATENED WOOD TURTLE

Already recognized for harboring a globally rare plant community—the woodland scour of the Potomac River floodplain—Riverbend Park also shelters a state-threatened reptile, the wood turtle. Park staff first documented this tortoise in 2008. Because it is known only in four Virginia counties, the state has listed it as a reptile whose existence is threatened. Biologists attribute its decline to habitat fragmentation, loss of wetlands, siltation of streams from human development, and collection by humans for the pet trade.

The wood turtle lacks flashy colors on its carapace (shell) like the similarly sized box turtle, but it does have one distinctive feature that could help you identify it. Look closely at the scutes (plates) on the turtle's carapace. A wood turtle's scutes down the center of the carapace are keeled; they literally rise up to a blunt point like small pyramids. This feature is the source of one of the turtle's nicknames: sculptured tortoise.

It lives both in dry forest and stream habitats, preferring the dry land during summer and moving to the stream in winter. Regardless of where it's found, the wood turtle always needs a stream or flooded wetland nearby to prevent drying out during heat spells.

One of its favorite food sources is fruit of the pawpaw tree, which means at Riverbend Park, as you walk the Paw Paw Passage Trail between the nature center and the Potomac River, you should keep a sharp eye and ear out for this small turtle scuffling through the leafy understory of the forest. If you see one, take a picture, note the location, and let park staff know about your discovery. Do not touch or otherwise disturb the turtles.

25 Sky Meadows State Park

On first approach, it's easy to see how Sky Meadows got its name and why amateur astronomers flock here to view the heavens. Hillside pastures offer expansive views in every direction. The views from Piedmont Overlook and the Ambassador Whitehouse Trails stir memories of alpine meadows. The Appalachian Trail passes through the park for 3 miles, and numerous house ruins and wagon roads tell the story of long-gone farmers.

Start: From a map trailboard 60 feet west of the visitor parking lot

Distance: 6.7-mile loop

Approximate hiking time: 3 hours

Difficulty: Moderate due to a mix of long uphill climbs through hillside meadows and level terrain along the ridge top. The forest trails are rocky with brief, but steep, inclines.

Trail surface: Forest trails, mowed meadow paths, gravel road

Seasons: Best spring and fall

Other trail users: Trails on this route are hiker-only. Other trails in the park allow bikes and horses.

Handicapped accessibility: Bathrooms, the visitor center, and the gift shop are accessible via a paved path and ramp. One picnic site with a grill is accessible, as is a flat, but not paved, trail to the fishing pond.

Canine compatibility: Leashed dogs permitted

Land status: State park, National Scenic Trail

Fees and permits: Entrance fee; camping fee

Schedule: Open daily 8:00 a.m. to dusk

Facilities: Restrooms, picnic tables, visitor center with small nature center and gift shop (sells firewood), beverage machine at picnic shelter. Primitive, hike-in camping has pit toilets and non-potable water that must be treated before drinking.

Maps: DeLorme *Virginia Atlas & Gazetteer:* Page 77 A5. USGS 7.5 minute series: Upperville, VA. See also National Geographic's TOPO! software, Mid-Atlantic Region, Disc 4: Washington, D.C. State park–issued trail maps are available at an interactive kiosk located in the picnic area next to the visitor center. A trail map can be downloaded from the park website.

Trail contacts: Sky Meadows State Park, 11012 Edmunds Lane, Delaplane, VA 20144; (540) 592-3556; www.dcr.virginia.gov/state-parks/sky-meadows

Special considerations: The park's hilly meadows have little shade, so in the summer bring sun protection and plenty of water. Gap Run is the only stream of any reliability. There is a well at the primitive campsite, but water must be treated before used for drinking.

Finding the trailhead: Distance from Washington, D.C.: 60 miles

From I-66: Take exit 23, following signs for US 17/VA 55 and Delaplane. Continue straight (north) on US 17 when VA 55 turns left (west). In 6.7 miles, turn left (west) on CR 710 (Edmunds Lane) and enter the state park. It is 0.5 mile on CR 710 to the park contact station, and 1.1 miles to the visitor center and trailhead parking. Trailhead GPS: N38 59.527' / W77 57.997'

The Hike

The impressive stone Mount Bleak House greets you when you pull into the parking lot, a tangible reminder that this young park is steeped in history. The famous philanthropist Paul Mellon donated the original property of 1,132 acres in 1975 expressly for development as a state park. In 1987, 245 acres were added for access to the Appalachian Trail, and in 1988, Mellon topped it off with another 486 acres.

The view inspired a resident of Mount Bleak during World War II to name it Skye Farm, in tribute to his native Isle of Skye in Scotland, and so the park became Sky Meadows.

The entire area of Loudoun County drips with the Civil War, with much of it focused around Col. John Singleton Mosby and his "rangers." He dominated this area during the Civil War so much that the surrounding countryside was dubbed "Mosby's Confederacy."

Headed for some high meadow hiking

On the morning of July 19, 1861, Abner Settle of Mount Bleak would have seen thousands of Union campfires, the soldiers camped there on their way to the First Battle of Bull Run (Manassas). Two of the Settle boys were among Mosby's Rangers.

Today, a line of replica cannon recalls those solemn times. Nearby, a trailboard lifts the mood. We're here for hiking, after all, not to re-hash old battles.

Begin walking on a dirt road built in the 1820s to connect the 3 miles between the village of Paris and Semper's Mill. Deeply rutted by wagon wheels, the road is flanked by fieldstone fences with cornfields and pastures beyond them.

The road leads to Snowden Manor, the ruins of which can still be seen. Here George S. Ayre lived with his wife and four daughters. A sign tells the sad tale: In summary, the last of the girls died here, an old woman in 1893. The house was sold for debts in 1902, and in 1913 the frame house burned, leaving the brick chimney and the flagstone foundations we see today.

Prolific spring wildflowers and naturalized daffodils lining the trail lift the mood again. In a little over 2 miles you reach the Appalachian Trail (AT), a trail sign helpfully informing you that Harper's Ferry, West Virginia, is only 32.8 miles to go! On this footpath highway you're as likely to meet grubby through-hikers on a 2,000-mile journey as you are day-tripping urbanites on a Saturday trail run.

The park's focal point, Mount Bleak House (in this case, *bleak* means "exposed to the weather"), was built in the 1840s by Abner and Mary Settle. The journal of their niece, Amanda Edmonds, gives a firsthand account of Civil War–era events that took place here. It is for sale in the gift shop.

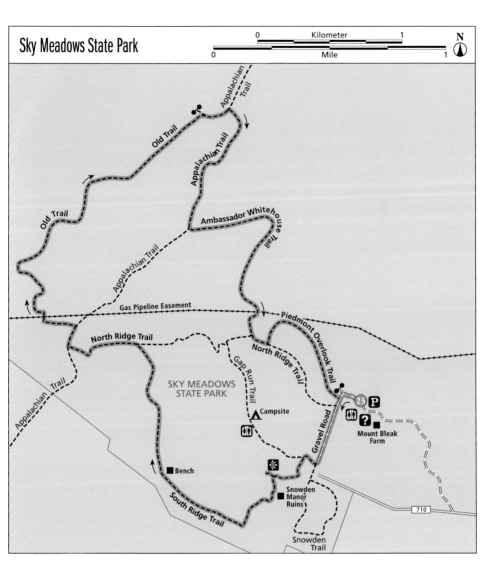

Sky Meadows State Park

0   Kilometer   1

0   Mile   1

N

Appalachian Trail

Old Trail

Appalachian Trail

Old Trail

Ambassador Whitehouse Trail

Appalachian Trail

Gas Pipeline Easement

North Ridge Trail

Piedmont Overlook Trail

North Ridge Trail

Appalachian Trail

SKY MEADOWS STATE PARK

Gap Run Trail

Campsite

Gravel Road

25 P

Mount Bleak Farm

Bench

Snowden Manor Ruins

South Ridge Trail

710

Snowden Trail

Miles and Directions

0.0   START at a large map board west of the visitor center parking lot. Follow a gravel-lined footpath 0.1 mile and turn left (south) on a dirt road. In 150 feet, continue straight past a junction for North Ridge Trail and Piedmont Overlook Trail on the right, marked by a set of stone steps. (*Note:* This junction marks the return point for this 6.7-mile loop.)

0.4   Turn right (west) on Gap Run Trail, which is a mowed grass path. In 260 feet, turn left onto the yellow-blazed South Ridge Trail.

0.7   A side trail forks right off South Ridge Trail and leads in 0.1 mile to a scenic overlook with views northeast across meadows and pastures.

Appalachian Trail day-hikers

0.8 Pass the stone ruins of Snowden Manor on the left side of the trail. A chimney and foundation—and bouquets of daffodils in the springtime—are visible remains of the home, which burned in 1913.

2.0 Turn left (west) on the blue-blazed North Ridge Trail.

2.3 Turn right (north) on the white-blazed Appalachian Trail (AT). Hike 0.1 mile and turn left (west) on the purple-blazed Old Trail. (*FYI:* Old Trail is the former route of the AT.)

2.6 Drop off the trail onto a dirt road and turn right (north). Cross a natural gas line easement and turn left (west) to reenter the woods on a dirt footpath.

3.6 Stay right as a dirt road merges with Old Trail. The road and trail share the same path for 0.1 mile. Thereafter, the jeep trail continues straight (east) while Old Trail veers left (north) as a single-track footpath.

4.2 Turn right (east) at a four-way intersection and follow Old Trail uphill. (*Note:* The road to the left (west) ends at a red metal gate marking the boundary of a private farm.)

4.3 Turn right (southeast) onto the AT.

4.9 Turn left (east) onto Ambassador Whitehouse Trail, a mowed grass path marked by light blue blazes.

5.8 Drop off the trail onto a natural gas line easement. Turn right (west) and briefly walk along this wide, mowed corridor, then turn left (south) at a light-blue–blazed junction. The trail reenters the woods and descends via switchbacks.

6.0 At a North Ridge Trail junction, turn left (east), descend 88 yards, and turn left (north) again onto the red-blazed Piedmont Overlook Trail. Within 0.1 mile, cross a fence stile and enter a spacious meadow.

6.4 After a long descent through the hillside meadows, the trail turns hard right and crosses a footbridge. There is an old livestock barn on the right.

6.6 At a North Ridge Trail junction, turn left (south), cross a fence stile, and descend to the gravel road (Gap Run Trail). Turn left again and walk 150 feet north to a red metal gate, where you turn right (east).

6.7 HIKE ENDS at the map board adjacent to the visitor parking lot.

OPTIONS

You can shorten this loop by 1.3 miles by skipping the Old Trail and staying straight (north) on the AT to its junction with the Ambassador Whitehouse Trail. Or, if you're in the mood for an open-air meadow hike, focus on the Piedmont Overlook Trail (0.6 mile), Ambassador Whitehouse Trail (1.1 miles), and the lower half of the North Ridge Trail.

Hike Information

Local information: Warrenton-Fauquier Visitor's Center, 33 N. Calhoun St., Warrenton, VA; (800) 820-1021; www.visitfauquier.com. Provides dining, museum, winery, and lodging information.

Local events/attractions: Astronomy Evenings at Sky Meadows State Park, Apr through Nov. The park hosts the Delaplane Strawberry Festival in late May. Call (540) 592-3556 for a schedule of events.

Good eats: Hunter's Head Tavern, 9048 John Mosby Hwy. (US 50), Upperville, VA; (540) 592-9020; www.huntersheadtavern.com. English-themed pub in a 1750 log cabin.

Local outdoor stores: Mountain Trails, 115 North Loudon St., Winchester, VA; (540) 667-0030; www.mountain-trails.com

Hike tours: Tours of Mount Bleak House are given.

Organizations: Friends of Sky Meadows State Park; (540) 592-3556; www.virginia parks.org/friends-sk

District of Columbia

Washington, D.C., hiking excursions can be divided into three broad categories: urban, stream valley, and public gardens. As our featured hikes show, when you can mix all three into select hikes, a special experience awaits.

And what a city! Pierre L'Enfant designed it in 1791 with an eye toward creating a new Rome, a beacon of freedom for the world. Yet the nation's capital remained a stagnant tidal backwater until massive public works campaigns of the late 1800s, and a visionary Beaux-Arts policy outlined by the McMillan Commission in 1902 laid the groundwork for the modern-day city. And when we say "laid the groundwork," we mean it literally. When you walk along West Potomac Park, you're stepping on filled land that was once a stagnant swampy backwater of the Potomac River, subject to tidal flooding.

Rock Creek Park is Washington's recreation epicenter, and rightly so. Advocates campaigned for its creation for more than twenty years, starting in the 1860s, before they ever saw their vision realized. It is the most rugged and expansive example of a peculiar D.C. outdoor recreation outlet: the stream valley park. So it is that a hiker can follow Foundry Branch and Battery Kemble Run, city streets, manicured gardens, and the C&O Canal National Historic Trail for an urban hike that is guaranteed to reshape your image of the city. It is ironic that the stream valley parks, oases of greenery, survived largely through indifference and were long abused by pollution. They now harbor some of the city's last vestiges of un-manicured natural beauty and diversity.

Even the National Mall, that great public space marked by larger and ever larger monuments to people and events in our history, is largely green space. Under the tall old oak trees that shade the World War I memorial, it is possible to re-imagine Washington not as an urban core, but as one great big outdoor playground.

◀ *Top: Paddle boats on the tidal basin*
Bottom: Biking past Peirce's Mill

181

26 Georgetown Loop (Rock Creek Park South)

Washington's stream valley parks are a world apart from the city streets that are within earshot throughout this 12-mile hike. The trails follow small brooks through centuries-old forests in a world where seeing a fox scoot across the trail is not unusual. It's a world well known to dog walkers and runners, but it's lesser known to hikers and naturalists. With that in mind, this route links ten different trails and city sidewalks for a full-day trek for the ambitious hiker. The route skirts community gardens, passes through old Georgetown neighborhoods, and crests near one of the highest points in the city.

Start: From Peirce Mill, 2401 Tilden Street

Distance: 12.3-mile loop

Approximate hiking time: 4 to 5 hours

Difficulty: Moderate due to length and numerous road crossings

Trail surface: Stone path, paved bike path, dirt path, paved city street, stairs, footbridge, tunnel, streambed, street crossings, stream crossings

Seasons: Summer

Other trail users: Some portions of this route are used by joggers, walkers, in-line skaters, bicyclists, cross-country skiers; other sections are hiker-only.

Handicapped accessibility: In general, the paved bike paths are accessible.

Canine compatibility: Leashed dogs permitted

Land status: National park

Fees and permits: None

Schedule: The park is open daily during daylight hours. The Nature Center is open Wed through Sun, 9:00 a.m. to 5:00 p.m. Peirce Barn at the old mill site is open noon to 5:00 p.m. on weekends.

Facilities: Bathrooms and a snack bar at Fletcher's Boat House; restrooms at Picnic Area 1 in Rock Creek Park, adjacent to Peirce Mill; planetarium

Maps: DeLorme *Maryland/Delaware Atlas & Gazetteer:* Page 46 C3. USGS 7.5 minute series: *Washington West, DC, MD, VA.* Also, the Potomac Appalachian Trail Club's (PATC) *Map N: Rock Creek Park Area.* The map inset details parks and trails used on this hike.

Trail contacts: Rock Creek Park, 5200 Glover Rd. NW, Washington, D.C. 20015; (202) 895-6000; www.nps.gov/rocr. PATC (see *Hike Information*) maintains the stream valley trails.

Special considerations: The Rock Creek and Potomac Parkway traffic flow is altered for weekday rush hour traffic. From Connecticut Avenue, it is one-way going south between 6:45 and 9:30 a.m., and one-way going north from 3:45 to 6:30 p.m. Also, access streets like Glover Road, Ross Drive, Bingham Drive, and Sherrill Drive are not maintained after heavy snowfall or in icy conditions.

Canal Road, which separates Battery Kemble Park from Fletcher's Boat House and the C&O Canal National Historic Park, is a significant obstacle on this route. A culvert passes beneath the road and is tall enough for walkers to pass. However, hikers must have the agility to scale a head-high fence at the far end. Fence slats are sturdy and widely spaced, and climbing it is akin to climbing up a stepladder. We recommend against crossing over Canal Road. There is virtually no road shoulder, and traffic moves past at full speed. The embankment is steep; slipping down into the roadway is a real possibility. If you cannot pass beneath Canal Road via the culvert, skip the lower leg of Battery Kemble Park. Instead, turn left and walk MacArthur Boulevard to Glover-Archibold Park's southern trailhead. Resume the hiking directions at the 6.7-mile cue.

Finding the trailhead: From Northern Virginia: Cross the Potomac on I-66 / US 50 via the Theodore Roosevelt Memorial Bridge. Take the Independence Avenue exit (right lane). After merging onto Independence, in quick succession turn right and merge onto Rock Creek and Potomac Parkway. In 0.7 mile, continue straight at an intersection with Virginia Avenue. As signs indicate that Connecticut Avenue is approaching, stay right and follow signs for the National Zoo and Beach Drive. (*Note:* The Rock Creek and Potomac Parkway ends at Connecticut Avenue; Beach Drive becomes the main north–south route through Rock Creek Park.) Continue straight on Beach Drive, with Klingle Avenue on the left and Piney Branch Parkway on the right. At the four-way stoplight with Beach Road, Park Road (on the right), and Tilden Street (on the left), turn left onto Tilden Street. Cross Rock Creek and turn right into the parking area for Peirce Mill.

From downtown Washington, D.C.: Follow directions above from the intersection of the Rock Creek and Potomac Parkway and Virginia Avenue. Or, follow Connecticut Avenue northwest from DuPont Circle for 2.3 miles and turn right on Tilden Street. In another 0.5 mile, turn left into Peirce Mill parking area.

From Maryland and I-495 (Capital Beltway): Take exit 33 (Connecticut Avenue, Chevy Chase, Kensington) and follow it south toward Chevy Chase. In 4.6 miles, turn right on Tilden Street. In another 0.5 mile, turn left into Peirce Mill parking area.

Public transportation: The Red Line offers three stops in proximity to this route. The closest are Cleveland Park and UDC–Van Ness. From either you can pick up the Melvin Hazen Trail where it crosses Connecticut Avenue (start Miles and Directions at 0.7 mile from the trailhead). Tenley-town–UA Metro is closer to Glover-Archibold Park. See Options below for a revised route if you use this Metro station. Trailhead GPS: N38 56.418' / W77 03.117'

The Hike

In a city of monuments and imposing edifices, Washington's stream valley parks persist as small oases of nature. Tree-shaded corridors form a loop around Georgetown, where inconspicuous streams pass through city neighborhoods en route to the Potomac River and Rock Creek. The forests shading them are much loved by their neighbors as running paths, community gardens, and dog-walking routes. Mature stands of tulip poplar, beech, and sycamore trees provide shelter for the urban wildlife quartet: raccoon, fox, opossum, and deer. Understory shrubs—many others exotic and invasive (and running riot)—attract songbirds that feast on the berry-producing plants.

The stream valley parks that surround Georgetown present the best opportunity to link many disparate parks and trails into a single route. It begins with Rock Creek Park, the granddaddy of them all. The Parkway Trail along Rock Creek, Glover-Archibold Trail along Foundry Branch, and Battery Kemble Trail along its namesake stream are the three pillars. These are north-to-south routes that follow streams winding through city neighborhoods to meet the slack waters of the Potomac beneath Georgetown Heights.

URBAN HIKING

Within the first mile into this route, hikers will confront the busy, four-lane-wide Connecticut Avenue. As the crow flies, the route continues straight across the street. But as city law dictates, our described route turns right (north) to the nearest traffic light and crosswalk. D.C. traffic laws state: "Between adjacent intersections controlled by traffic control signal devices or by police officers, pedestrians shall not cross the roadway at any place except in a crosswalk." And so it is with all of our city walking directions: Where there is an option between the shortcut or the law, we chose the law. Not every road crossing on this route is controlled by signal devices or other means. In these instances, traffic laws dictate that pedestrians outside a crosswalk must yield the right-of-way to vehicles, and they should cross at right angles to the sidewalk. Learn more about laws related to pedestrians and traffic laws at http://dmv.dc.gov/info/DMV Municipal Regulations.shtm.

Linking them are small east–west connectors: the Melvin Hazen Trail, the Wesley Heights Trail, the Chesapeake and Ohio National Historic Trail, the Whitehaven Trail, and the Dumbarton Oaks Trail. These routes cross the grain of terrain. They're hilly and winding, where the stream valley trails are straight and descending. It is on these routes that you'll get your exercise as you climb out of one valley and descend into the next.

Exhibit A for how unpredictable this walk will be: Within the first 0.5 mile, you will start the hike at Peirce Mill in Rock Creek Park, a gristmill and one of the earliest industries of the Washington, D.C., area. Pass through open fields at Picnic Area 1.

Enter the woods along Melvin Hazen Branch, the first stream valley park of this route. (It's a beauty: narrow, steep, and windy.) Follow a trail that rock-hops the stream and, after the last picture-perfect wading pool, climb up the stream slope. Skirt the back wall of an apartment building and emerge onto Connecticut Avenue. In quick order, navigate four lanes of zip-zip-zip traffic and walk up Rodman Street and its row of tidy single-family homes. Where the sidewalk ends, keep walking, and there, on the right, spy a wood sign with yellow words. (Here, when we took this hike, we re-entered the cool shade of the wood and watched, mouths agape, as a fox coolly padded downhill to the stream. Our exclamations startled the small canine, and it scooted out of sight. For the next 0.5 mile, until the trail rose once more out of wooded stream valley to another city street, this flash of wildlife consumed our imagination.)

▶ **KID APPEAL**

The restored Peirce Mill in Rock Creek Park demonstrates how colonial-era millers ground wheat into flour. The mill's wooden parts are restored, and there's a millstone powered from a stream. Next door in Peirce Barn, kids can try on old-fashioned clothes and play with nineteenth-century toys.

These urban trails cross roadways.

The city's stream valley parks hold moments of beauty. As the days lengthen and temperatures rise, spring beauty and cut-leaved toothwort will poke up through the leaf litter of the forest floors. Six or seven months later, in autumn, tulip poplar leaves turn yellow, and maple leaves turn red. In late winter, the American beech tree still clings to its paper-thin leaves that sound like a gentle maraca when the wind rustles the branches.

Exotic non-native species cloak trees along Glover-Archibold Trail.

Glover-Archibold Park is named for two icons of Washington, D.C., society, Charles Carroll Glover and Anne Archibold. Charles Carroll Glover was a banker and philanthropist better known for spearheading the creation of Rock Creek Park and construction of the National Cathedral in the late 1800s. Anne Archibold was a Standard Oil heiress who bequeathed the land for public use.

DUMBARTON OAKS

You've descended through stream valleys, crossed roads, and passed through culverts, but the landscaped trail through Dumbarton Oaks is something altogether different. Here, stone benches line little nooks etched into the hillside. The streambed is channeled with precise masonry work. All of it is the legacy of Mildred and Robert Bliss, he a career diplomat, she a garden aficionado. They developed the Dumbarton Oaks property after buying it in the 1920s. Today their estate is divided between the National Park Service and a Harvard University research center for the study of gardens and the history of landscape architecture. More than twenty gardens on the property are open for public enjoyment.

It wasn't always this pretty. Washington's stream valley parks are holdovers from an era when a creek, any creek, was a city sewer. The raw waste dumped into them was swept away downstream. Smelly and foul, a potential source of disease and generally unpleasant, they were largely ignored. From this abuse, unintended consequences—unforeseen, you might argue—arose. As woodlands were cleared to accommodate a growing Washington and Georgetown community, trees in the stream valleys were spared. As hikers, we can enjoy the results.

Miles and Directions

0.0 START at Peirce Mill, a colonial-era gristmill. Follow a stone path down past the mill to a bike path that parallels the stream. Turn right (south) on the bike path, which is Western Ridge Trail. Pass beneath a bridge and walk past Picnic Area 1 on the right. Where the bike path crosses Rock Creek on a pedestrian bridge, turn right (west) and walk across a grass field to the edge of the forest.

0.2 Enter the woods on the Melvin Hazen Trail, a dirt footpath marked by a yellow blaze on a wooden post. (*Note:* Western Ridge Trail heads left [south] from this junction and is the return portion of this hike.)

0.7 Exit the woods onto Connecticut Avenue. Cross the street at a traffic light to the right, then double back on Connecticut as far as Rodman Street NW. Turn right (west) on Rodman and walk up the residential street.

0.9 Beyond where the sidewalk ends on Rodman Street, look right for a wooden sign marking the Melvin Hazen Trail. Reenter the woods here and immediately turn left at a T junction to descend to the stream on a single-track dirt path.

1.3 Emerge from the woods at Reno Road and Tilden Street NW. Turn left, cross Reno Road, and walk up Springland Lane.

1.5 Springland Lane ends in a cul-de-sac. Find a stone-laid path at the back of the paved circle and follow it up a small set of stairs. Turn right on a wide grass easement. This strip empties onto Idaho Avenue NW, a short residential street. Where Idaho ends, turn left onto Tilden Street. At Tilden and 37th Street, turn right and walk 2 blocks to Van Ness Street (crossing over Upton Street en route).

1.8 Turn left (west) on Van Ness Street.

2.0 Cross Wisconsin Avenue and walk downhill. In 0.1 mile, turn left onto a well-worn dirt path and cross a grassy field. There is a sign at this junction for Glover-Archibold Park. At the far end of the field, the park enters the woods and descends into the Foundry Branch stream valley.

2.7 Emerge from the woods and follow the dirt path across a grass field to Massachusetts Avenue. Cross diagonally right and reenter woods on the opposite side. The trail descends as a dirt footpath.

3.2 Cross Cathedral Avenue. Drop off the roadside on a set of stairs with handrails.

3.3 Cross New Mexico Avenue diagonally left at the intersection with Garfield Street. Descend back into the stream valley park on wide steps. When the trail levels, cross a footbridge.

3.5 Stay straight at a junction with a trail that intersects on the right.

3.7 Turn right (west) onto the Wesley Heights Trail. Cross Foundry Branch on stream rocks. The trail follows a small tributary of Foundry Branch as it climbs.

3.8 Cross the stream and climb the embankment to a T junction. Turn right and continue on the Wesley Heights Trail.

3.9 Exit the woods onto 44th Street, cross, and turn right (north) on the sidewalk. Walk 200 feet and turn left to descend a short flight of stairs. The trail thereafter is a dirt footpath. (*Note:* Trail markings here are scant; avoid an unmarked footpath that enters the woods directly opposite where you exit onto 44th Street.)

4.1 Cross Foxhall Road and reenter to descend into the woods at a wooden trail sign and a National Park Service boundary stick.

4.4 Cross 49th Street diagonally left and enter Battery Kemble Park. A lone yellow blaze on a tree marks the trailhead here, but the dirt trail is wide and self-evident. Descend to Battery Kemble Run, cross on a footbridge with railings, and climb the stream embankment to a T junction. Turn left (south) and follow a dirt footpath.

4.8 Cross MacArthur Boulevard to the Conduit Road Schoolhouse, a red building. Re-enter the woods on a dirt path to the left of this building. (*Note:* Built in 1864 and operational until the 1920s, the schoolhouse is on the National Register of Historic Places and presently houses the Discovery Creek Children's Museum of Washington.)

5.0 Rock-hop Battery Kemble Run to where it passes beneath Canal Road via a culvert. Where it emerges on the other side of the road, climb over a wooden barrier fence and enter Fletcher's Boat House in C&O Canal National Historic Park. Cross the C&O Canal on a footbridge. Turn left (east) onto the canal towpath. (*FYI:* There is a concession stand that sells hot dogs and drinks at Fletcher's Boat House.)

6.7 Descend off the towpath via a long flight of stairs, turn right, and pass beneath the canal via a pedestrian tunnel. Follow the paved path around and up to Canal Road. At the sidewalk, turn right, cross a bridge, and then turn right again onto a dirt path etched into a grass field. This is the southern end of Glover-Archibold Park. Within a few hundred yards, the trail passes beneath an old trestle and enters the woods.

7.2 Climb through an open field to Reservoir Road at 44th Street. Cross Reservoir Road and reenter the park. The dirt footpath descends and follows Foundry Branch.

7.6 Turn right onto Whitehaven Trail.

7.8 Veer left at a fork in the trail. In the next 0.1 mile, turn left and avoid an unmarked, but well-traveled, path that splits right.

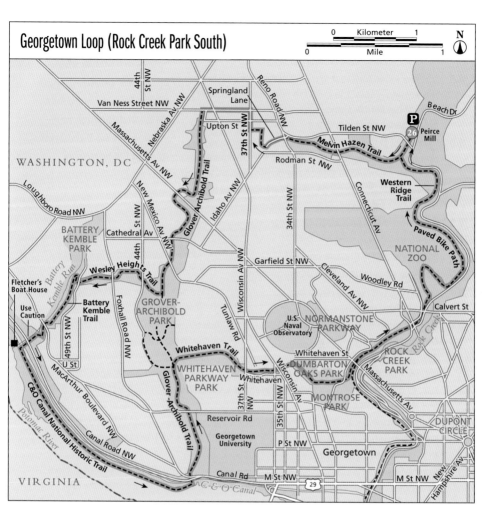

Kilometer
0   1

Mile
0   1

N

8.0   Enter a field after passing a fenced-in community garden. Cross the field diagonally right and, at the far end, beyond a water fountain, reenter the woods. Immediately after, watch for a trail that enters from the right, and pass straight through a four-way trail intersection.

8.2   Enter a small park and follow a well-worn footpath to the sidewalk on 37th Street. Cross the road, keeping a Metro bus shelter to your right. Reenter the woods between Whitehaven on the right and U Street on the left. Pass beneath a residential power line easement and climb a long set of stairs up a steep hillside. (*Stay alert:* The 0.2 mile of trail between 37th Street to Wisconsin Avenue is not well marked. At the top of the steps, avoid an unmarked left-branching trail. A few feet past this, turn left at an unmarked trail junction. Only after this turn are the yellow trail blazes visible. If you miss this turn, the trail drops steeply down to Whitehaven Parkway.)

8.4   Cross 35th Street, pass through a field, and cross Wisconsin Avenue. Walk down Whitehaven Street and, at the base of this dead-end street, look diagonally right across the street for a wooden sign that marks the entrance to Dumbarton Oaks Park.

8.6 Enter Dumbarton Oaks Park on a yellow-blazed dirt footpath.

8.7 Stay straight at a junction with the Normanstone Trail.

8.8 At a fork in the trail, veer right and cross a stream on two wooden planks. The trail from here features masonry walls, stone benches, and small alcoves. The stream, too, has its banks lined with stone.

9.0 Pass out of Dumbarton Oaks Park onto a paved road. Swing left and downhill, cross the road, and reenter the woods on the opposite side on a wide dirt road. As you descend through the woods, the stream is on your left side.

9.1 Cross the stream on a wood footbridge with railings. Descend to Rock Creek and swing left (north) to follow the stream valley on the Parkway Trail, which is a narrow dirt footpath.

9.3 Pass beneath the massive bridge that carries Massachusetts Avenue across Rock Creek.

9.5 Continue straight past the Normanstone Trail.

9.7 Exit the dirt path onto a paved bike trail. Turn left (north) and follow the paved walkway, which is used by joggers, walkers, in-line skaters, and bikers.

10.0 Cross a ramp road that rises left to Connecticut Avenue. Past here, the path crosses beneath Taft Bridge, which carries Connecticut Avenue over Rock Creek.

10.2 Turn left just before Rock Creek Parkway enters a tunnel. Pass through a gate marking the entrance to the National Zoo. (*Note:* From May through August, this gate is open from 6:00 a.m. to 8:00 p.m. From September through April, the gate is open 6:00 a.m. to 6:00 p.m. It is closed on Christmas.)

11.8 Veer left off the paved bike path onto Western Ridge Trail, which follows the streamside as a dirt path. The route is blazed green. Within 0.1 mile of this split, Western Ridge splits into a "strenuous" or "moderate" route. A trail sign indicates each route. Choose either.

12.0 Exit the woods in the grass field of Picnic Area 1. Turn right and walk across grass to the paved bike path. Turn left (north) on the path (avoiding the bridge that carries the bike path south across Rock Creek).

12.3 HIKE ENDS at Peirce Mill.

The name Dumbarton dates back to the original land patent of 1703 in what is today Georgetown, given to Ninian Beall, a Scotsman. He named the high rock promontory for Dumbarton Rock in his homeland.

OPTIONS

The Red Line stop at Tenleytown–AU Metro lands you on Wisconsin Avenue. Walk south to the intersection with Tilden Avenue, turn right, and walk down Tilden 0.1 mile to the north entrance to Glover-Archibold Park. (Pick up *Miles and Directions* at mile 2.0.) If you choose this start option, you can shorten the loop by eliminating Whitehaven Parkway, Dumbarton Oaks, and the West Ridge Trail. After turning north from the C&O Canal National Historic Trail onto Glover-Archibold Trail, stay straight on G-A Trail until you return to Tilden Avenue. Retrace your steps to the Tenleytown–AU Metro.

Hike Information

Local information: Destination DC, Washington, D.C.; (202) 789-7000; www.washington.org

Local events/attractions: The National Zoo, 3001 Connecticut Ave. NW, Washington, D.C.; (202) 633-4888; http://nationalzoo.si.edu. The nation's zoo is adjacent to the hike and is part of the Smithsonian Institution.

Good eats: The National Zoo has several cafes and snack carts where you can get hamburgers, salads, pizza, and subs.

Local outdoor stores: Patagonia Washington DC, 1048 Wisconsin Ave. NW, Washington, DC, (202) 333-1776; www.patagonia.com

REI Washington DC Flagship Store, 201 M Street NE, Washington, DC; (202) 543-2040; www.rei.com

Hike tours: Rock Creek Park rangers lead programs throughout the year.

Organizations: Potomac Appalachian Trail Club (PATC), 118 Park St. SE, Vienna, VA; (703) 242-0315; www.patc.net. Maintains many of the trails and produces a map.

27 National Mall Monuments

Nearly 2 miles in length, anchored by memorials from end to end, the National Mall today embodies the spirit, if not the exact design, of Pierre-Charles L'Enfant's original vision for Washington, D.C.: a grand lawn and boulevard that is both a gathering place and a symbol of American democracy. There are as many ways to explore the Mall as there are visitors. Our route, from first footsteps to last, traces the evolution of "America's front lawn" from yesteryear's dirt roads and open canals to today's green space and iconic monuments. By trip's end, you'll have visited thirteen memorials and monuments—a monumental feat unto itself.

Start: From the Tidal Basin Inlet bridge on Ohio Drive SW. *Alternate start:* If arriving on the Mall via Metro, start at the Washington Monument ticket office on 15th Street NW.

Distance: 4.6-mile loop, with an option of adding a 4.3-mile loop through East Potomac Park

Approximate hiking time: 2 hours for each loop

Difficulty: Easy due to paved paths, no elevation gain, and services like snack bars, bathrooms, park benches, and water fountains

Trail surface: Paved footpaths and roads

Seasons: May through Nov. Expect larger than normal crowds on weekends, and in May when the cherry blossoms bloom.

Other trail users: Pedestrians, joggers, bike riders, tourists

Handicapped accessibility: Most of the Mall is handicapped accessible. The Big Three memorials—Jefferson, Washington, and Lincoln—have elevators.

Canine compatibility: Leashed dogs are allowed on the National Mall, but not inside specific monuments or memorials. The lone exception is the Franklin Delano Roosevelt Memorial. Dogs are not allowed on the walkways through the Vietnam Veterans, World War II, or Korean War Veterans National Memorial.

Land status: National park

Fees and permits: None

Schedule: 24 hours a day

Facilities: The Jefferson, Washington, and Lincoln Memorials have public restrooms, visitor centers, and gift shops. The official visitor center for the entire National Mall & Memorial Park is located on 17th Avenue near the intersection with Independence.

Maps: DeLorme *Maryland/Delaware Atlas & Gazetteer:* Page 46 D3. USGS 7.5 minute series: *Washington West, DC, MD, VA.* National Park Service map of the downtown Mall is available at the park visitor center or any information booth at the Jefferson and Washington Memorials.

Trail contacts: National Mall & Memorial Parks, 900 Ohio Dr. SW, Washington, D.C. 20024; (202) 426-6841; www.nps.gov/nama

Finding the trailhead: From I-395 (Virginia): Drive north on combined I-395/US 1 across the Potomac River. Bear right to stay on I-395 where the highways split and US 1 goes straight. Take the next exit, on the right, for Potomac Park and Park Police (commercial trucks are prohibited). At the bottom of the ramp, turn right on Buckeye Drive SW. In 0.1 mile, turn right on Ohio Drive SW. Park in any one of the large parking lots on the right in the next 0.3 mile. After parking, walk north on a paved footpath along the Potomac River. Reach the trailhead, at the Tidal Basin Inlet bridge, in 0.2 mile.

Alternate parking: If the parking lots are full, continue straight (north) on Ohio Drive SW. Cross the Tidal Basin Inlet. The section of Ohio Drive SW between the Tidal Basin and Independence Drive SW features on-street parking. After parking, walk south on a paved path along the Potomac to reach the trailhead at the Tidal Basin Inlet bridge.

Public transportation: Orange and Blue Lines have service to Smithsonian Station. Exit the station onto the National Mall, turn south, and walk toward the Washington Monument. Begin *Miles and Directions* from the Washington Monument. Trailhead GPS: Tidal Basin Inlet: N38 52.808' / W77 02.420'; Washington Monument: N38 53.364' / W77 01.993'

The Hike

Electric describes the scene as you explore the National Mall. Throngs move in seemingly all directions. Kites swoop, soar, and swoop again overhead. On huge open lawns, kids kick a soccer ball. Bike riders and joggers weave in between people whose eyes are cast upward, soaking in monuments and memorials. The Mall is big enough to accommodate this activity—and much more. Yet if explored thoroughly, it turns out to be a place dotted with small curiosities and quiet, tucked-away spots that make it feel personal and intimate.

Like moths drawn to the light, our footsteps carry us to the base of the Washington Monument. This is not just the defining architecture of the Mall, but of all Washington. Whether from the heights of Georgetown or the Potomac River's edge in Virginia, it dominates the skyline. That's no accident. City ordinances dictate that no building can be built to exceed the monument's 555-foot height.

The story of its construction could occupy a television miniseries. Pierre L'Enfant, the French engineer who designed the capital city in 1791, envisioned a monument to Washington as part of his "monument core." His idea of a bronze sculpture—Washington on a horse—gave way to the obelisk. From afar, you might notice the stone is two different shades, lighter below and darker on top. It's about 150 feet up from the ground and marks the spot where construction stopped for twenty years, from 1858 to 1878 (including the Civil War years). When construction resumed, the quarry stone could not be matched, resulting in the different shades.

Walking around the base of the Washington Monument, we experienced a sense of vertigo as we looked skyward, and it seemed as if it was leaning, leaning . . . leaning. Forcing our eyes toward the ground, we spotted a small piece of square granite sticking out of the ground. A sign on this 2-foot-by-2-foot stone identified it as Jefferson Pier. If, in looking around, you wonder why a docking pier was located in this landlocked spot, you're not alone.

When we did research about the National Mall later, it became the thread that unraveled the long history of the National Mall and its evolution.

Jefferson Pier once stood on the banks of Tiber Creek, a small tributary that flowed south past Capitol Hill and emptied into the Potomac in an area known as Potomac Flats (or, as one congressman once declared, a "damn swamp"). If, in

World War II Memorial

THE TWO HALVES OF THE NATIONAL MALL

The National Mall, 2 miles in length, is anchored on the east end by the U.S. Capitol and on the west by the Lincoln Memorial. Halfway between is the Washington Monument. Bounding it to the north is the White House, and to the south, the Jefferson Memorial. It's easily divided into two parts. The eastern half from the Capitol to the Washington Monument is Museum Row, where more than ten museums line the Mall, including the Smithsonian Institute. The bulk of this hike takes place in the western half of the Mall, the monument core, more formally known as West Potomac Park. The long, skinny Reflecting Pool is the centerpiece; around it stand all the well-known memorials, from the oldest (Washington) to the newest (the Martin Luther King Jr. Memorial).

the mid-1800s, you stood at the pier and looked west, you would be looking out over a swamp that was part of the tidal Potomac. The creek soon became a canal, and for a time it served as an open sewer. The roads around it were dirt and the homes shanties and shacks. Starting in 1872, under an ambitious public works program, the canal was enclosed in concrete (its route today is approximated by Constitution Avenue). Then, in 1882, the U.S. Army Corps of Engineers began filling in Potomac Flats. The swampland turned into land that would later become West Potomac Park.

Tiber **is a name that harkens back to the Tiber River in Italy, and Rome, the city that was built on its banks. Tiber Creek, the small tributary that flowed through Washington, D.C., was called Goose Creek in colonial times, but** *Tiber* **better captured the grandeur L'Enfant envisioned for America's capital city—the new Rome.**

The pier itself? Although it was on the banks of a navigable creek, it was not meant as a boat tie-up. Rather, Jefferson ordered it installed to mark a Prime Meridian for the new United States. It marks the spot where a line drawn due south from the White House intersects with a line drawn due west from the U.S. Capitol. This was mile marker zero, the point from which miles east and, more significantly, west were measured. (The Prime Meridian now is in Greenwich, England.)

It is somehow fitting for a hike that celebrates men and women, their contributions and sacrifices, to be entirely on man-made ground (this including the optional East Potomac Park leg down to Hains Point). One of the latest grand monuments to be erected here is the World War II Memorial. Set at the east end of the Reflecting Pool, the memorial is all white marble, dramatic sculptures, and powerfully wrought inscriptions of patriotism, sacrifice, and duty set amid pools and fountains. A different sort of inspiration awaits in nearby Constitution Gardens, a tree-shaded oasis on the north side of the Reflecting Pool. This memorial, grassy and passive, has a small pool and an island reached via a footbridge. Here, big willow trees droop long wavy branches over a modest display honoring the fifty-six signers of the Declaration of Independence. Canada geese cruise the pond waters near to shore.

If, after hitting the Vietnam Veterans, Lincoln, and Korean War Veterans Memorials—and with the Franklin Delano Roosevelt still to come—you start feeling monument fatigue, follow our footsteps to the D.C. War Memorial. It is on the south side of the Reflecting Pool. A microforest of tall oak trees shades a small rotunda supported by Roman-like columns. It was built in honor of Washington, D.C.'s, World War I veterans, of which 26,000 served. It is set off from both road and sidewalk, and therefore it is less noticeable. As if transported, we walked actual dirt paths through the trees and emerged in the bright sunshine that lighted and warmed the rotunda.

If there was ever a place on the National Mall to read a book beneath a tree, this would be it. And if we could recommend a title, it would be *Spring in Washington* by Louis J. Halle, a natural history of how a city springs to life anew each year.

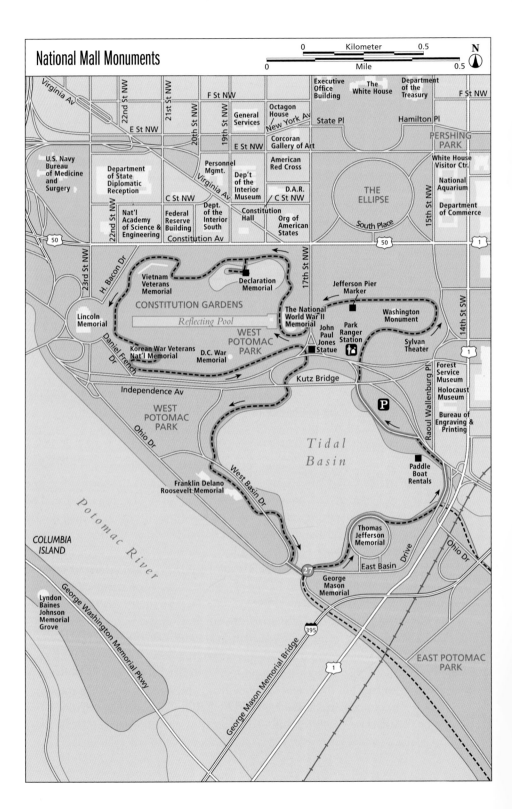

National Mall Monuments

0   Kilometer   0.5
0   Mile   0.5

N

Virginia Av

22nd NW

21st St NW

20th St

19th St NW

F St NW

E St NW

General
Services

Octagon
House
New York Av

Executive
Office
Building

The
White House

Department
of the
Treasury

F St NW

State Pl

Hamilton Pl

PERSHING
PARK

Corcoran
Gallery of Art

E St NW

U.S. Navy
Bureau
of Medicine
and
Surgery

Department
of State
Diplomatic
Reception

Personnel
Mgmt.

American
Red Cross

White House
Visitor Ctr.

Virginia Av

Dep't
of the
Interior
Museum

D.A.R.

National
Aquarium

THE
ELLIPSE

15th St NW

C St NW

22nd St NW

C St NW

Department
of Commerce

Nat'l
Academy
of Science &
Engineering

Federal
Reserve
Building

Dept.
of the
Interior
South

Constitution
Hall

Org of
American
States

South Place

Constitution Av

50

50

1

23rd St NW

H. Bacon Dr

Vietnam
Veterans
Memorial

Declaration
Memorial

17th St NW

Jefferson Pier
Marker

14th St SW

CONSTITUTION GARDENS

Reflecting Pool

The National
World War II
Memorial

Washington
Monument

Lincoln
Memorial

WEST
POTOMAC
PARK

John
Paul
Jones
Statue

Park
Ranger
Station

Sylvan
Theater

Daniel French Dr

Korean War Veterans
Nat'l Memorial

D.C. War
Memorial

Forest
Service
Museum

Independence Av

Kutz Bridge

Raoul Wallenburg Pl

Holocaust
Museum

WEST
POTOMAC
PARK

P

Bureau of
Engraving &
Printing

Ohio Dr

Tidal
Basin

Paddle
Boat
Rentals

West Basin Dr

POTOMAC RIVER

Franklin Delano
Roosevelt Memorial

COLUMBIA
ISLAND

Thomas
Jefferson
Memorial

Drive

Ohio Dr

27

East Basin

George Washington Memorial Pkwy

Lyndon
Baines
Johnson
Memorial
Grove

George
Mason
Memorial

395

EAST POTOMAC
PARK

George Mason Memorial Bridge

1

Miles and Directions

0.0 START from the Tidal Basin Inlet bridge on Ohio Drive SW. At the east end of the bridge, turn right (north) and cross East Basin Drive to enter the George Mason Memorial.

0.1 Recross East Basin Drive SW, walking north, then veer right on a sidewalk that skirts the edge of the Tidal Basin beneath the shade of cherry trees.

0.4 Enter the Jefferson Memorial at the base of a large flight of stairs leading to the rotunda. After exploring, return to the base of these stairs and turn right on the sidewalk that encircles the Tidal Basin. As you circle toward Independence Avenue, pass over the Tidal Basin outlet and a paddleboat concession.

1.0 Cross straight over Independence Avenue and walk past the National Park Service offices for the National Mall and Memorial Garden. (*Note:* This office is not the main visitor center for the park.)

1.2 Turn right (east) and begin a long walk around the base of the Washington Monument.

1.4 Pass the ticket office for the Washington Monument. Continue circling the north side of the monument. Walk straight (west) down the Mall toward the World War II Memorial. Pass the Jefferson Pier marker en route. (*FYI:* There are restrooms in the ticket office building.)

1.8 Cross straight over 17th Street and enter the World War II Memorial. After exploring, exit the memorial on its right (north) side and follow a sidewalk that leads up a gentle slope.

2.0 Enter the Constitution Gardens. Bear right (north) on a path that circles a pond on your left.

2.2 Reach the 56 Signers of the Declaration of Independence Memorial by turning left (south) and crossing a footbridge onto a small island. After exploring, retrace your footsteps over the bridge and turn left (west).

2.6 Enter the Vietnam Veterans Memorial near the Vietnam Women's Memorial. Exit at the west end of the memorial, near the *Three Servicemen* sculpture. Follow Harry Bacon Drive west toward the Lincoln Memorial.

2.9 Reach the base of the Lincoln Memorial. A long flight of stairs leads up to the portico. After exploring, return to this spot, turn right (south), and follow a sidewalk that crosses a road. Your route parallels Daniel French Drive, but you veer left, following signs for the Korean War Veterans Memorial.

3.1 Reach the Korean War Veterans Memorial. After exploring, return to Daniel French Drive and follow a sidewalk left. At an intersection with Independence Avenue, turn left (east) and continue walking.

3.3 Veer left off the sidewalk onto a dirt path.

3.5 Reach the D.C. War Memorial, a circular portico lined with Roman-style arches and shaded by large oak trees. After exploring, exit the memorial by following a sidewalk past the bathrooms.

3.7 Reach the National Mall Visitors Center on 17th Street. Turn right (south) and head toward Independence Avenue.

3.8 In succession, cross the westbound and eastbound lanes of Independence Avenue. (*Note:* That's a statue of John Paul Jones in a traffic island at the junction of 17th Street and Independence Avenue.)

3.9 Turn right on a sidewalk that skirts the Tidal Basin. (*FYI:* On the left you'll find the first Japanese cherry tree given to the United States as a gesture of friendship by the city of Tokyo, in 1912. It grows in a small grove on the right, marked by a small stone.)

4.2 Turn right and climb a staircase into the Franklin Delano Roosevelt Memorial. After exploring, exit the memorial at the east end and resume walking along the Tidal Basin.

4.6 HIKE ENDS at the bridge over the Tidal Basin inlet.

OPTIONS

East Potomac Park is a narrow peninsula that extends southeast along the Potomac River. It's best known for the public golf course and as a bike-riding circuit. You can add another 4.3 miles to your walk by including a loop through the park. Trails are on paved sidewalks, which you'll share with anglers and parents with strollers. Hains Point, at the southern tip, is named for Maj. Peter Conover Hains of the U.S. Army Corps, who oversaw creation of East and West Potomac Parks out of the mudflats of the Potomac River.

Hike Information

Local information: Destination DC, Washington, D.C.; (202) 789-7000; www.washington.org

Local events/attractions: The National Cherry Blossom Festival at the height of the blooms in mid-March to mid-April. The Blossom Kite Festival is held annually during the festival at the Washington Monument. www.nationalcherryblossomfestival.org

Eastern Market, 7th Street and North Carolina Avenue SE, Washington, D.C.; www.easternmarket-dc.org. Local merchants offer produce, flowers, baked goods, and meats, inside during the week and in an open-air farmers' market on weekends, year-round.

Good eats: There are refreshment stands and food trucks outside the monuments,, or you can have lunch inside one of the Smithsonian museum cafes.

Local outdoor stores: Patagonia Washington DC, 1048 Wisconsin Ave. NW, Washington, DC, (202) 333-1776; www.patagonia.com

REI Washington DC Flagship Store, 201 M Street NE, Washington, DC; (202) 543-2040; www.rei.com

Hike tours: The park offers ranger-led walking tours, as do many private tour companies. Dates and times for NPS walks and programs are found in the *Mall Times,* a monthly newspaper issued by the National Park Service.

Other resources: *City of Trees: The Complete Field Guide to the Trees of Washington, D.C.,* by Melanie Choukas-Bradley and Polly Alexander

28 Rock Creek Park North

As far back as 1866, people recognized Rock Creek's natural beauty and fought to protect it. It would be another quarter century before an actual park came into being. Long, narrow, and heavily wooded, this 10-mile-long park is a twisty green stripe through a sea of urbanism. It is also a magnet for hikers, joggers, horseback riders, and others. The spacious northern section of the park is big enough to hold them all. Here, it is hilly and wooded, with room to roam.

Start: From the Rock Creek Nature Center

Distance: 7.1-mile loop

Approximate hiking time: 3 hours

Difficulty: Moderate due to distance and some confusing trail junctions

Trail surface: Paved paths, dirt woodland paths, roads

Seasons: Best in summer

Other trail users: Horseback riders, joggers, walkers, in-line skaters, and bikers

Handicapped accessibility: The Edge of Wood Trail at the nature center is paved and has a rope guide for the visually impaired.

Canine compatibility: Leashed dogs permitted

Land status: National park

Fees and permits: No entrance fee or permits, although a fee and permit are required for groups using the picnic area

Schedule: The park is open daily during daylight hours. The nature center is open Wed through Sun 9:00 a.m. to 5:00 p.m. and closed Thanksgiving, Christmas, and New Year's Day.

Facilities: There are restrooms at the nature center and a chemical toilet at the Boundary Bridge parking area. The nature center features natural-history displays and a planetarium. Throughout Rock Creek Park are historic buildings, tennis courts, a golf course, and an equestrian center.

Maps: DeLorme *Maryland/Delaware Atlas & Gazetteer:* Page 46 B3. USGS 7.5 minute series: *Washington West, DC, MD, VA.* Also, the Potomac Appalachian Trail Club's (PATC) *Map N: Rock Creek Park Area.*

Trail contacts: Rock Creek Park, 5200 Glover Rd., Washington, D.C. 20008; (202) 895-6000; www.nps.gov/rocr

Special considerations: The park closes sections of Beach Drive to cars from 7:00 a.m. to 7:00 p.m. on weekends and federal holidays for recreational use by hikers, bicyclists, runners, and in-line skaters. Closed sections are: Beach Drive north from Broad Branch Road to Military Road; from Picnic Area 10 to Wise Road; and from West Beach Drive to the Boundary Bridge parking area. Bingham Drive and Sherrill Drive are also closed to cars on weekends and federal holidays.

In the south region of the park, the Rock Creek and Potomac Parkway traffic flow is altered for weekday rush hour traffic. From Connecticut Avenue it is one-way going south between 6:45 and 9:30 a.m., and one-way going north from 3:45 to 6:30 p.m. Also, access streets like Glover Road, Ross Drive, Bingham Drive, and Sherrill Drive are not maintained after heavy snowfall or in icy conditions.

Finding the trailhead: From Northern Virginia: Cross the Potomac on I-66/US 50 (the Theodore Roosevelt Memorial Bridge). Take the Independence Avenue exit (right lane) and, after merging onto Independence, in quick succession turn right and merge onto Rock Creek and Potomac Parkway.

In 0.7 mile, continue straight at an intersection with Virginia Avenue. As road signs indicate Connecticut Avenue approaching, stay right and follow signs for the National Zoo and Beach Drive. (*Note:* The Rock Creek and Potomac Parkway ends at Connecticut Avenue; Beach Drive becomes the main north–south route through Rock Creek Park.) Continue straight on Beach Drive at Klingle Avenue on the left and Piney Branch Parkway on the right. There is a traffic light at Beach Drive and Park Road/ Tilden Street. In 0.3 mile past this, bear left at an intersection with Blagden Avenue. One hundred yards past this, turn left off Beach Drive onto Broad Branch Road. (*Note:* Beach Drive from this point north to Military Road is closed on weekends and holidays.) Cross Rock Creek and immediately turn right on Glover Road, following signs for the Rock Creek Nature Center. In less than a mile, fork left and uphill, avoiding Ross Drive, which forks right and downhill. In 0.8 mile past this fork, turn right into the nature center parking area.

From downtown Washington, D.C.: Follow directions above from the intersection of the Rock Creek and Potomac Parkway and Virginia Avenue. Or, take New Hampshire Avenue north from DuPont Circle for 0.6 mile. Turn left onto 16th Street NW and, in 3 miles, turn right onto an entrance ramp for Military Road. In 1 mile, turn left onto Glover Road. In 0.5 mile, turn left into the nature center parking area.

From Maryland and I-495 (Capital Beltway): Take exit 31B / Georgia Avenue, following signs for Georgia Avenue South and Silver Spring. Once on Georgia Avenue, stay in either of the two right lanes so that, in 0.3 mile from I-495, you can exit right onto 16th Street. In 3.1 miles, turn right and merge onto Military Road. In 1 mile, turn left onto Glover Road. In 0.5 mile, turn left into the nature center parking area. Trailhead GPS: N38 57.594' / W77 03.103'

The Hike

Rock Creek Park, at its broadest, is only a mile wide. It is a nearly 10-mile-long narrow stream valley park that passes in this Google Earth age as the long green swath of trees separating downtown Washington, D.C., and Georgetown. But to look at it as a single homogenous unit is to miss the small details that make moving between the upland woods and the streamside floodplains a joy.

Unmarked, but well used, are several fishermen's paths through floodplains along Rock Creek. If you're hiking the Valley Trail, you'll find one in a wide bend in the river north of Riley Spring Bridge; the other is between West Beach Drive and Boundary Bridge. They are the proverbial low road, alternatives to the higher, drier route of the official Valley Trail.

One advantage in following them is personal satisfaction. These unmarked paths bring you close to the creek. On a sandbar, a few tree logs that washed downstream in a long-ago high flood sit high and dry, perfect perches for a snack and relaxing. The stream is a melodious riffle, not so loud that you can't hear bird chatter. A hiker told us that come autumn, there's a hint of Monet in the air. Rock Creek in calm water reflects back yellow and red leaves on overhanging trees, making a shimmering mirage of color.

In terms of plants, the floodplain just feels different from the upland. Here, there is more smooth alder but less holly, which is abundant in the understory of the drier forests that cover the stream valley's sloping hills. There is American hornbeam, a skinny tree whose rippling trunk and tight gray bark give the appearance of muscles. It's an apt comparison; this tough, heavy wood was preferred for making the handles of axes and sledgehammers. Yellow poplar and American beech are two of the main trees you'll find in an upland forest, but in the floodplain, they're replaced by eastern black walnut. Donald Culross Peatttie, in his book *A Natural History of Trees,* ranks black walnut second only behind pecan in usefulness. The nontimber forest product program at Virginia Tech lists a number of uses for the tree: Indians chewed the bark to ease toothaches, and processed eastern black walnut shells are "soft grit abrasives" perfect for "cleaning jet engines, electronic circuit boards, ships, and automobile gear systems."

The northern section of Rock Creek Park is the perfect spot to "converse" with both the upland woods and streamside floodplains. A long stretch of Western Ridge Trail, north from Bingham Drive to Beach Drive, covers hilly terrain. It is the largest chunk of unspoiled woodland in the park, with only Wise Road bisecting it. This is the territory of the great horned owl and the screech owl.

The park's namesake: "Rock Creek"

A detour from this heavy upland forest down along Pinehurst Branch leads to other discoveries. By October, hackberry trees are in fruit along the Pinehurst Branch Trail, offering songbirds, like the cedar waxwing, valuable fuel. There are three shallow-water fords across the branch on our route; the last is a scramble up the stream bank to dry ground. The trail uphill is a narrow path that in summer almost disappears beneath the crowded shrub understory. In no time, you're standing atop a knoll amid red oak and tulip poplar. In this spot, in a park that records two million recreational visits annually, you can hear an acorn drop.

Miles and Directions

0.0 START from the front entrance of the Rock Creek Nature Center. Follow a paved path west past the Edge of Woods Trail on the right. Where the path splits into a T, turn right (north) onto the green-blazed Western Ridge Trail, which here shares the route with a paved bike path. A small sign at this junction points the way to Fort DeRussy, which is also to the right. Walk downhill to four-lane Military Road and cross straight over.

0.2 Turn right at an interpretive sign for Fort DeRussy. In the next 0.1 mile, you will veer left off the paved path as Western Ridge Trail becomes a wide dirt trail. Soon after this, make a right (north) turn at a double green blaze as Western Ridge Trail becomes a narrow woods trail. (*Side trip:* The wide dirt path that continues straight from this double green blaze is a horse trail. In 200 yards or so, it passes the ruins of Fort DeRussy, a Civil War–era defense. This is also the return leg of this hike.)

0.5 Turn left at a double green blaze for Western Ridge Trail. (*Note:* Straight ahead is Cross Trail 5 [CT 5], which descends to Millerhouse Ford on Rock Creek.)

0.6 Emerge from the woods and trace a horse pasture fence on your right. At the end of the fence line, turn right (north) and walk between the horse pasture and a community garden on the right. The trail meets a paved road. Turn left (west) on the road, keeping a line of stubby wooden posts on your right.

0.7 Turn right onto a paved path marked by a wooden post with a green blaze for Western Ridge Trail. (*Note:* This path is immediately past a gated road that will parallel the trail for a few hundred yards.)

0.9 Cross Bingham Drive diagonally left. On the far side, Western Ridge Trail is still a paved path. Within a hundred yards, follow Western Ridge Trail as it forks left. Walk another 20 feet and turn right (north) on Western Ridge, which is now a path of dirt and crushed rock.

1.1 Stay straight on green-blazed Western Ridge Trail at a junction with Cross Trail 3 (CT 3).

1.3 Western Ridge Trail veers right at a fork in the trail. Follow it a few feet downhill to a four-way trail junction. Turn right (east) onto the Pinehurst Branch Trail and descend to cross

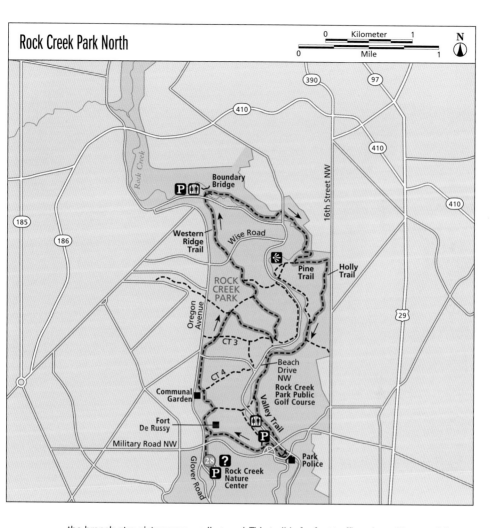

Rock Creek Park North

the branch at a picturesque wading pool. This trail is for foot traffic only and is one of the most scenic in the park.

1.6   Cross Pinehurst Branch again at another scenic spot. The stream, now on your left side, makes a wide bend. At low water, exposed stream rocks are a nice place to perch and soak in the scenery.

1.7   Pinehurst Branch Trail reaches a four-way trail junction. Turn left (east) and descend the stream bank and cross Pinehurst Branch. On the opposite side, turn left (north) and start to climb an unnamed, unmarked footpath. The route is steep on a narrow footpath that in summer is nearly overrun by shrubs and small trees.

1.8   At a T junction with another unnamed, unmarked trail, turn left (west).

2.1   Turn right (north) onto the green-blazed Western Ridge Trail.

2.2   Stay straight (north) on Western Ridge Trail at a junction with Cross Trail 2 (CT 2), which heads downhill to the right to Riley Spring Bridge on Rock Creek.

Bicyclists

2.5 Cross Wise Road and reenter the woods on Western Ridge Trail, which here is a dirt footpath.

2.9 Western Ridge Trail ends at Beach Drive. Walk straight across the road, reentering the woods at a wood trail sign that marks the trailhead for the blue-blazed Valley Trail. Briefly, this dirt footpath skirts the Boundary Bridge parking area on your left. (*Note:* There is a chemical toilet at the parking area.)

3.0 Turn right (north) and follow Valley Trail, now a wide, graded path of dirt and crushed rock, across Rock Creek on the Boundary Bridge. A few feet past the bridge, veer right (east) off Valley Trail onto a well-trod, but unmarked, fisherman's path. (*Note:* The fisherman's path and Valley Trail are near West Beach Drive. We prefer the fisherman's path—the low road, if you will—because it keeps us close to the creek and is good for sightings of birds like great blue heron.)

3.6 Merge with the Valley Trail just before a bridge on West Beach Drive. Veer right onto the blue-blazed Valley Trail and pass beneath the bridge.

4.2 Climb the Valley Trail to a junction with the yellow-blazed Pine Trail. Turn left (east) onto Pine Trail and begin climbing. (*Side trip:* At this junction, turn right instead and walk 0.1 mile to an overlook onto Rock Creek. After enjoying the view, return to Pine Trail and resume this route.)

4.4 Pine Trail levels at a junction with Holly Trail. Turn right (south) onto Holly Trail and immediately begin to descend on a narrow dirt footpath. You'll climb into and out of a seasonal stream in a steep-sided gully. (*Note:* Straight uphill on Pine Trail leads to 16th Street.)

5.0 After a steep descent on Holly Trail, reach a T junction with the blue-blazed Valley Trail. Turn left (south) onto Valley Trail. Soon after, the trail passes beneath Sherrill Drive Bridge. Keep an eye out for a blue blaze on the bridge abutment.

5.1 Stay straight (south) on Valley Trail as Whittier Trail branches left (east). For the next 1.5 miles, it is a wide, flat streamside dirt path.

5.6 *Stay alert:* Follow the Valley Trail as it veers left (southeast) and uphill as a narrow, rocky footpath. (*Note:* The streamside trail that continues straight from this junction is Cross Trail 5 [CT 5]. It crosses Rock Creek at Milkhouse Ford.)

5.8 Pass by a park service bathroom on the right side of Valley Trail.

6.0 A series of switchbacks carries the Valley Trail off the hillside and down to Beach Drive. Turn left (south) and walk along the road shoulder beneath the Military Road bridge. When you see the road shoulder getting pinched into a narrow strip of grass by the looming hillside on your left, cross Beach Road and continue south on the paved bike path.

6.2 Reach the intersection of Joyce Road and Beach Drive. Turn right (west) onto Joyce Road. Cross Rock Creek and immediately, on the other side, turn right (north) onto a paved bike path. Follow it as it passes beneath Military Road. Rock Creek is through the trees off to the right.

6.4 Turn right (north) onto an unnamed horse trail that crosses the bike path. Walk a few feet to where the horse trail forks. Here, bear left and begin an uphill climb. (*Note:* The right fork of the trail goes north alongside Rock Creek to CT 5 and eventually Milkhouse Ford.)

6.8 Pass the spur trail to Fort DeRussy on the right. Within 200 yards, merge onto the green-blazed Western Ridge Trail by continuing to walk straight on the dirt trail. Avoid the green-blazed leg of Western Ridge Trail that heads right (north) at this merge. After walking a few hundred feet more, veer right onto a paved bike path, which shares the route with Western Ridge Trail.

6.9 Turn left (south) on the combined bike path/Western Ridge Trail. Walk downhill to Military Road and cross over. The path then climbs uphill alongside Glover Road.

7.0 Turn left at a sign for the nature center.

7.1 HIKE ENDS at the Rock Creek Nature Center.

Hike Information

Local information: Destination DC, 901 7th Street NW, 4th Floor, Washington, D.C.; (202) 789-7000; www.washington.org

Good eats: The Parkway Deli, 8317 Grubb Road, Silver Spring, MD; (301) 587-1427; www.theparkwaydeli.com

The Daily Dish, 8301 Grubb Road, Silver Spring, MD; (301) 588-6300; www.thedailydishrestaurant.com

Local outdoor stores: Patagonia Washington DC, 1048 Wisconsin Ave. NW, Washington, DC; (202) 333-1776; www.patagonia.com

REI Washington DC Flagship Store, 201 M Street NE, Washington, DC; (202) 543-2040; www.rei.com

Hike tours: Ranger-led horseback tours are offered in the park. There are also a host of ranger and Junior Ranger programs led from the nature center.

Organizations: Potomac Appalachian Trail Club (PATC), 118 Park St. SE, Vienna, VA; (703) 242-0315; www.patc.net. Maintains the Valley Trail, Western Ridge Trail, and the connecting trails.

The Art of Hiking

When standing nose to nose with a black bear, you're probably not too concerned with the issue of ethical behavior in the wild. No doubt you're just terrified. But let's be honest. How often are you nose to nose with a black bear? For most of us, a hike into the "wild" means loading up the SUV with expensive gear and driving to a toileted trailhead. Sure, you can mourn how civilized we've become—how GPS units have replaced natural instinct and Gore-Tex, true grit—but the silly gadgets of civilization aside, we have plenty of reasons to take pride in how we've matured. With survival now on the back burner, we've begun to realize—and it's about time—that we have a responsibility to protect, no longer just conquer, our wild places; that they, not we, are at risk. So please, do what you can. The following section will help you understand better what it means to "do what you can" while still making the most of your hiking experience. Anyone can take a hike, but hiking safely and well is an art requiring preparation and proper equipment.

Trail Etiquette

Zero impact. Always leave an area just like you found it—if not better than you found it. Avoid camping in fragile, alpine meadows and along the banks of streams and lakes. Use a camp stove versus building a wood fire. Pack out all of your trash and extra food. Bury human waste at least 100 feet from water sources under 6 to 8 inches of topsoil. Don't bathe with soap in a lake or stream—use prepackaged moistened towels to wipe off sweat and dirt, or bathe in the water without soap.

Stay on the trail. It's true, a path anywhere leads nowhere new, but purists will just have to get over it. Paths serve an important purpose: They limit impact on natural areas. Straying from a designated trail may seem innocent, but it can cause damage to sensitive areas—damage that may take years to recover, if it can recover at all. Even simple shortcuts can be destructive. So please, stay on the trail.

Leave no weeds. Noxious weeds tend to overtake other plants, which in turn affects animals and birds that depend on them for food. To minimize the spread of noxious weeds, hikers should regularly clean their boots, tents, packs, and hiking poles of mud and seeds. Also brush your dog to remove any weed seeds before heading off into a new area.

Keep your dog under control. You can buy a flexi-lead that allows your dog to go exploring along the trail, while allowing you the ability to reel him in should another hiker approach or should he decide to chase a rabbit. Always obey leash laws, and be sure to bury your dog's waste or pack it out in resealable plastic bags.

Respect other trail users. Often you're not the only one on the trail. With the rise in popularity of multiuse trails, you'll have to learn a new kind of respect beyond the nod and "hello" approach you may be used to. First investigate whether you're on a multiuse trail, and assume the appropriate precautions. When you encounter motorized vehicles (ATVs, motorcycles, and 4WDs), be alert. Though they should always

Jug Bay overlook (hike 8)

yield to the hiker, often they're going too fast or are too lost in the buzz of their engine to react to your presence. If you hear activity ahead, step off the trail just to be safe. Note that you're not likely to hear a mountain biker coming, so be prepared and know ahead of time whether you share the trail with them. Cyclists should always yield to hikers, but that's little comfort to the hiker. Be aware. When you approach horses or pack animals on the trail, always step quietly off the trail, preferably on the downhill side, and let them pass. If you're wearing a large backpack, it's often a good idea to sit down. To some animals, a hiker wearing a large backpack might appear threatening. Many national forests allow domesticated grazing, usually for sheep and cattle. Make sure your dog doesn't harass these animals, and respect ranchers' rights while you're enjoying yours.

Getting into Shape

Unless you want to be sore—and possibly have to shorten your trip or vacation—be sure to get in shape before a big hike. If you're terribly out of shape, start a walking program early, preferably eight weeks in advance. Start with a 15-minute walk during your lunch hour or after work and gradually increase your walking time to an hour. You should also increase your elevation gain. Walking briskly up hills really strengthens your leg muscles and gets your heart rate up. If you work in a storied office building, take the stairs instead of the elevator. If you prefer going to a gym, walk the treadmill or use a stair machine. You can further increase your strength and endurance by walking with a loaded backpack. Stationary exercises you might consider are squats, leg lifts, sit-ups, and push-ups. Other good ways to get in shape include biking, running, aerobics, and, of course, short hikes. Stretching before and after a hike keeps muscles flexible and helps avoid injuries.

Preparedness

It's been said that failing to plan means planning to fail. So do take the necessary time to plan your trip. Whether going on a short day hike or an extended backpack trip, always prepare for the worst. Simply remembering to pack a copy of the U.S. Army Survival Manual is not preparedness. Although it's not a bad idea if you plan on entering truly wild places, it's merely the tourniquet answer to a problem. You need to do your best to prevent the problem from arising in the first place. In order to survive— and to stay reasonably comfortable—you need to concern yourself with the basics: water, food, and shelter. Don't go on a hike without having these bases covered. And don't go on a hike expecting to find these items in the woods.

    Water. Even in frigid conditions, you need at least two quarts of water a day to function efficiently. Add heat and taxing terrain and you can bump that figure up to one gallon. That's simply a base to work from—your metabolism and your level of conditioning can raise or lower that amount. Unless you know your level, assume that you need one gallon of water a day. Now, where do you plan on getting the water?

    Preferably not from natural water sources. These sources can be loaded with intestinal disturbers, such as bacteria, viruses, and fertilizers. *Giardia lamblia*, the most common of these disturbers, is a protozoan parasite that lives part of its life cycle as a cyst in water sources. The parasite spreads when mammals defecate in water sources. Once ingested, *Giardia* can induce cramping, diarrhea, vomiting, and fatigue within two days to two weeks after ingestion. Giardiasis is treatable with prescription drugs. If you believe you've contracted giardiasis, see a doctor immediately.

Treating water. The best and easiest solution to avoid polluted water is to carry your water with you. Yet, depending on the nature of your hike and the duration, this may not be an option—one gallon of water weighs 8.5 pounds. In that case you'll need to look into treating water. Regardless of which method you choose, you should always carry some water with you in case of an emergency. Save this reserve until you absolutely need it.

There are three methods of treating water: boiling, chemical treatment, and filtering. If you boil water, it's recommended that you do so for 10 to 15 minutes. This is often impractical because that exhausts a great deal of your fuel supply. You can opt for chemical treatment, which will kill *Giardia* but will not take care of other chemical pollutants. Another drawback to chemical treatments is the unpleasant taste of the water after it's treated. You can remedy this by adding powdered drink mix to the water. Filters are the preferred method for treating water. Many filters remove *Giardia*, organic and inorganic contaminants, and don't leave an aftertaste. Water filters are far from perfect as they can easily become clogged or leak if a gasket wears out. It's always a good idea to carry a backup supply of chemical treatment tablets in case your filter decides to quit on you.

Food. If we're talking about survival, you can go days without food, as long as you have water. But we're also talking about comfort. Try to avoid foods that are high in sugar and fat like candy bars and potato chips. These food types are harder to digest and are low in nutritional value. Instead, bring along foods that are easy to pack, nutritious, and high in energy (e.g., whole-grain bagels, nutrition bars, dehydrated fruit, gorp, and jerky). If you are on an overnight trip, easy-to-fix dinners include rice mixes with dehydrated potatoes, corn, pasta with cheese sauce, and soup mixes. For a tasty breakfast, you can fix hot oatmeal with brown sugar and reconstituted milk powder topped off with banana chips. If you like a hot drink in the morning, bring along herbal tea bags or hot chocolate. If you are a coffee junkie, you can purchase coffee that is packaged like tea bags or instant coffee in individual servings. You can prepackage all of your meals in heavy-duty resealable plastic bags to keep food from spilling in your pack. These bags can be reused to pack out trash.

Shelter. The type of shelter you choose depends less on the conditions than on your tolerance for discomfort. Shelter comes in many forms—tent, tarp, lean-to, bivy sack, cabin, cave, and so forth. If you're camping in the desert, a bivy sack may suffice, but if you're above the tree line and a storm is approaching, a better choice is a three- or four-season tent. Tents are the logical and most popular choice for most backpackers because they're lightweight and packable—and you can rest assured that you always have shelter from the elements. Before you leave on your trip, anticipate what the weather and terrain will be like and plan for the type of shelter that will work best for your comfort level (see "Equipment" later in this section).

Finding a campsite. If there are established campsites, stick to those. If not, start looking for a campsite early—around 3:30 or 4 p.m. Stop at the first decent site you see. Depending on the area, it could be a long time before you find another suitable location. Pitch your camp in an area that's level. Make sure the site is at least 200 feet from fragile areas like lakeshores, meadows, and stream banks. And try to avoid areas thick in underbrush, as they can harbor insects and provide cover for approaching animals.

If you are camping in stormy, rainy weather, look for a rock outcrop or a shelter in the trees to keep the wind from blowing your tent all night. Be sure that you don't camp under trees with dead limbs that might break off on top of you. Also, try to find an area that has an absorbent surface, such as sandy soil or forest duff. This, in addition to camping on a surface with a slight angle, will provide better drainage. By all means, don't dig trenches to provide drainage around your tent—remember you're practicing zero-impact camping.

If you're in bear country, steer clear of creek beds or animal paths. If you see any signs of a bear's presence (e.g., scat, footprints), relocate. You'll need to find a campsite near a tall tree where you can hang your food and other items that may attract bears, such as deodorant, toothpaste, or soap. Carry a lightweight nylon rope with which to hang your food. As a rule you should hang your food at least 20 feet from the ground and 5 feet away from the tree trunk. You can put food and other items in a waterproof stuff sack and tie one end of the rope to the stuff sack. To get the other end of the rope over the tree branch, tie a good-size rock to it and gently toss the rock over the tree branch. Pull the stuff sack up until it reaches the top of the branch and tie it off securely. Don't hang your food near your tent! If possible, hang your food at least 100 feet away from your campsite. Alternatives to hanging your food are bear-proof canisters (required in some national parks) and metal bear boxes.

Lastly, think of comfort. Lie down on the ground where you intend to sleep and see if it's a good fit. For morning warmth (and a nice view to wake up to), have your tent face east.

First Aid

I know you're tough, but get 10 miles into the woods and develop a blister and you'll wish you had carried that first-aid kit. Face it, it's just plain good sense. Many companies produce lightweight, compact first-aid kits. Just make sure yours contains at least the following:

- ❑ adhesive bandages
- ❑ moleskin or duct tape
- ❑ various sterile gauze and dressings
- ❑ white surgical tape
- ❑ Ace bandage

- ❏ antihistamine
- ❏ aspirin
- ❏ Betadine solution
- ❏ first-aid book
- ❏ antacid tablets
- ❏ tweezers
- ❏ scissors
- ❏ antibacterial wipes
- ❏ triple-antibiotic ointment
- ❏ plastic gloves
- ❏ sterile cotton tip applicators
- ❏ syrup of ipecac (to induce vomiting)
- ❏ thermometer
- ❏ wire splint

Here are a few tips for dealing with and hopefully preventing certain ailments.

Sunburn. Take along sunscreen or sunblock, protective clothing, and a wide-brimmed hat. If you do get a sunburn, treat the area with aloe vera gel, and protect it from further sun exposure. At higher elevations, the sun's radiation can be particularly damaging to skin. Remember that your eyes are vulnerable to this radiation as well. Sunglasses can be a good way to prevent headaches and permanent eye damage from the sun, especially in places where light-colored rock or patches of snow reflect light up in your face.

Blisters. Be prepared to take care of these hike-spoilers by carrying moleskin (a lightly padded adhesive), gauze and tape, or adhesive bandages. An effective way to apply moleskin is to cut out a circle of moleskin and remove the center—like a doughnut—and place it over the blistered area. Cutting the center out will reduce the pressure applied to the sensitive skin. Other products can help you combat blisters. Some are applied to suspicious hot spots before a blister forms to help decrease friction to that area, while others are applied to the blister after it has popped to help prevent further irritation.

Insect bites and stings. You can treat most insect bites and stings by applying 1% hydrocortisone cream topically and taking a pain medication such as ibuprofen or acetaminophen to reduce swelling. If you forgot to pack these items, a cold compress or a paste of mud and ashes can sometimes assuage the itching and discomfort. Remove any stingers by using tweezers or scraping the area with your fingernail or a knife blade. Don't pinch the area as you'll only spread the venom.

Some hikers are highly sensitive to bites and stings and may have a serious allergic reaction that can be life threatening. Symptoms of a serious allergic reaction can include wheezing, an asthma attack, and shock. The treatment for this severe type of reaction is epinephrine. If you know that you are sensitive to bites and stings, carry a prepackaged kit of epinephrine, which can be obtained only by prescription from your doctor.

Ticks. Ticks can carry diseases such as Rocky Mountain spotted fever and Lyme disease. The best defense is, of course, prevention. If you know you're going to be hiking through an area littered with ticks, wear long pants and a long-sleeved shirt. You can apply a permethrin repellent to your clothing and a Deet repellent to exposed skin. At the end of your hike, do a spot check for ticks (and insects in general). If you do find a tick, coat the insect with petroleum jelly or tree sap to cut off its air supply. The tick should release its hold, but if it doesn't, grab the head of the tick firmly—with a pair of tweezers if you have them—and gently pull it away from the skin with a twisting motion. Sometimes the mouthparts linger, embedded in your skin. If this happens, try to remove them with a disinfected needle. Clean the affected area with an antibacterial cleanser and then apply triple antibiotic ointment. Monitor the area for a few days. If irritation persists or a white spot develops, see a doctor for possible infection.

Poison ivy, oak, and sumac. These skin irritants can be found most anywhere in North America and come in the form of a bush or a vine, having leaflets in groups of three, five, seven, or nine. Learn how to spot the plants. The oil they secrete can cause an allergic reaction in the form of blisters, usually about 12 hours after exposure. The itchy rash can last from ten days to several weeks. The best defense against these irritants is to wear clothing that covers the arms, legs and torso. For summer, zip-off cargo pants come in handy. There are also nonprescription lotions you can apply to exposed skin that guard against the effects of poison ivy/oak/sumac and can be washed off with soap and water. If you think you were in contact with the plants, after hiking (or even while on the trail during longer hikes) wash with soap and water. Taking a hot shower with soap after you return home from your hike will also help to remove any lingering oil from your skin. Should you contract a rash from any of these plants, use an antihistamine to reduce the itching. If the rash is localized, create a light bleach/water wash to dry up the area. If the rash has spread, either tough it out or see your doctor about getting a dose of cortisone (available both orally and by injection).

Snakebites. Snakebites are rare in North America. Unless startled or provoked, the majority of snakes will not bite. If you are wise to their habitats and keep a careful eye on the trail, you should be just fine. When stepping over logs, first step on the log, making sure you can see what's on the other side before stepping down. Though your chances of being struck are slim, it's wise to know what to do in the event you are.

If a *nonpoisonous* snake bites you, allow the wound to bleed a small amount and then cleanse the wounded area with a Betadine solution (10% povidone iodine). Rinse the wound with clean water (preferably) or fresh urine (it might sound ugly, but it's sterile). Once the area is clean, cover it with triple antibiotic ointment and a clean bandage. Remember, most residual damage from snakebites, poisonous or otherwise, comes from infection, not the snake's venom. Keep the area as clean as possible and get medical attention immediately.

Trailside first aid

If you are bitten by a poisonous snake, remove the toxin with a suctioning device, found in a snakebite kit. If you do not have such a device, squeeze the wound—*do not* use your mouth for suction, as the venom will enter your bloodstream through the vessels under the tongue and head straight for your heart. Then clean the wound just as you would a nonpoisonous bite. Tie a clean band of cloth snugly around the afflicted appendage, about an inch or so above the bite (or the rim of the swelling). This is *not* a tourniquet—you want to simply slow the blood flow, not cut it off. Loosen the band if numbness ensues. Remove the band for a minute and reapply a little higher every 10 minutes.

If it is your friend who's been bitten, treat him or her for shock—make the person comfortable, lying down with elevated legs, and keep him or her warm. Avoid applying anything cold to the bite wound. Immobilize the affected area and remove any constricting items such as rings, watches, or restrictive clothing, as swelling may occur. Once your friend is stable and relatively calm, hike out to get help. The victim should get treatment ideally within 12 hours, which usually consists of a tetanus shot, antivenin, and antibiotics.

If you are alone and struck by a poisonous snake, stay calm. Hysteria will only quicken the venom's spread. Follow the procedure above, and do your best to reach help. When hiking out, don't run—you'll only increase the flow of blood throughout your system. Instead, walk calmly.

Dehydration. Have you ever hiked in hot weather and had a roaring headache and felt fatigued after only a few miles? More than likely you were dehydrated. Symptoms of dehydration include fatigue, headache, and decreased coordination and judgment. When you are hiking, your body's rate of fluid loss depends on the outside temperature, humidity, altitude, and your activity level. On average, a hiker walking in warm weather will lose 4 liters of fluid a day. That fluid loss is easily replaced by normal consumption of liquids and food. However, if a hiker is walking briskly in hot, dry weather and hauling a heavy pack, he or she can lose 1 to 3 liters of water an hour. It's important to always carry plenty of water and to stop often and drink fluids regularly, even if you aren't thirsty.

Heat exhaustion is the result of a loss of large amounts of electrolytes and often occurs if a hiker is dehydrated and has been under heavy exertion. Common symptoms of heat exhaustion include cramping, exhaustion, fatigue, lightheadedness, and nausea. You can treat heat exhaustion by getting out of the sun and drinking an electrolyte solution made up of 1 teaspoon of salt and 1 tablespoon of sugar dissolved in a liter of water. Drink this solution slowly over a period of 1 hour. Drinking plenty of fluids (preferably an electrolyte solution/sports drink) can prevent heat exhaustion. Avoid hiking during the hottest parts of the day, and wear breathable clothing, a wide-brimmed hat, and sunglasses.

Hypothermia is one of the biggest dangers in the backcountry, especially for day hikers in the summertime. That may sound strange, but imagine starting out on a hike in midsummer when it's sunny and 80 degrees out. You're clad in nylon shorts and a cotton T-shirt. About halfway through your hike, the sky begins to cloud up, and in the next hour a light drizzle begins to fall and the wind starts to pick up. Before you know it, you are soaking wet and shivering—the perfect recipe for hypothermia. More advanced signs include decreased coordination, slurred speech, and blurred vision. When a victim's temperature falls below 92 degrees F, the blood pressure and pulse plummet, possibly leading to coma and death.

To avoid hypothermia, always bring a windproof/rainproof shell, a fleece jacket, tights made of a breathable, synthetic fiber, gloves, and hat when you are hiking in the mountains. Learn to adjust your clothing layers based on the temperature. If you are climbing uphill at a moderate pace you will stay warm, but when you stop for a break you'll become cold quickly, unless you add more layers of clothing.

If a hiker is showing advanced signs of hypothermia, dress the victim in dry clothes and make sure he or she is wearing a hat and gloves. Place the person in a sleeping bag in a tent or shelter that will provide protection from the wind and other elements. Give the person warm fluids to drink and keep him or her awake.

Frostbite. When the mercury dips below 32 degrees F, your extremities begin to chill. If a persistent chill attacks a localized area, say, your hands or your toes, the circulatory system reacts by cutting off blood flow to the affected area—the idea being to protect and preserve the body's overall temperature. And so it's death by attrition for the affected area. Ice crystals start to form from the water in the cells of the neglected tissue. Deprived of heat, nourishment, and now water, the tissue literally starves. This is frostbite.

Prevention is your best defense against this situation. Most prone to frostbite are your face, hands, and feet, so protect these areas well. Wool is the material of choice because it provides ample air space for insulation and draws moisture away from the skin. Synthetic fabrics, however, have recently made great strides in the cold-weather clothing market. Do your research. A pair of light silk liners under your regular gloves is a good trick for keeping warm. They afford some additional warmth, but more importantly they'll allow you to remove your mitts for tedious work without exposing the skin.

If your feet or hands start to feel cold or numb due to the elements, warm them as quickly as possible. Place cold hands under your armpits or bury them in your crotch. If your feet are cold, change your socks. If there's plenty of room in your boots, add another pair of socks. Do remember, though, that constricting your feet in tight boots can restrict blood flow and actually make your feet colder more quickly. Your socks need to have breathing room if they're going to be effective. Dead air provides insulation. If your face is cold, place your warm hands over your face, or simply wear a head stocking.

Should your skin go numb and start to appear white and waxy, chances are you've got or are developing frostbite. Don't try to thaw the area unless you can maintain the warmth. In other words, don't stop to warm up your frostbitten feet only to head back on the trail. You'll do more damage than good. Tests have shown that hikers who walked on thawed feet did more harm, and endured more pain, than hikers who left the affected areas alone. Do your best to get out of the cold entirely and seek medical attention—which usually consists of performing a rapid rewarming in water for 20 to 30 minutes.

The overall objective in preventing both hypothermia and frostbite is to keep the body's core warm. Protect key areas where heat escapes, like the top of the head, and maintain the proper nutrition level. Foods that are high in calories aid the body in producing heat. Never smoke or drink when you're in situations where the cold is threatening. By affecting blood flow, these activities ultimately cool the body's core temperature.

Hantavirus Pulmonary Syndrome (HPS). Deer mice spread the virus that causes HPS, and humans contract it from breathing it in, usually when they've disturbed an area with dust and mice feces from nests or surfaces with mice droppings or urine. Exposure to large numbers of rodents and their feces or urine presents the greatest risk. As hikers, we sometimes enter old buildings, and often deer mice live in these places. We may not be around long enough to be exposed, but do be aware of this disease. About half the people who develop HPS die. Symptoms are flu-like and appear about two to three weeks after exposure. After initial symptoms, a dry cough and shortness of breath follow. Breathing is difficult. If you even think you might have HPS, see a doctor immediately!

Natural Hazards

Besides tripping over a rock or tree root on the trail, there are some real hazards to be aware of while hiking. Even if where you're hiking doesn't have the plethora of poisonous snakes and plants, insects, and grizzly bears found in other parts of the United States, there are a few weather conditions and predators you may need to take into account.

Lightning. Thunderstorms build over the mountains almost every day during the summer. Lightning is generated by thunderheads and can strike without warning, even several miles away from the nearest overhead cloud. The best rule of thumb is to start leaving exposed peaks, ridges, and canyon rims by about noon. This time can vary a little depending on storm buildup. Keep an eye on cloud formation, and don't underestimate how fast a storm can build. The bigger they get, the more likely a thunderstorm will happen. Lightning takes the path of least resistance, so if you're the high point, it might choose you. Ducking under a rock overhang is dangerous, as you form the shortest path between the rock and ground. If you dash below tree line, avoid standing under the only or the tallest tree. If you are caught above tree line, stay away from anything metal you might be carrying, Move down off the ridge slightly to a low, treeless point and squat until the storm passes. If you have an insulating pad, squat on it. Avoid having both your hands and feet touching the ground at once and never lie flat. If you hear a buzzing sound or feel your hair standing on end, move quickly because an electrical charge is building up.

Flash floods. On July 31, 1976, a torrential downpour dumped tons of water into the Big Thompson watershed near Estes Park, Colorado. Within hours, a wall of water moved down the narrow canyon, killing 139 people and causing more than $30 million in property damage. The spooky thing about flash floods, especially in western canyons, is that they can appear out of nowhere from a storm many miles away. While hiking or driving in canyons, keep an eye on the weather. Always climb to safety if danger threatens. Flash floods usually subside quickly, so be patient and don't cross a swollen stream.

Bears. Most of the United States (outside of the Pacific Northwest and parts of the Northern Rockies) does not have a grizzly bear population, although some rumors exist about sightings where there should be none. Black bears are plentiful, however. Here are some tips in case you and a bear scare each other. Most of all, avoid scaring a bear. Watch for bear tracks (five toes) and droppings (sizable with leaves, partly digested berries, seeds, and/or animal fur). Talk or sing where visibility or hearing is limited. Keep a clean camp, hang food and toiletries, and don't sleep in the clothes you wore while cooking. Be especially careful in spring to avoid getting between a mother and her cubs. In late summer and fall bears are busy eating berries and acorns to fatten up for winter, so be extra careful around berry bushes. If you do encounter a bear, move away slowly while facing the bear, talk softly, and avoid direct eye contact. Give the bear room to escape. Since bears are very curious, it might stand upright to get a better whiff of you, and it may even charge you to try to intimidate you. Try to stay calm. If a bear does attack, fight back with anything you have handy. Unleashed dogs have been known to come running back to their owners with a bear close behind. Keep your dog on a leash or leave it at home.

Other considerations. Hunting is a popular sport in the United States, especially during rifle season in October and November. Hiking is still enjoyable in those months in many areas, so just take a few precautions. First, learn when the different hunting seasons start and end in the area in which you'll be hiking. During this time frame, be sure to wear at least a blaze orange hat, and possibly put an orange vest over your pack. Don't be surprised to see hunters in camo outfits carrying bows or muzzleloading rifles around during their season. If you would feel more comfortable without hunters around, hike in national parks and monuments or state and local parks where hunting is not allowed.

Navigation

Whether you are going on a short hike in a familiar area or planning a weeklong backpack trip, you should always be equipped with the proper navigational equipment—at the very least a detailed map and a sturdy compass.

Maps. There are many different types of maps available to help you find your way on the trail. Easiest to find are US Forest Service maps. These maps tend to cover large areas, so be sure they are detailed enough for your particular trip. You can also obtain national park maps as well as high-quality maps from private companies and trail groups. These maps can be obtained either from outdoor stores or ranger stations.

U.S. Geological Survey (USGS) topographic maps are particularly popular with hikers—especially serious backcountry hikers. These maps contain the standard map symbols such as roads, lakes, and rivers, as well as contour lines that show the details of the trail terrain like ridges, valleys, passes, and mountain peaks. The 7.5-minute series (1 inch on the map equals approximately ⅔ mile on the ground) provides the closest inspection available. USGS maps are available by mail (U.S. Geological Survey, Map Distribution Branch, P.O. Box 25286, Denver, CO 80225) or at www .usgs.gov.

If you want to check out the high-tech world of maps, you can purchase topographic maps on CD-ROM. These software-mapping programs let you select a route on your computer, print it out, then take it with you on the trail. Some software mapping programs let you insert symbols and labels, download waypoints from a GPS unit, and export the maps to other software programs.

The art of map reading is a skill that you can develop by first practicing in an area you are familiar with. To begin, orient the map so it is lined up in the correct direction (i.e., north on the map is lined up with true north). Next, familiarize yourself with the map symbols and try to match them up with terrain features around you such as a high ridge, mountain peak, river, or lake. If you are practicing with a USGS map, notice the contour lines. On gentler terrain these contour lines are spaced farther apart, and on steeper terrain they are closer together. Pick a short loop trail and

Essential navigation tools: compass and map

stop frequently to check your position on the map. As you practice map reading, you'll learn how to anticipate a steep section on the trail or a good place to take a rest break, and so on.

Compasses. First off, the sun is not a substitute for a compass. So, what kind of compass should you have? Here are some characteristics you should look for: a rectangular base with detailed scales, a liquid-filled, protective housing, a sighting line on the mirror, luminous alignment and back-bearing arrows, a luminous north-seeking arrow, and a well-defined bezel ring.

You can learn compass basics by reading the detailed instructions included with your compass. If you want to fine-tune your compass skills, sign up for an orienteering class or purchase a book on compass reading. Once you've learned the basic skills of using a compass, remember to practice these skills before you head into the backcountry.

If you are a klutz at using a compass, you may be interested in checking out the technical wizardry of the GPS (Global Positioning System) device. The GPS was developed by the Pentagon and works off twenty-four NAVSTAR satellites, which were designed to guide missiles to their targets. A GPS device is a handheld unit that calculates your latitude and longitude with the easy press of a button. The Department of Defense used to scramble the satellite signals a bit to prevent civilians (and spies!) from getting extremely accurate readings, but that practice was discontinued in May 2000, and GPS units now provide nearly pinpoint accuracy (within 30 to 60 feet).

There are many different types of GPS units available and they range in price from $100 to $400. In general, all GPS units have a display screen and keypad where you input information. In addition to acting as a compass, the unit allows you to plot your route, easily retrace your path, track your traveling speed, find the mileage between waypoints, and calculate the total mileage of your route.

Before you purchase a GPS unit, keep in mind that these devices don't pick up signals indoors, in heavily wooded areas, on mountain peaks, or in deep valleys.

Pedometers. A pedometer is a small, clip-on unit with a digital display that calculates your hiking distance in miles or kilometers based on your walking stride. Some units also calculate the calories you burn and your total hiking time. Pedometers are available at most large outdoor stores and range in price from $20 to $40.

Trip Planning

Planning your hiking adventure begins with letting a friend or relative know your trip itinerary so they can call for help if you don't return at your scheduled time. Your next task is to make sure you are outfitted to experience the risks and rewards of the trail. This section highlights gear and clothing you may want to take with you to get the most out of your hike.

Day Hikes

- ❑ camera/film
- ❑ compass/GPS unit
- ❑ pedometer
- ❑ daypack
- ❑ first-aid kit
- ❑ food
- ❑ guidebook
- ❑ headlamp/flashlight with extra batteries and bulbs
- ❑ hat
- ❑ insect repellent
- ❑ knife/multipurpose tool
- ❑ map
- ❑ matches in waterproof container and fire starter
- ❑ fleece jacket
- ❑ rain gear
- ❑ space blanket
- ❑ sunglasses
- ❑ sunscreen
- ❑ swimsuit

- ❑ watch
- ❑ water
- ❑ water bottles/water hydration system

Overnight Trip

- ❑ backpack and waterproof rain cover
- ❑ backpacker's trowel
- ❑ bandanna
- ❑ bear repellent spray
- ❑ bear bell
- ❑ biodegradable soap
- ❑ pot scrubber
- ❑ collapsible water container (2–3 gallon capacity)
- ❑ clothing—extra wool socks, shirt, and shorts
- ❑ cook set/utensils
- ❑ ditty bags to store gear
- ❑ extra plastic resealable bags
- ❑ gaiters
- ❑ garbage bag
- ❑ ground cloth
- ❑ journal/pen
- ❑ nylon rope to hang food
- ❑ long underwear
- ❑ permit (if required)
- ❑ rain jacket and pants
- ❑ sandals to wear around camp and to ford streams
- ❑ sleeping bag
- ❑ waterproof stuff sack
- ❑ sleeping pad
- ❑ small bath towel
- ❑ stove and fuel
- ❑ tent
- ❑ toiletry items
- ❑ water filter
- ❑ whistle

Equipment

With the outdoor market currently flooded with products, many of which are pure gimmickry, it seems impossible to both differentiate and choose. Do I really need a tropical-fish-lined collapsible shower? (No, you don't.) The only defense against the maddening quantity of items thrust in your face is to think practically—and to do so before you go shopping. The worst buys are impulsive buys. Since most name brands will differ only slightly in quality, it's best to know what you're looking for in terms of function. Buy only what you need. You will, don't forget, be carrying what you've bought on your back. Here are some things to keep in mind before you go shopping.

Clothes. Clothing is your armor against Mother Nature's little surprises. Hikers should be prepared for any possibility, especially when hiking in mountainous areas. Adequate rain protection and extra layers of clothing are a good idea. In summer, a wide-brimmed hat can help keep the sun at bay. In the winter months the first layer you'll want to wear is a "wicking" layer of long underwear that keeps perspiration away from your skin. Wear long underwear made from synthetic fibers that wick moisture away from the skin and draw it toward the next layer of clothing, where it then evaporates. Avoid wearing long underwear made of cotton, as it is slow to dry and keeps moisture next to your skin.

The second layer you'll wear is the "insulating" layer. Aside from keeping you warm, this layer needs to "breathe" so you stay dry while hiking. A fabric that provides insulation and dries quickly is fleece. It's interesting to note that this one-of-a-kind fabric is made out of recycled plastic. Purchasing a zip-up jacket made of this material is highly recommended.

The last line of layering defense is the "shell" layer. You'll need some type of waterproof, windproof, breathable jacket that will fit over all of your other layers. It should have a large hood that fits over a hat. You'll also need a good pair of rain pants made from a similar waterproof, breathable fabric. Some Gore-Tex jackets cost as much as $500, but you should know that there are more affordable fabrics available that work just as well.

Now that you've learned the basics of layering, don't forget to protect your hands and face. In cold, windy, or rainy weather you'll need a hat made of wool or fleece and insulated, waterproof gloves that will keep your hands warm and toasty. As mentioned earlier, buying an additional pair of light silk liners to wear under your regular gloves is a good idea.

Footwear. If you have any extra money to spend on your trip, put that money into boots or trail shoes. Poor shoes will bring a hike to a halt faster than anything else. To avoid this annoyance, buy shoes that provide support and are lightweight and flexible. A lightweight hiking boot is better than a heavy leather mountaineering boot for most day hikes and backpacking. Trail running shoes provide a little extra cushion and are made in a high-top style that many people wear for hiking. These running shoes are lighter, more flexible, and more breathable than hiking boots. If you know you'll be hiking in wet weather often, purchase boots or shoes with a Gore-Tex liner, which will help keep your feet dry.

When buying your boots or trail shoes, be sure to wear the same type of socks you'll be wearing on the trail. If the footwear you're buying are for cold-weather hiking, try them on while wearing two pairs of socks. Speaking of socks, a good cold-weather sock combination is to wear a thinner sock made of wool or polypropylene covered by a heavier outer sock made of wool. The inner sock protects the foot from the rubbing effects of the outer sock and prevents blisters. Many outdoor stores have some type of ramp to simulate hiking uphill and downhill. Be sure to take advantage of this test, as toe-jamming shoe fronts can be painful and debilitating on the down-hill trek.

Once you've purchased your footwear, be sure to break them in before you hit the trail. New footwear is often stiff and needs to be stretched and molded to your foot.

Hiking poles. Hiking poles help with balance and, more importantly, take pressure off your knees. The ones with shock absorbers are easier on your elbows and knees. Some poles even come with a camera attachment for use as a monopod. And heaven forbid you meet a mountain lion, bear, or unfriendly dog, the poles can make you look a lot bigger.

Backpacks. No matter what type of hiking you do, you'll need a pack of some sort to carry the basic trail essentials. There are a variety of backpacks on the market, but let's first discuss what you intend to use it for: day hikes or overnight trips.

If you plan on doing a day hike, a daypack should have some of the following characteristics: a padded hip belt that's at least 2 inches in diameter (avoid packs with only a small piece of nylon webbing for a hip belt); a chest strap, which helps stabilize the pack against your body; external pockets to carry water and other items that you want easy access to; an internal pocket to hold keys, a knife, a wallet, and other miscellaneous items; an external lashing system to hold a jacket; and a hydration pocket for carrying a hydration system, which consists of a water bladder with an attachable drinking hose.

For short hikes some hikers like to use a fanny pack to store just a camera, food, a compass, a map, and other trail essentials. Most fanny packs have pockets for two water bottles and a padded hip belt.

If you intend to do an extended, overnight trip, there are multiple considerations. First off, you need to decide what kind of framed pack you want. There are two backpack types for backpacking: the internal frame and the external frame. An internal frame pack rests closer to your body, making it more stable and easier to balance when hiking over rough terrain. An external frame pack is just that, an aluminum frame attached to the exterior of the pack. An external frame pack is better for long backpack trips because it distributes the pack weight better and you can carry heavier loads. It's easier to pack, and your gear is more accessible. It also offers better back ventilation in hot weather.

The most critical measurement for fitting a pack is torso length. The pack needs to rest evenly on your hips without sagging. A good pack will come in two or three sizes and have straps and hip belts that are adjustable according to your body size and characteristics. Other features that are nice to have on a backpack include a removable day pack or fanny pack, external pockets for extra water, and extra lash points to attach a jacket or other items.

When you purchase a backpack, go to an outdoor store with salespeople who are knowledgeable in how to properly fit a pack. Once the pack is fitted for you, load the pack with the amount of weight you plan on taking on the trail. The weight of the pack should be distributed evenly, and you should be able to swing your arms and walk briskly without feeling out of balance. Another good technique for evaluating a pack is to walk up and down stairs and make quick turns to the right and to the left to be sure the pack doesn't feel out of balance.

Sleeping bags and pads. Sleeping bags are rated by temperature. You can purchase a bag made of synthetic fiber, or you can buy a goose down bag. Goose down bags are more expensive, but they have a higher insulating capacity by weight and will keep their loft longer. You'll want to purchase a bag with a temperature rating that fits the time of year and conditions you are most likely to camp in. One caveat: The techno-standard for temperature ratings is far from perfect. Ratings vary from manufacturer to manufacturer, so to protect yourself you should purchase a bag rated 10 to 15 degrees below the temperature you expect to be camping in. Synthetic bags are more resistant to water than down bags, but many down bags are now made with a Gore-Tex shell that helps to repel water. Down bags are also more compressible than synthetic bags and take up less room in your pack, which is an important consideration if you are planning a multiday backpack trip. Features to look for in a sleeping bag include a mummy-style bag, a hood you can cinch down around your head in cold weather, and draft tubes along the zippers that help keep heat in and drafts out.

You'll also want a sleeping pad to provide insulation and padding from the cold ground. There are different types of sleeping pads available, from the more expensive self-inflating air mattresses to the less expensive closed-cell foam pads. Self-inflating air mattresses are usually heavier than closed-cell foam mattresses and are prone to punctures.

Tents. The tent is your home away from home while on the trail. It provides protection from wind, snow, rain, and insects. A three-season tent is a good choice for backpacking and can range in price from $100 to $500. These lightweight and versatile tents provide protection in all types of weather, except heavy snowstorms or high winds, and range in weight from 4 to 8 pounds. Look for a tent that's easy to set up and will easily fit two people with gear. Dome-type tents usually offer more headroom and places to store gear. Other tent designs include a vestibule where you can store wet boots and backpacks. Some nice-to-have items in a tent include interior pockets to store small items and lashing points to hang a clothesline. Most three-season tents also come with stakes so you can secure the tent in high winds. Before you purchase a tent, set it up and take it down a few times to be sure it is easy to handle. Also, sit inside the tent and make sure it has enough room for you and your gear.

Cell phones. Many hikers are carrying their cell phones into the backcountry these days in case of emergency. That's fine and good, but please know that cell phone coverage is often poor to nonexistent in valleys, canyons, and thick forest. More importantly (and concerning), people have started to call for help because they're tired or lost. Let's go back to being prepared. You are responsible for yourself in the backcountry. Use your brain to avoid problems, and if you do encounter one, first use your brain to try to correct the situation. Only use your cell phone, if it works, in true emergencies.

Hiking with Children

Hiking with children isn't a matter of how many miles you can cover or how much elevation gain you make in a day; it's about seeing and experiencing nature through their eyes.

Kids like to explore and have fun. They like to stop and point out bugs and plants, look under rocks, jump in puddles, and throw sticks. If you're taking a toddler or young child on a hike, start with a trail that you're familiar with. Trails that have interesting things for kids, like piles of leaves to play in or a small stream to wade through during the summer, will make the hike much more enjoyable for them and will keep them from getting bored.

You can keep your child's attention if you have a strategy before starting on the trail. Using games is not only an effective way to keep a child's attention, it's also a great way to teach him or her about nature. Play hide and seek, where your child is the mouse and you are the hawk. Quiz children on the names of plants and animals. If your children are old enough, let them carry their own daypack filled with snacks and water. So that you are sure to go at their pace and not yours, let them lead the way. Playing follow the leader works particularly well when you have a group of children. Have each child take a turn at being the leader.

With children, a lot of clothing is key. The only thing predictable about weather is that it will change. Especially in mountainous areas, weather can change dramatically in a very short time. Always bring extra clothing for children, regardless of the season. In the winter, have your children wear wool socks and warm layers such as long underwear, a fleece jacket and hat, wool mittens, and good rain gear. It's not a bad idea to have these along in late fall and early spring as well. Good footwear is also important. A sturdy pair of high-top tennis shoes or lightweight hiking boots are the best bet for little ones. If you're hiking in the summer near a lake or stream, bring along a pair of old sneakers that your child can put on when he or she wants to go exploring in the water. Remember when you're near any type of water, always watch your child at all times. Also, keep a close eye on teething toddlers who may decide a rock or leaf of poison oak is an interesting item to put in their mouth.

From spring through fall, you'll want your kids to wear a wide-brimmed hat to keep their face, head, and ears protected from the hot sun. Also, make sure your children wear sunscreen at all times. Choose a brand without PABA—children have sensitive skin and may have an allergic reaction to sunscreen that contains PABA. If you are hiking with children younger than six months, don't use sunscreen or insect repellent. Instead, be sure that their head, face, neck, and ears are protected from the sun with a wide-brimmed hat, and that all other skin exposed to the sun is protected with the appropriate clothing.

Remember that food is fun. Kids like snacks, so it's important to bring a lot of munchies for the trail. Stopping often for snack breaks is a fun way to keep the trail interesting. Raisins, apples, granola bars, crackers and cheese, cereal, and trail mix all make great snacks. If your child is old enough to carry his or her own backpack, fill it with treats before you leave. If your kids don't like drinking water, you can bring boxes of fruit juice.

Avoid poorly designed child-carrying packs—you don't want to break your back carrying your child. Most child-carrying backpacks designed to hold a 40-pound child will contain a large carrying pocket to hold diapers and other items. Some have an optional rain/sun hood.

Hiking with Your Dog

Bringing your furry friend with you is always more fun than leaving him behind. Our canine pals make great trail buddies because they never complain and always make good company. Hiking with your dog can be a rewarding experience, especially if you plan ahead.

Getting your dog in shape. Before you plan outdoor adventures with your dog, make sure he's in shape for the trail. Getting your dog into shape takes the same discipline as getting yourself into shape, but luckily, your dog can get in shape with you. Take your dog with you on your daily runs or walks. If there is a park near your house, hit a tennis ball or play Frisbee with your dog.

Swimming is also an excellent way to get your dog into shape. If there is a lake or river near where you live and your dog likes the water, have him retrieve a tennis ball or stick. Gradually build your dog's stamina up over a two- to three-month period. A good rule of thumb is to assume that your dog will travel twice as far as you will on the trail. If you plan on doing a 5-mile hike, be sure your dog is in shape for a 10-mile hike.

Training your dog for the trail. Before you go on your first hiking adventure with your dog, be sure he has a firm grasp of the basics of canine etiquette and behavior. Make sure he can sit, lie down, stay, and come. One of the most important commands you can teach your canine pal is to "come" under any situation. It's easy for your friend's nose to lead him astray or possibly lost. Another helpful command is the "get behind" command. When you're on a hiking trail that's narrow, you can have your dog follow behind you when other trail users approach. Nothing is more bothersome than an enthusiastic dog that runs back and forth on the trail and disrupts the peace of the trail for others. When you see other trail users approaching on the trail, give them the right of way by quietly stepping off the trail and making your dog lie down and stay until they pass.

Equipment. The most critical pieces of equipment you can invest in for your dog are proper identification and a sturdy leash. Flexi-leads work well for hiking because they give your dog more freedom to explore but still leave you in control. Make sure your dog has identification that includes your name and address and a number for your veterinarian. Other forms of identification for your dog include a tattoo or a microchip. You should consult your veterinarian for more information on these last two options.

The next piece of equipment you'll want to consider is a pack for your dog. By no means should you put all of your dog's essentials in your pack—let him carry his own gear! Dogs that are in good shape can carry 30 to 40 percent of their own weight.

Most packs are fitted by a dog's weight and girth measurement. Companies that make dog packs generally include guidelines to help you pick out the size that's right for your dog. Some characteristics to look for when purchasing a pack for your dog include a harness that contains two padded girth straps, a padded chest strap, leash attachments, removable saddle bags, internal water bladders, and external gear cords.

You can introduce your dog to the pack by first placing the empty pack on his back and letting him wear it around the yard. Keep an eye on him during this first introduction. He may decide to chew through the straps if you aren't watching him closely. Once he learns to treat the pack as an object of fun and not a foreign enemy, fill the pack evenly on both sides with a few ounces of dog food in resealable plastic bags. Have your dog wear his pack on your daily walks for a period of two to three weeks. Each week add a little more weight to the pack until your dog will accept carrying the maximum amount of weight he can carry.

You can also purchase collapsible water and dog food bowls for your dog. These bowls are lightweight and can easily be stashed into your pack or your dog's. If you are hiking on rocky terrain or in the snow, you can purchase footwear for your dog that will protect his feet from cuts and bruises.

Always carry plastic bags to remove feces from the trail. It is a courtesy to other trail users and helps protect local wildlife.

The following is a list of items to bring when you take your dog hiking: collapsible water bowls, a comb, a collar and a leash, dog food, plastic bags for feces, a dog pack, flea/tick powder, paw protection, water, and a first-aid kit that contains eye ointment, tweezers, scissors, stretchy foot wrap, gauze, antibacterial wash, sterile cotton tip applicators, antibiotic ointment, and cotton wrap.

First aid for your dog. Your dog is just as prone—if not more prone—to getting in trouble on the trail as you are, so be prepared. Here's a rundown of the more likely misfortunes that might befall your little friend.

❑ *Bees and wasps.* If a bee or wasp stings your dog, remove the stinger with a pair of tweezers and place a mudpack or a cloth dipped in cold water over the affected area.

❑ *Porcupines.* One good reason to keep your dog on a leash is to prevent him from getting a nose full of porcupine quills. You may be able to remove the quills with pliers, but a veterinarian is the best person to do this nasty job because most dogs need to be sedated.

❑ *Heat stroke.* Avoid hiking with your dog in really hot weather. Dogs with heat stroke will pant excessively, lie down and refuse to get up, and become lethargic and disoriented. If your dog shows any of these signs on the trail, have him lie down in the shade. If you are near a stream, pour cool water over your dog's entire body to help bring his body temperature back to normal.

❑ *Heartworm.* Dogs get heartworms from mosquitoes that carry the disease in the prime mosquito months of July and August. Giving your dog a monthly pill prescribed by your veterinarian easily prevents this condition.

❑ *Plant pitfalls.* One of the biggest plant hazards for dogs on the trail are sand spurs. Sand spurs are pointed grass seed heads that bury themselves in your friend's fur and between his toes, and even get in his ear canal. If left unattended, these nasty seeds can work their way under the skin and cause abscesses and other problems. If you have a long-haired dog, consider trimming the hair between his toes and giving him a summer haircut to help prevent sand spurs from attaching to his fur. After every hike, always look over your dog for these seeds—especially between his toes and his ears.

Other plant hazards include burrs, thorns, thistles, and poison oak. If you find any burrs or thistles on your dog, remove them as soon as possible before they become an unmanageable mat. Thorns can pierce a dog's foot and cause a great deal of pain. If you see that your dog is lame, stop and check his feet for thorns. Dogs are immune to poison oak, but they can pick up the sticky, oily substance from the plant and transfer it to you.

❑ *Protect those paws.* Be sure to keep your dog's nails trimmed so he avoids getting soft tissue or joint injuries. If your dog slows and refuses to go on, check to see that his paws aren't torn or worn. You can protect your dog's paws from trail hazards such as sharp gravel, foxtails, lava scree, and thorns by purchasing dog boots.

❑ *Sunburn.* If your dog has light skin he is an easy target for sunburn on his nose and other exposed skin areas. You can apply a nontoxic sunscreen to exposed skin areas that will help protect him from overexposure to the sun.

❑ *Ticks and fleas.* Ticks can easily give your dog Lyme disease, as well as other diseases. Before you hit the trail, treat your dog with a flea and tick spray or powder. You can also ask your veterinarian about a once-a-month pour-on treatment that repels fleas and ticks.

❑ *Mosquitoes and deer flies.* These little flying machines can do a job on your dog's snout and ears. Best bet is to spray your dog with fly repellent for horses to discourage both pests.

- ❏ *Giardia.* Dogs can get giardiasis, which results in diarrhea. It is usually not debilitating, but it's definitely messy. A vaccine against the *Giardia lamblia* bacteria is available.

- ❏ *Mushrooms.* Make sure your dog doesn't sample mushrooms along the trail. They could be poisonous to him, but he doesn't know that.

When you are finally ready to hit the trail with your dog, keep in mind that national parks and many wilderness areas do not allow dogs on trails. Your best bet is to hike in national forests, BLM lands, and state parks. Always call ahead to see what the restrictions are.

Hike Index

About the Authors: Bill & Mary Burnham

We began hiking together more than twenty-five years ago. Our first trip as a couple was in Shenandoah National Park (we can attest to the state slogan: Virginia truly is for Lovers!). *Hiking Virginia* was our very first book, published in 2001, and the first edition of *Best Hikes Near Washington, D.C.* came out in 2010.

In the last decade, we've added outdoor outfitting to our efforts, guiding people to our favorite places: Winter kayak expeditions in the Florida Keys and Everglades from the pages of our *Florida Keys Paddling Atlas*, and paddling and hiking in Virginia Spring through Fall.

We call home the Eastern Shore of Virginia, within easy reach of both sources of inspiration: ocean and mountains.

You can reach us and follow our adventures at www.burnhamguides.com or on Facebook. We'd love to hear about your adventures!